THE BUCOLIC PLAGUE

ALSO BY JOSH KILMER-PURCELL

FICTION

Candy Everybody Wants

NONFICTION

I Am Not Myself These Days

THE BUCOLIC PLAGUE

HOW TWO MANHATTANITES

BECAME GENTLEMEN FARMERS

AN UNCONVENTIONAL MEMOIR

JOSH KILMER-PURCELL

HARPER

An Imprint of HarperCollins*Publishers*
www.harpercollins.com

HarperCollins books may be purchased for educational, business,
or sales promotional use. For information, please write: Special
Markets Department, HarperCollins Publishers, 10 East 53rd
Street, New York, NY 10022.

FIRST EDITION

Designed by William Ruoto

Library of Congress Cataloging-in-Publication Data has been ap-
plied for.

ISBN 978-0-06-133698-0

10 11 12 13 14   OV/RRD   10 9 8 7 6 5 4 3 2

For the Honorable William Beekman and all of the past and present citizens of Sharon Springs, who have the old-fashioned decency not to laugh at us to our faces

This is a memoir of a certain time in my life. The names of some characters have been changed, and some are composites of various people, experiences, and conversations I had then. If you think that's unfair, you've obviously never lived in a small town and written a memoir about your neighbors.

Author's Caution

This book is not about living your dream. It will not inspire you. You will not be emboldened to attempt anything more than making a fresh pot of coffee.

The author reminds you that there are plenty of other memoirs out there written by courageous souls who have broken with their past, poetically leaving behind things such as:

1. Drugs and/or Drinking
2. Career Ennui
3. Bad Relationships

. . . and have successfully achieved goals such as:

1. Creative Fulfillment
2. The Simple Life
3. Jesus's Approval

The author notes that those memoirs are generally full of more shit than a barn at the end of a long winter.

The Judge built a spacious mansion west of Beekman's Corners in 1802–'04, which is still standing, having the appearance of a "baronial hall," in which he lived in princely style until his death, which occurred on the 26th of November, 1845, at the age of seventy-eight. His remains were deposited in the family vault, near the residence, and lying near are five of his first children, the eldest being born in the year 1789. Mrs. Beekman lies beside him, having died in December, 1835, at the age of seventy.

    —*History of Schoharie County, New York,*
       William E. Roscoe, 1882

THE BUCOLIC PLAGUE

Prologue

The last time I saw 4 A.M., I was tottering home in high heels and a matted wig sipping from the tiny bottles of Absolut I always kept in my bag for emergencies. Emergencies like "last call."

Now, a little more than a decade later, I'm digging through the backpack I've propped up on the front fender of my pickup truck, counting baby bottles of fresh milk.

"Thirteen . . . fourteen . . . fifteen. I've got fifteen bottles," I report to Farmer John, who, as a lifelong farmer, has seen every single 4 A.M. of his life with considerably more dignity than I ever had. I wonder if farm parents start to panic when their infants first attempt to sleep through the night. "What's wrong with our child?! It just lays there not working for eight hours at a time!"

"That should be enough. Just ration it out," John advises. "They don't know when to stop. They'll drink whatever you give them, and you don't want them to have upset stomachs."

"How do I know if they have upset stomachs?"

"You'll know."

"Now you're sure I don't need any permits or anything?" I ask John. "What if I get pulled over?"

"I looked online," John answers, wedging the oversize dog cage containing five three-week-old baby goats farther into the pickup's backseat. "I didn't see any laws about transporting live-stock. You're not crossing state lines or anything."

It's not the state lines I'm worried about. It's the city one. I think it's safe to say that I'll be the only commuter hauling five baby goats across the George Washington Bridge into New York City this morning for their daytime television debut.

As I pull out of the driveway of the farm, I adjust the rearview mirror to check on the five tiny napping goats. They inhale and exhale in unison in a tight pile in their cage on the backseat. The windshield begins to fog over as their breaths warm up the chilly April morning interior of the truck.

In the mirror I also see Farmer John still standing outside the barn watching me drive over the hill with his most pre-cious possessions—the first five kids born in 2008. As with most of the adventures my partner, Brent, and I cook up, the reticent and gentle John is dubious. As our "co-farmer" (liberal guilt keeps me from calling him our "caretaker"), John is of-ten rightfully wary of our big-city ways. It's risky to transport livestock this young. Everything from feeding to exposure to drafts and jostling must be monitored. All of the savings of John's forty-plus-year life have been invested in his eighty-head goat herd. And here I am, chief city slicker, driving off with this year's potential profits.

I flick on the truck's heat to dissipate the condensation on the windshield. With all of the milk tankers that speed along our country road during the wee hours of the morning, I need to be able to see the hilly road clearly. It's been a lifelong goal of mine never to die ironically. I need to be alert, even though it's a struggle. It's Wednesday morning, and I'd made the three-and-a-half-hour trip to our weekend farm from the city last night after work, arriving around midnight. And now, after only three hours of sleep, I'm on my way back into the city. Destination: *The Martha Stewart Show* studio. And then, after the taping, I have to head straight to the advertising agency where I work for a meeting with our most important client.

For weeks I'd been dreading the logistics of this trip as much as I'd been excited about it. But in the end, it was too good of an opportunity to pass up.

Brent, who as "Dr. Brent" works with Martha as her resident health and wellness expert, had given Martha several bars of our handmade goat milk soap for Christmas. She enjoyed it so much that she suggested that Brent and she do a segment together on her television show teaching viewers how to make their own soap at home.

Brent, with his MBA background, and me, with my advertising résumé, realized what an amazing opportunity had fallen into our laps. Companies like GE and Procter & Gamble pay fortunes for a mere mention on Martha's popular daytime show. Here we had two entire segments to promote a product. Sure, it wasn't a product we'd actually begun manufacturing yet, but we had three weeks from the day Martha extended the invitation until the day of the filming. With our combined expertise, we could launch a company in that short time, couldn't we? Overachievers that we are, we jumped into it without question. But secretly I had another motivation. Maybe, just maybe, it could be successful enough for me to finally slow down my life a little. Running a farm on the weekends, in addition to being a partner in a booming ad agency as well as writing books and magazine columns, was beginning to tally up to a colossal midlife crisis.

So I buckled down and got to work designing a logo and packaging, and spent hours online figuring out how to build a Web site for the farm. While online farming might not seem to be the most obvious route to riches, I was inspired by William Beekman himself, who had built our historic farm in 1802. He became successful not simply as a farmer, but also as a businessman who owned and ran a neighboring mercantile and a grain mill. On top of it all, he'd been appointed by the governor as the first judge of Schoharie County. He was a nineteenth-century multitasker. Brent and I could relate. Then again, he had an army of slaves to help him. All we had was Farmer John and the Internet.

An hour into the three-and-a-half-hour drive to the studio, I'm amazed at how docile the kids are. The truck's movement seems to be keeping them in a lulled sleep. Checking my watch, I pull over into a rest stop on the New York State thruway to give them their morning bottle-feeding at the exact hour John had instructed. I pull the cage out of the backseat and set it on the open tailgate of the pickup bed.

Even at that early hour I soon draw a small crowd of onlookers, cooing at the sight of five tiny goats lining up to poke their heads through the cage to fight over the bottles in my hands. Though I was only supposed to split two bottles between them, I go ahead and pass out three more so that the onlookers can feed them as well.

"Look at them drink! They're *adorable!*" one burly trucker comments. "Can I touch them?"

"Sure," I answer, as a rush of hands squeezes through the cage to caress their silken coats. The kids love the attention and leap around playfully. As semis and cars whiz by on the nearby thruway, the crowd surrounding the truck seems to have forgotten wherever it had been in a rush to get to this morning.

The morning feeding has completely woken up the kids, and once back on the road, I laugh at the playful bleating and wrestling I hear from the seat behind me. Passing truckers look down into my backseat and smile. A few even wave. This trip, contrary to everything I'd anticipated, is *fun.*

And then the smell hits me.

Oh God. The smell. What's happening back there? I've never smelled anything this horrifically pungent in my life. It reeks like a cross between rotting potatoes and sun-baked roadkill. Despite the fact that I'm cruising along at 80 mph in rush-hour thruway traffic, I crane my neck around to see what gate of hell had opened up in my backseat.

My five small passengers are leaping around in their cage, completely ignorant of the fact that they're energetically smearing their own poo over one another. And it's not the quaintly round manure pellets they generally expel. It's diarrhea, and lots of it. Just as John warned me against, I've overfed them.

I begin gagging. The goats continue playfully bleating. Though it's still a chilly 45 degrees outside, I roll down all the windows. This doesn't seem to do anything other than swirl the stench around the truck's cab and shove it further up my nose. This is horrible. I still have two hours of driving left to go.

I lean my head out the driver's-side window gasping for fresh air. How long can I drive with my head out the window? I take a deep breath and hold it. For the next three hours I alternate between plunging my head into the 80 mph windstream outside the window and ducking back inside, holding my breath until the road begins blurring in front of my eyes.

By the time I hit the George Washington Bridge, traffic is at a complete standstill. Without the wind blowing through the truck, the stench seems to concentrate even more. I've already thrown up twice into my Dunkin' Donuts coffee cup, and once down the front of the dress shirt I'm wearing to the important presentation at the agency later this morning.

The kids continue to frolic unabated in their puddle of poo.

I check my watch. Damn. I'm twenty minutes late and the studio is way down on Twenty-sixth Street. Brent is going to kill me.

It takes me an additional forty minutes to crawl the 154 blocks to the studio, making me exactly one hour late for a TV program that goes live in half an hour. Brent's waiting for me, frantically pacing up and down the sidewalk by the loading dock outside the studio.

"Where were you?" he yells as I step out of the cab, gasping for air.

"Traffic . . . *gasp* . . . rush hour . . . *gasp* . . . kids . . . *retch* . . . feeding . . ."

Brent whips open the back door of the truck and immediately recoils. I try to explain.

"Poo . . . *gasp* . . . jumping . . . *gasp* . . ."

"Oh my God. What happened to them?!"

Brent is standing back from the truck, staring at the five caged kids who bleat playfully back at him. They're covered head to toe with their own waste. Not that they notice. They wrestle over top of one another hoping that Brent is the next kind stranger who'll feed them a bottle of ammunition.

"I can't take them inside like this," Brent says.

I stagger across the sidewalk and lean against the side of the studio. Never did I think I'd be so thankful to take in deep breaths of New York City air.

"Isn't there a sink or something inside?" I wheeze.

"I can't take them into the studio kitchen. There's a cooking segment today!"

"A hose maybe?"

Brent paces back and forth next to the truck. The pedestrians walking by on their way to work pause briefly once they notice the cage full of baby goats that Brent had removed—at arm's length—and placed on the sidewalk. The second they lean in for a closer look, however, they too recoil and continue quickly on their way. I can almost see them standing around the coffeemaker telling their colleagues about the poor, neglected shit-covered baby goats they saw on the sidewalk on their way to work. Except that they'll probably call them sheep, because they're New Yorkers. A year ago they would've been me.

I have an idea.

"Is there a deli around here?" I ask Brent.

"Up there. On the corner of Tenth Ave." He points. "Don't leave me here with these."

"Baby wipes. I'll go get some baby wipes."

"That won't work—they're *covered*."

"Do you have a better idea? Maybe something out of *Martha Stewart Living*? Ten Tips for Removing Goat Shit Stains?"

"Just go," he says, waving me off. "And *hurry*. They're already rehearsing inside.

"*And get the unscented ones!*" Brent yells after me.

"*Why?*" I yell back, wondering if I've missed some simple farm logic.

"*Martha doesn't like fragrance!*"

Jogging down the street with the sun just breaking over the buildings in the east, I suddenly realize that it's the same street and the same morning sun that used to guide me home nearly a decade ago, drunkenly staggering from streetlamp to streetlamp after another endless night performing as a drag queen at a nearby dance club.

With the reminiscently familiar stench of my own vomit-covered shirt filling my nose, I ask myself:

Is this progress?

Book 1

Chapter One

October 13, 2006

"Don't panic," Brent said, "but there's a huge spider on your shoulder."

Not panicking seemed like the least pragmatic reaction under the circumstances. So I went ahead and panicked with unabashed exuberance. Limbs flailed. My head hit the passenger-side window. My waving hands nearly shifted the rental car into reverse at 65 mph.

"*Is it gone?!*" I screamed.

"For the moment," Brent answered calmly, rationally, predictably Brent-like. "But it's still in here somewhere."

"Let's pull over," I said. "I'm not going to drive all the way back to the Red Roof Inn with a black widow waiting to suck out all my blood."

"Black widows don't suck blood," Brent said, sighing. "They bite."

"I bet it came from the apples," I said. "There are probably more, lying in wait."

I was afraid to turn around and look at the five full bushels of apples lined up across the backseat. In my mind they were all teeming with blood-sucking arachnids. Other than this brush with death, it had been the perfect weekend so far—our seventh annual apple-picking weekend. Each fall since we'd first met, we put on our best Ralph Lauren plaids, rented a car from the Hertz on Sixty-fourth Street, and drove north until we found an orchard that we liked. Our only criteria were that it made its own doughnuts on site, and wasn't crawling with similar Manhattan escapees such as ourselves. Which meant we usually had to travel pretty far north. After picking more apples than we could ever possibly consume, we would spend the night in a budget motel, preferably just off a major highway—not because we couldn't afford a cozy inn, but because cheap hotels reminded Brent of vacations from his youth. They reminded me of Fleet Week, so it worked out well for both of us.

"Come on, pull over," I said again.

"Let's wait until we hit the next town," Brent said. "We need to get more gas anyway before it gets dark. What are we close to?" He nodded at the map I had in my lap, which was more to keep the draft from the car vents off my legs than for any sort of navigation. I looked down, squinting in the rapidly fading late fall afternoon light.

"We're two pinkie fingernails away from the next red dot."

"That's not very helpful."

"Well, it's better than being two thumbnails away, that's for damn sure."

I turned to look out the window. This was the farthest north we'd ever driven. It was even more beautiful here than in the Hudson River Valley, where we usually ventured. The sky was wide and rolling, and the hills were dotted with tumbledown farms, picturesque in an abandoned, gray Andrew Wyeth kind of way. The winding road led us into a wide gulley of some sort, with silvery slate walls on either side of us. Bright yellow birch leaves stuck to the rocks, made wet with what looked to be a spring gushing from inside the rocks themselves. As we drove around a slight bend, it looked as if we were coming on a village. It seemed like every hollow in these parts was populated by a few houses (badly in need of paint), a post office, and one or two boarded-up stores. This one, though, felt different, and as we drove on it became apparent exactly how different it was.

"Wow," Brent said. "Where's this?"

I looked down at the map, and then realized that Brent was right—I wasn't very good with navigation. I didn't see this village, or any other, within several pinkie fingernails of where I presumed we were. I looked back out the window. This town was unlike any other that we'd driven through that day—or any day for that matter. It was hauntingly beautiful.

As we entered the village, on the left we could just make out a hulking old hotel with an almost Spanish-looking facade. From the looks of the sumac and scrub trees that had grown up through the driveway, it had long been abandoned. On our right we passed a low-slung structure with a faded painted sign indicating that it was once THE IMPERIAL BATHS. We passed a second abandoned bathhouse, and then a little farther up the road we spotted yet another huge hotel—this one right on the main street, with a block-long front porch, five stories of white clapboard, and darkened, very empty windows. The sign out front read THE ROSEBORO.

We were speechless as Brent slowed to a crawl and turned up a side street. This village was incredible. The road was in as much disrepair as the buildings. Every street was lined with abandoned summer hotels and boardinghouses. There wasn't a light on in the windows of any of them. The only sign of life was a hunched woman in a babushka who walked along the frost-heaved, uneven sidewalk. She didn't even glance at us as we slowly drove past her.

"All these empty old hotels and boardinghouses," I said. "It's like *The Shining* meets *Petticoat Junction*."

"Ugh. Do you smell that?" Brent asked, wrinkling his nose. "Eggs. Rotten Eggs."

"Well, obviously the whole town is way past its expiration date." The air did smell awful.

We wound our way up and down the hilly backstreets of this near ghost town in a valley. The wind picked up a little and the yellow and orange leaves scuttered across the empty streets. It was downright eerie.

"Did you find where we are yet?" Brent asked again.

"Hang on. Slow down—I see a plaque or something."

Brent pulled the car over to the side of the main street, though that was just a formality. We could've stopped right in the middle of the street and no one would've had to drive around us. There simply wasn't any sign of life anywhere. We got out of the car and walked over to a sign planted next to the sidewalk. Someone had a wood fire burning somewhere. Other than the old woman, who seemed to have disappeared into thin air, the smell of smoke was the only indication that anyone else was in the vicinity.

"Welcome to Historic Sharon Springs," Brent said, reading from the metal sign.

I leaned in to read over his shoulder. I noticed that there were similar historical society signs all up and down the main street— practically one in front of each abandoned building. It had the effect of making the entire street look like a series of dioramas in a Natural History Museum. With the sun nearly vanished, and most of the streetlights not working, it was nearly getting too dark to read.

The Town of Sharon (originally called New Dorlach) has lived with a dual identity for two centuries, home both to families with agricultural and rural roots, and to visitors and proprietors with visions of resorts and spas. Sharon is one of six original towns to form Schoharie County in 1797. Sharon's dual identity is also about ethnicity and social tradition. Native Americans

were lured here by the healing qualities of the sulphur, mag-
nesia and chalybeate springs. . . . During the second half of the
19th Century, Sharon Springs was home to over sixty hotels and
rooming houses accommodating over 10,000 visitors each summer. By the early 1900s, Sharon's indigenous Christian mix had
become distanced from the summer clientele with the influx of
European visitors, primarily from Judaic tradition.

"Sulphur water. Hence the smell," Brent mused. "This is
where people used to 'take the waters.'"

"It looks like somebody took the people."

"It's beautiful, though, isn't it?"

"Yes," I said. "In a very odd way. It doesn't feel as dead as it
looks."

"Martha would love this town," Brent said. "The old architecture is amazing."

"Well, she better get here quick. One good snowstorm and
it'll be a pile of rubble."

We climbed back into the car and slowly made our way to
the other end of the main street, taking in all of the abandoned
glory. Before the hill that led out of town, the road bent slightly,
enough to hide one final old hotel from our view until we were
right in front of it. It was ablaze with light. And people moving about in the windows. After all of the abandoned darkness, I
nearly had to shield my eyes.

"Whoa. People!" I said.

"The American Hotel," Brent read from the sign out front.

Neither of us actually had to suggest stopping. Brent automat-
ically turned into the gravel driveway. It was full of cars—so full
that we had to park on the grass. We got out and walked around
to the front entrance. The front porch stretched the length of the
white wooden building, punctuated with black shutters at each
window. It was lined with comfortable old wicker rockers and

meticulously decorated with piles of pumpkins and cornstalks. If Norman Rockwell were gay and owned a hotel, this would have been it.

There was another porch above our heads, running along the length of the second floor, and there looked to be a floor above that as well. There must have been several dozen rooms in this place.

"Do you think—" I started.

"No way. A place like this has got to be booked months ahead of time."

"Way out here?"

Brent opened the front door and warm air flooded onto both of our chilled faces.

"A woodstove," he remarked happily.

"A full bar," I added happily-er.

The burning stove and carved wooden bar were located at the far end of the cozy lobby decorated with well-worn antiques and memorabilia from Sharon Springs in its spa heyday.

It almost felt like an episode of *The Twilight Zone.* Had we stepped across a threshold to a different era? This was the one building in town that looked as if it had anyone in it, and now that we were inside, it looked as if it had *everyone* in it. Connected to the lobby was a restaurant, in which every table was set formally and full of patrons. The noise, after driving around those deserted streets, was almost too much to bear.

A voice bellowed from behind the host stand, near the hotel desk complete with little cubbyholes for keys.

"Hello! Welcome to the American!"

It was a bear of a man, tall, broad shouldered and chested, dark haired, with a full beard and mustache to match. He reminded me of a drawing of Paul Bunyan in a picture book I had as a child. After greeting us, he held up a friendly finger motioning for us to wait as he turned back to chat with one of the waitresses who had come up to ask him a question.

Brent studied a framed postcard of the American Hotel that looked as if it had been printed a hundred years ago. It was summertime when the photo was taken, and the sidewalk outside was lined by a row of stately trees. The grass and trees were both manicured to perfection, and several horses were tied to hitching posts. The men and women on the porch were all smiling broadly and were wearing suits and ties, or full dark skirts. It's rare to see a photo of that era in which the people are smiling. Sharon Springs must have been a very popular place at one time.

"Okay! Sorry about that . . . Do you guys have a dinner reservation?"

I turned back around to see Paul Bunyan stepping out from behind the host stand wearing . . . a kilt.

Not that Brent and I were the least bit secretive about our relationship, but whenever we traveled around small rural areas, we were always a little self-conscious of appearing gay. We did this less out of concern for our own safety, but more out of respect for communities that may not have had a fair chance to grapple with the subject beyond the occasional *Jerry Springer* episode.

And there stood Paul Bunyan in a kilt.

"Ah no," Brent said. "We didn't make a reservation. We were just driving by. But if we can get dinner, we'd like to."

Paul Bunyan winced and sucked in his breath.

"Gosh." He looked down at the reservation book. "We're really booked tonight. I'm very sorry."

My heart dropped into my stomach—in which there was plenty of room. I'd been looking over the menu posted by the front desk and had already picked out my three-course meal. Everything looked delicious and local.

"But you can eat here, in the bar area, if you'd like," Paul Bunyan offered brightly. We quickly accepted.

Our dinner plates arrived and were taken away in a satisfied blur. I'd eaten in restaurants around the globe, but I didn't think I'd ever eaten a better meal. It wasn't simply the food—it was the warmth of the fire, the coziness of the bar, and the slight mysterious air of this Brigadoon.

As the last course was being cleared away, Paul Bunyan came by our table. We motioned for him to join us, and he pulled up a comfy leather chair.

"I'm Doug," Paul Bunyan said. He squinched his eyes at us, inspecting. "You guys are from the city," he deduced accurately. "What brings you way out here?"

"We got lost," Brent said.

Doug laughed a big hearty guffaw. "So did I," he said. "Twelve years ago. And I still can't find my way back. *Take me with you!*"

"Please do," another man said as he approached the table. This man was a bit leaner, with a scruffier beard than Doug's and thinner, lighter hair that was graying at the temples. "Is he bothering you?" he asked, putting his hand on Doug's shoulder.

"Am I bothering *them*?" Doug said. "Here I was, literally minding my own business, when in walk these city slickers demanding a meal."

I could already tell that I liked the brash Doug.

"Table twelve wants you to drop by," this second man said.

"My public can wait," Doug said. "I'm hatching an escape plan."

The second man rolled his eyes and pulled up a wooden chair beside Doug's.

"I'm Garth," he said. "How was your meal?"

Garth seemed very gentle and sincere. It had been a long time since I actually believed that someone truly cared how my meal was.

I quickly pieced together that they were the owners of the American Hotel, and that they were, in fact, "together," as my mother euphemistically says. The four of us chatted the evening away. They told us how they'd fled the city in 1996 and wound up first opening a café and bakery up the street. Garth had been a Broadway musician, and Doug had been an actor. We told them about ourselves, that I worked in advertising and wrote on the side, and how Brent had quit being a doctor to work with Martha Stewart. By the time there was a lull in the conversation the giant grandfather clock in the bar was chiming midnight. I looked around only to notice that there were no other customers left. I cast a wary glance at Brent, and then to the clock. Doug picked up on my signaling.

"You two heading out?"

"I suppose we should," I said. Ugh. The Red Roof Inn awaits. "We're going to try to make it to Albany tonight and get a room."

"Why—and I would ask this of any living being—*why* would you want to stay in *Albany*?" Doug asked.

I'd been eyeing the keys in the cubbyholes by the front desk all night. Each time I'd gotten up to use the restroom, more and more of them were missing. There was no way this place would have an extra room in the middle of peak leaf-peeping season, would it? But even as of fifteen minutes ago when I went to the bar for yet another Riesling, cubbyhole number eleven still had its very own shiny key in it. I'd always desperately wanted to stay in the type of place that kept its keys in cubbyholes. It makes me think of movies like *Holiday Inn* and *Same Time, Next Year*. If an establishment cared enough to keep its keys cozy, just imagine how its guests felt. But I'd promised myself I wouldn't inquire about vacancies. The deal between Brent and I was that the day's driver always gets to pick the hotel. And I knew he'd choose the Red Roof Inn.

"You don't have a room here, do you?" Brent asked of Doug.

I couldn't believe what I was hearing. Brent was willing to give up noisy ice machines, fuzzy HBO, and fiberglass shower stalls for cubbyhole number eleven? Brent must have been under the spell of this place too.

Doug shouted at Garth, who was cashing out the dinner receipts at the front desk.

"Did the Schmitters ever show?"

Garth looked into number eleven.

"Nope."

Doug turned back to us.

"Good news, bad news," Doug said. "Good news is that we have a room." He paused for dramatic effect. "Bad news is that there's only one double bed." His face turned serious for the first time in the evening. "And we don't go for homosexualists in these parts."

His tone was so sober that I almost believed him. But an instant later he broke out in his heartiest laugh of the evening as he rose to bring us the treasure of cubbyhole number eleven.

Chapter Two

"They were nice," Brent said once we'd settled into the car the next morning.

"Yep," I said curtly.

"What's wrong?" Brent asked.

"Nothing."

"Nothing big, or nothing small?"

"Nothing-nothing."

"Well, *I* had a good time," he said.

"Me too."

"Then what's bothering you?"

"I don't know," I said. "It just seems like the weekend flew by so quickly. I'm not ready to go back into the city."

It's been said that whenever New Yorkers leave the city, they can't fathom how they live there. But as soon as they return, they get caught right back up in the pace of it all and egotistically proclaim that they could never live anywhere else.

Doug and Garth were kind enough to show us exactly where we were on the map and to trace out the most picturesque route back to the city. It seemed to be pretty much a straight line down Route 10 into a town called Cobleskill and then another forty-five minutes or so until we would hit the New York State Thruway. Then it was a straight two-and-a-half-hour ride right back into the hectic hustle and hassles of the greatest city in the world.

I wasn't ready to go back. I never was after our apple-picking weekends. They gave me just the slightest familiar taste of the slow rural life I enjoyed growing up in a small farm town in Wisconsin. Our five bushels of McIntoshes in the backseat may as well have been from the Garden of Eden. Each bite reminded me of how good it used to be, but how doomed we were to our stressful urban careers and lifestyle.

We didn't need to talk much, thankfully, as we drove down the pretty route that Doug and Garth had picked out for us. Just out of town we passed a picturesque pond and witnessed a flock of geese splash down for a pit stop on its way south. A little farther beyond we passed a herd of Holstein cows on a hill—black and white polka dots against the brilliant orange sugar maples. About four miles away we passed a tiny outcropping of farmhouses punctuated by an archetypal gleaming white wooden church. The Sunday service had just let out. Here was the church. Here was the steeple. Open up the doors and out came the people.

"Wait. Slow down. Here's another historical sign." I would stop for anything to prolong our idyllic getaway. Luckily the entire area seemed to be saturated with state historical society roadside plaques. Whoever the local state senator was, he was certainly bringing home the bronze.

This particular sign was planted on the road in front of an elaborate white house. It was unlike any house that we'd seen in the area. Most of the other homes in the vicinity were either simple turn-of-the-century farmhouses or prefabricated beige boxes.

"What's the sign say?" Brent asked. I rolled down the window and stuck my head out.

"The Beekman Mansion. Built 1802. William Beekman was first judge of court held in Schoharie County. Died here on November 26, 1845. Buried on this farm."

"Is it a museum?"

"I don't know." It looked like a museum. I wasn't exactly an architecture buff, but I remembered enough from when my parents dragged me to Williamsburg, Virginia, as a child to recognize the structure as vaguely Federal. Maybe with a slight Georgian twist. It had white balustrades around the roofline and intricately carved arched moldings above each window. Even in the shade of the double row of centuries-old sugar maples in formation across the front yard, the white clapboard seemed to glow. But the most amazing feature was a massive forty-five-paned arched Palladian window smack in the center of the second floor.

"It's gorgeous," Brent said. I knew that he was appreciating entirely different features than I was. Being from the South, he was probably staring at the ornate balustrades and what looked to be a porch with pillars that wrapped around the back and sides. It definitely had a plantation gene somewhere in its bones.

Being more northern, I loved its elegant but simple symmetry—its four hidden chimneys built right into the boxy home, the ornate but understated carvings painted white against the white background.

With its peculiar and unique details, the house was like a perfect combination of Brent and me—both southern and northern in equal complementary measures.

"Drive up farther," I said. "We'll see if it's open." A building this beautiful had to be a museum. Nobody had a right to own it all to themselves.

As we inched forward, we realized there was a barn just to the south of it—a perfect red barn in the architectural style of Fisher-Price. The white house with the red barn, with the green manicured grass, with the orange maples . . . It was like something out of a Disney movie. I half expected an animatronic milkmaid to stick her head out of the hayloft door and wave at us.

This was nothing like the farms I grew up around in Wisconsin, where the house was generally an afterthought to the outbuildings, and a yard was considered to be whatever patches of grass grew up through the mud. Farms are messy, I'd learned. Really messy. When your business is dependent on inventory that shits wherever it feels like, you can't really be a stickler for neatness.

This farm had style—loads of it. It was, if there was such a thing, a New York City farm.

"I have to see the inside of this place," I said to Brent. He nodded his head in agreement. "Pull in the driveway."

We both sucked in our breath at the same time.

Just behind one of the stone pillars on either side of the driveway was another sign:

REALTY USA. 518-555-3423, MICHELLE CURRAN.
REDUCED.

I read it over at least three times. I was afraid to speak, in case it might break some spell and the sign would disappear. I looked over. Brent was staring at it just as intently.

Then he turned to stare at me.

There was no reason to say anything. We both knew what was coming next. Brent reached for his phone, while I found a pencil and paper to take down whatever information he relayed. He dialed the number and put the phone to his ear. I'm pretty sure his hand was shaking.

"There's no answer," Brent said. *"Shit."*

I'd never heard Brent swear before—or "cuss" as he phrased it with his southern idiom. Being from a family who built and started their own fundamentalist church, Brent was still afflicted with a few good habits he couldn't shake.

"Here, call the guys at the hotel. They know everything about this town," I said, trying to disguise the desperation in my voice. I handed him the hotel's brochure that I'd taken as I left. I knew that if we didn't see this house today, we never would. Not only was there a good chance that I could never find Sharon Springs on a map again, but there was also the reality that the moment we returned to the city we would be sucked back into our respective whirlwinds and completely forget to click our heels to come back to the farm.

"Hi, Doug?" Brent said into the phone. "It's Josh and Brent. We were guests of the hotel last night?" Doug apparently remembered us, and Brent continued. "We were taking the road you told us to take out of town, and we saw this house for sale—it's white, with a red b— Yes, the Beekman Mansion."

People call it by its name: the Beekman Mansion. As beautiful as it was, I wasn't sure I would call it a mansion. Although I supposed when it was built in 1802, it was an even more impressive structure than it was today.

While Brent talked with Doug, I was already imagining my life at the Beekman Mansion. I concluded that Brent and I would probably be known as the Beekman Boys. Or at least I hoped so. It would be far better than, say, the Fag Farmers.

Yes, I thought to myself, I'd like to live in a mansion, even part-time on the weekends. A weekend mansion. A mansion in which to relax, unwind, and do other mansion-y things that I didn't even know about yet. How could I? I'd never lived in a mansion. I wondered if there was a magazine I could get tips from. *Mansion Living.* Or *Today's Mansion.*

And then there was the whole farm aspect of the mansion. Looking around, there seemed to be a great deal of land included with it. I could put in a vegetable garden. There'd be no more hoofing it down to Union Square to buy fifteen-dollar organic frisée. We could get a cow. Every farm needs a cow. Surely someone would help us take care of it during the week in exchange for free milk. And chickens! We'd get the kind that laid the blue eggs, like Martha had. We'd make our houseguests rise with the roosters and go get their own eggs for breakfast.

I stopped myself. This was ludicrous. We were twice as far away from the city as Fire Island or the Hamptons. Even if, by some chance, we could afford a mansion, how would we get up here every week? How would we take care of things?

Brent hung up the phone.

"What did he say?" I asked.

"Well, it's been for sale for over four years. That little house over there is the caretaker's house." He pointed to a small modular home I hadn't even noticed on the far side of the barn.

"Did they know how much it's selling for?"

"A lot."

"A *lot* a lot? Or just 'a lot.'"

"A *lot* a lot. A million."

"You're kidding me. Who would pay a million dollars for something way out here?"

"Still, can we see inside?" The fact that we couldn't afford it in no way dampened my enthusiasm. It was probably completely run down on the inside anyway. A house this old probably had its rooms cut up, with each one remodeled during a different decade. And while owning a mansion was now firmly on my life's wish list, a fixer-upper mansion certainly wasn't.

"Michelle, the real estate agent, happens to be filling in for one of the brunch hostesses at the hotel," Brent said. "It's slow so they said she could be here in five minutes."

Of course she could, I thought. If I were a real estate agent in the middle of nowhere with a million-dollar mansion to unload, I wouldn't care how many people were waiting for their eggs Benedict.

Brent and I passed the time silently while we waited for Michelle to arrive. We were both too afraid to mention our thoughts aloud. They were too far-fetched to deserve being spoken. We weren't sure if the caretaker was home or not, so we didn't want to risk getting out to scout around the place. But simply sitting there at the end of the driveway with Brent gave me a sense of calm. The only noise was the occasional orange leaf that wafted down onto the car's roof. It was the same sort of relaxed as last night's relaxed, back at the hotel. Maybe even *more* relaxed. I wasn't sure of the last time I felt this way.

Michelle pulled her SUV behind us and honked. As she stepped out of her car, I wondered how someone like her wound up selling real estate way the hell out here. She was incredibly stylish, wearing a hot-pink-and-orange-patterned wrap dress. It screamed "fashion magazine editor" far more than "part-time brunch hostess." She was impossibly thin and tall—though maybe no taller than average once out of her knee-high, four-inch-heeled leather boots. The only thing that gave her away as a real estate agent was the way she immediately pushed her sunglasses up on top of her head. They must teach that in real estate school. Look 'em in the eye. Don't let 'em get away.

"Hi there," she sang. "Doug and Garth told me all about you." That's a good sign, I thought. We're already a gear in the local rumor mill. Up close, it was hard to tell Michelle's age. She could have been anywhere from thirty to sixty—another common real estate trait. "What do you think?" she continued. "Pretty impressive, huh?"

Impressive, yes. Attainable, no. Part of me felt horrible for having brought her out here. Having moved around so much in my life, I think that leading on a real estate agent adds some of the deepest chinks to one's karma.

"It's nice," Brent said, poker-faced. "Can we get inside?"

"Sure, that's why I'm here." Michelle smiled. "Follow me around to the side entrance."

As we walked across the yard, Michelle told us much of the same history that we'd learned from the sign out front. Stepping under the ancient maples made me feel historic myself. Old Judge Beekman probably planted these trees with his own hands.

Michelle jiggled the keys in the lock. The door looked to be new or at least well taken care of. I'd expected to see the real flaws of such an old house once we got up close. But like Michelle's face, it appeared timeless. Almost new.

"There we go," Michelle said, swinging open the side door and stepping aside for us to enter. "Most people come in this side door," she continued. "It enters directly into the library."

I couldn't believe my eyes. It *was* just like Williamsburg. Everything I could see had been restored to its original state— or even better, if that's possible. The library had bright yellow wallpaper and ebony floors that shone so brightly that the view from the windows reflected off them. The windows looked to be original too, with wavy uneven glass. At the far side of the room were built-in bookshelves on either side of an ornate, carved arch that led to another large, bright room—probably the formal living room.

There wasn't a speck of dust or cobweb in sight. The ancient house smelled like lemon-scented Pledge. Everything sparkled: the brass chandeliers, the wavy old panes in the windows. The only sign of negligence was the smattering of dead flies underneath each and every window. Michelle caught me looking at them.

"Even though the owner rarely visits, there is a housekeeper who comes once a week," she explained. "Perhaps the vacuum is broken." She quickly changed the subject. "There are seven fireplaces—all in working order. Two of them are completely original, and the others were rebuilt in their original locations." As she narrated the way through the first floor, I had a hard time listening. There were incredible details everywhere that diverted my attention.

"This center hall is over fifteen feet wide," she went on. "As you can see, it runs the entire length of the house, with exits at the front door and onto the wraparound porch. There is a second hall just like it directly upstairs."

Everything in the house looked as if it must have looked on the day that William Beekman and his family moved in. I could tell that the wallpaper and paint choices had been meticulously researched, as were the hardware on the doors, which also looked to be original. The swooping banister on the main stairway in the center hall was carved out of a single piece of cherry wood, according to Michelle. As I ran my hand across its perfectly smooth surface, she confirmed that it too was original. It had been found in the barn while the previous owners were doing the renovation.

"Who were the previous owners?" I asked, thinking that whoever they were, they were flush enough to spend far more than a million dollars renovating a house they were willing to sell for only a million dollars.

"They live down in the city," Michelle answered. "Or at least the widow does. This renovation was really her husband's passion. They have houses all over. He died six years ago."

"Where in the city?" Brent asked. I thought he was being a little too nosy, but since he rarely asked a question without a reason, I was willing to let him go on to see where he was heading.

"The east seventies, I think," Michelle answered.

"Maybe I know her," he said. "I used to be a geriatrician at Mount Sinai. We had a lot of patients from that area of town." When Brent still worked at the hospital, he often tended to VIP patients—i.e., those who had donated large sums of money in hopes of one day dying with better service. We'd get calls at home at all hours of the night. I grew accustomed to being woken up from a deep sleep by a hospital phone call informing Brent that a 104-year-old billionaire patient had died "unexpectedly" in his sleep. Nowadays I was woken up by Brent's BlackBerry, which buzzed all night with a stream of e-mails from Martha, who only slept four hours a day.

"Her name is Edith. Edith Selzner," Michelle added.

"Nope," Brent said, "doesn't ring a bell." But I saw where Brent was going with this. Now that we'd gotten the owner's name and neighborhood, we could look her up and contact her. If anyone could work over an Upper East Side widow till she caved in on price, it was a good-looking "single" geriatrician. These women always had some daughter/niece/cousin they needed to marry off. And for this place, I'd actually let Brent get married to a nice Waspy girl . . . as long as I could come visit.

The tour continued through the second floor, where there were five immaculate bedrooms, each of which had its own bathroom. The wide center hallway on the second floor was identical to the one below, except that it ended with the massive Palladian window overlooking the ancient maple trees. The fiery leaves outside made the entire cavernous hallway—large enough for ballroom dancing—glow.

"That's everything inside," Michelle said. "Would you like to see the crypt?"

"The what?" I said.

"The crypt," she repeated. "The Beekman Family Crypt. It's just in the side yard."

Of course I wanted to see the crypt. Who wouldn't? I wondered how she described that in the real estate listing. "Historic Mansion, 5BRM / 5BA / 7 FP / 1 CRPT."

Michelle led us out the kitchen doorway, down a slight slope past a row of apple trees, which were perfectly hung with bright red fruit—even bigger and shinier than the ones we'd picked yesterday. Does the caretaker shine the apples? I wondered.

We turned the corner around a slight hill and were met with a double stone–walled entry, ending at a solid iron door. There was a giant white obelisk at the entry, carved with the names and pertinent dates of Judge Beekman, his wife, and his children.

"Um, are they still inside?" I asked, not really wanting to know the answer.

"Go ahead and look," Michelle said, gesturing toward the iron door.

"It's unlocked?"

"Yes. This whole area was overgrown during the time the mansion was abandoned," she explained. "This entryway itself had completely collapsed. High school kids used to climb in through a hole on the roof and throw the bones around."

I made a mental note not to hire any local high school kids to do yard work. Once we owned the mansion, of course. And by now I was convinced that we would own this house.

"But Mr. Selzner had it completely restored. Here, look at this," Michelle said as she pulled what looked like a thick stick from between the cracks of the stone entry wall. "It's a bone. There are lots of them around."

Oh God, she was right. In nearly every large crack in the wall was a protruding bone—arm bones, leg bones, unidentifi-able bones. Whoever repaired this wall was one creepy mother-fucker.

"C'mon, let's go in," Michelle said cheerily.

Brent slowly pulled open the heavy iron door and disappeared into the darkness, followed by Michelle. I wasn't quite ready yet. I listened to their voices inside.

"I've always thought this would make a great wine cellar," I heard Michelle telling Brent.

"Or a great place for a Halloween party," Brent offered.

Call me superstitious, but I didn't think Old Judge Beekman

would have appreciated sharing his final resting place with a case of Sutter Home.

"Come on in, Josh," Brent called out. "It's cool."

I took a calming breath and stepped into the darkness. There was a slight step down, and immediately the temperature dropped at least 10 degrees. It took a few seconds for my eyes to adjust to the near complete darkness. My skin felt wet.

In the dim light I began to make out shapes. The crypt was larger than I'd expected. It was difficult to tell how cavernous it was from the outside since it was built into a hill. The interior looked to be about ten feet by fifteen feet. It was entirely made of stone, and the ceiling was constructed in a graceful barrel arch. From it hung an iron candle chandelier. At the far end of the wall were what looked to be shelving. I deduced that that was where the coffins were once stacked.

"What happened to the caskets?" I asked.

"Dunno," Michelle said. "Long gone."

Not everything was long gone I quickly realized, as I rested my hand on the shelf only to discover I was petting a human jawbone.

I gasped. "It's someone's head!" I said.

Brent, the doctor, immediately inspected my find and offered positive identification—as if a bone that looked like someone's chin could have been anything other than a jaw.

"Yep," Brent concurred. "And here's a tooth. And here's a sheet of lead left over from someone's coffin." He tried to hand me the tooth. I politely declined.

"The workers found a lot of bones around here when they were restoring the grounds," Michelle explained. "Most of them were reburied under the slate floor. But some they found later, I guess, and just put them inside. Rumor has it Beekman went through a lot of slaves."

As if it wasn't bad enough to have been desecrating some rich white guy's bones, we were also fondling the remains of people who had good reason to hold a grudge.

"And now let's see the pool," Michelle called out, exiting back into the light. "It's right next to the crypt," she added, "so if any of your guests drown, you won't have far to drag them."

I assumed she was joking. Then again, we were dealing with people who live in a veritable ghost town. Death and dying probably didn't faze them much.

The rest of the tour went by quickly—too quickly. I forgot to take any pictures of the interior, or the crypt, or the pool, or the historic barn, or anything, really. I had nothing to remember the place by—the place that for a couple of hours at least, I imagined would be mine.

But it was all too grand anyway. I couldn't think of a single reason why I deserved to have a place like this. This was not a place where I would live. This was a place where Martha would live.

I was the first to head back to the car while Brent and Michelle pointlessly exchanged e-mails and whatnots. I rolled down the window to breathe in the country air one last time. Now we'd have to race to get back to the city in time for Brent's dinner meeting.

Brent slid into the driver's seat.

"We are going to own this place," he proclaimed with steely determination.

"We can't afford a million dollars."

"Then we'll talk her down."

"To what? Half?"

"To whatever we need to," Brent said. "Don't you like it?"

"That's not really the issue," I answered.

"Just answer the question."

"Yes, I like it. Of course I like it. I love it, in fact."

"Then we're going to get it," Brent answered. I still looked dubious. "Look, I get paid a lot of money. You get paid a lot of money. We're very fortunate that way."

He was right. We were very, very fortunate. I worked hard to get to where I was. I'd worked my way up the corporate ladder after having started out by dancing on speakers in clubs in order to pay the rent. He'd worked even harder. Seven years of study to become a doctor, and then three more for his MBA. We had the money. We just weren't used to living like we had it. We were still packed into the same small apartment we'd had for the last seven years; the same small apartment we'd moved into while he was still a resident.

Wasn't it time to splurge a little? Everyone else we knew had been buying up weekend places in the Hamptons or Fire Island. Maybe it was time to relax, to cut our pace a bit. If we had a nice weekend place in the country, I could write even more.

I could write a book about a high-powered advertising executive and his vice president boyfriend who cashed it all in to lead simpler lives as gentlemen farmers.

It would be a bestseller.

I'd get rich.

I'd live in a mansion.

Three weeks later, we made a lowball offer and it was accepted.

Chapter Three

We delayed the closing until spring—partially to enjoy one last winter without heating bills, and partially to be sure that we weren't experiencing a sort of conjoined temporary insanity. There wasn't much in either Brent's or my résumé that would have indicated that we were destined for either a farm or a mansion—and certainly not a combo.

We were both raised without much money. We both went to work as soon as the laws in our respective states allowed. In fact, if my first job at age twelve was any predictor, the last place I wanted to spend my middle-age years was a farm. In my rural Wisconsin, the summer of sixth grade didn't mean summer camp and pool parties; it meant "detassling corn." Dozens of us would be dropped off by our parents each morning outside the gates of Waukesha County's largest farm. We stood there in the beating sun, or pouring rain, like pint-size illegal alien itinerant workers clutching Smurf lunch boxes. Eventually a parade of massive tractors hauling flatbed wagons would roar down the road. Once they reached us, they would slow to about 15 mph— just enough for us to run alongside in a mad scramble, chuck our lunch boxes aboard, and swing ourselves up onto the wagon like miniature hobos.

The wagons would take us out into the cornfields where we

would walk dozens of miles down rows of five-foot-high corn plants, reaching over our heads to strip the stalks of their deceptively fuzzy tassles at the top. In reality, the tassles were like prom corsages made of razor wire, which, over the course of weeks, turned our soft preteen pink hands into the calloused mitts of steelworkers.

For all this, we earned $1.65 an hour, and we were to be grateful since it was a dime over "agricultural juvenile minimum wage." The fact that Wisconsin even had such a designation should explain why the state is now complaining that it doesn't have enough young farmers left to take over its agricultural industry. Drinking warm milk from a thermos cup held by bleeding hands at high noon four miles deep in a cornfield makes even the most dedicated Future Farmer of America fantasize about an exciting career in accounting or insurance adjustment. Or drag queen turned ad guy, as the case may be.

Brent's upbringing was in many ways similar to my own. He worked at McDonald's through high school in North Carolina, and put himself through college, med school, and business school while working full time. He completely paid his own way and walked away with every degree without a penny of debt.

But even though our combined industriousness had paid off with rewarding careers, we still weren't accustomed to spending much of the money we made on anything other than necessities. During the winter following our discovery of the Beekman Mansion, Brent and I debated whether we should really go through with the closing. We padded around our cozy 850-square-foot urban apartment questioning what could prepare us for owning a 4,500-square-foot historical mansion and 100-year-old barn located on 60 acres. How would we possibly be able to take care of all that? Our home repair tool kit consisted of a hammer and two screwdrivers—one of which was for eyeglasses.

But for every argument I had one unbudgeable rebuttal: I was in love with the Beekman. Having spent a good part of my child-hood growing up relatively poor, the prospect of owning a man-sion complete with pool and formal flower gardens represented some sort of recognition for the hard work I'd done to get to the place where I could afford it. And the fact that the Beekman was also a farm brought my dreams in a strange full circle. I often felt my hard-won advertising career came at the expense of the values with which I was raised. It's no secret that American ad-vertising sometimes stretches truth to the point of breaking, just like the slow-motion cheese-pull shot in a Pizza Hut commer-cial. While I'd somehow avoided typical career conundrums like shilling cigarettes to children, I had to occasionally readjust my moral compass in the pursuit of a paycheck. Early on in my ca-reer, for example, I'd been assigned to the U.S. Marines account. At the time I'd managed to convince my staunchly pacifist and gay self that recruiting disadvantaged young men and women into a life-threatening and homophobic environment was a fair tradeoff for their prospect of free tuition down the road. A few years later, when challenged with the task of making horse rac-ing sexy again for the National Thoroughbred Racing Associa-tion, I enlisted Hollywood celebrities and recruited fashionistas to the nation's horse tracks, knowing full well that what I was re-ally doing was making those with gambling problems feel cool.

Owning a farm, I felt, would at least bring me back in the direc-tion of my Wisconsin roots. I could grow my own food, support a hard-hit local economy, and metaphorically raise my middle finger at the factory farm industry that was causing so many of our nation's ills—from high-fructose-corn-syrup-induced diabe-tes and obesity, to hormone-injected meat that caused nine-year-old girls to grow breasts.

Of course nine-year-old girls with breasts sounded like some-thing I might dream up to help sell hormone-injected meat had I been assigned the challenge.

My weariness with advertising had been growing over the years, but particularly lately during my agency's regular status meetings. Each week, the creative department gathered around the large conference room table to report on its progress on current assignments.

During one of these meetings that February, I realized that I'd been working on one particular project—a print campaign for a medium-size health insurance company—for exactly one year. All that was needed were three quarter-page newspaper ads. Three. I'd presented dozens of campaigns over the previous twelve months, flown to six different cities across the United States to sell them, worked over the Christmas holidays, and sat in five rounds of focus groups, and was now rereading the same exact status report as I had one year ago.

And I'd gotten a huge bonus because of it. But I hadn't, as one of my colleagues was fond of saying, "moved the ball down the field" even an inch. I was working nights, weekends, and holidays and getting nowhere. All that mattered, though, was that I kept the clients happy. Success to many clients equals working hard and ending up with nothing. You can only get fired for doing something wrong if you've done something in the first place.

I guess I really am good at what I do.

But I knew—I knew—there was more I was born to do. There had to be something else—something I could show for my life other than a clutch of television commercials and some magazine ads. Even a fistful of corn tassles seemed more substantial.

At the Beekman, I could plant corn again. And detassle it myself (even though twenty-five years later, I still had no idea why corn needed to be detassled in the first place). And perhaps eventually, as we paid the mortgage down, we could sell our apartment in the city and live a full-time life of stylish agrarian subsistence at the Beekman. My days as a corporate shill could be over sooner than I'd planned.

By the time we'd settled on a closing date, I'd sold myself on the idea that I was only a few years away from penning my last tagline, which was one of the biggest pitfalls of a life in advertising. If you start buying your own bullshit, you risk becoming management material.

Chapter Four

"You first."

"No, you first."

"I'll carry you."

"Like hell you will," I said. "You're not going to drop me and break my neck on my very first day as a mansion owner."

We'd barely made it to the Beekman Mansion's front door while there was still light outside. The days were growing longer as the spring was progressing, but the sun still disappeared around 6 P.M. It was remarkable how far behind the seasons were in Sharon Springs compared to the city, a scant four hours south. While the trees were in full leaf back home in Central Park, in Sharon Springs the majestic oaks we stood under the previous fall barely had visible buds. It still felt more like February than the end of April.

"Okay, I'll go first," I relented. "I'm fucking freezing."

Only ten hours ago we'd woken up exclusively urban dwellers. It had been a busy day for both of us. Brent stayed behind in the city to finalize the mortgage, while I took the train to Albany to go see about buying a car. It'd been years since I'd purchased a car . . . thirteen, in fact—the entire time I've lived in New York City. And I'd certainly never purchased a pickup truck before. Everything I knew about trucks could fit on a lesbian's pinkie finger. But as new farmers, I reckoned that we would need one, as well as begin "reckoning" rather than merely thinking. So the moment I arrived at the Albany train station, I took a taxi to a random used car dealership with an envelope containing $20,000 cash. I had no illusions that I could possibly outwit a seasoned used car salesman, so in the end I drove away with a 2004 used Ford something-or-other and the reassuring conviction that I'd been completely ripped off.

None of that mattered though when I picked Brent up at the train station. Still in his suit and tie, I thought he looked hilarious climbing up into the passenger seat of our "gently pre-owned" truck. He was grinning wider than I'd ever seen.

"Let's go!" he said, holding up the signed mortgage papers. *"We're officially gentlemen farmers!"*

"Hurry up," Brent said. "It's like January out here."

The wind had picked up, and my fingers were growing numb as I tried to jiggle the key every which way in the lock.

"Maybe it's the wrong key," I said. Michelle had left the key under the mat for us.

"Nope," Brent replied. "I asked her at the closing. She'd just used it yesterday."

I was beginning to debate whether the bed of the pickup truck or the shelf in the crypt would be a more comfortable place to pass the night when the key finally caught and the door swung open.

"It's ours!" I shouted, stepping inside. My cry echoed through the bare rooms for a millisecond before it was joined by a shrieking, high-pitched alarm.

"What's that?" Brent shouted over the ear-shattering noise.

"It must be the burglar alarm."

"What burglar alarm?" Brent yelled.

"Exactly," I replied, searching the dark walls near the door for either the light switch or alarm panel. I found both, and flipped on the library light. The digital alarm control, however, wasn't as simple to figure out.

"Looks like we need a code," I shouted. *"What's the code?"*

"How would I know?" Brent shrugged.

"Didn't they give you anything at the closing?"

Brent dug through his briefcase and handed me a two-inch-thick sheaf of official-looking papers. The alarm was deafening. I prayed it wasn't hooked up to the local police precinct. What a fine impression that would make. "Those two new city boys—you know, the girly ones—couldn't figure out how to break into their own house."

A minute later and both Brent and I were on the floor with the hundred sheets of official closing documents fanned out in front of us. We had to find the damn code. The alarm continued its wail. Compounding our difficulty were the damn dead flies that covered the wood floors in a dark carpet of carcasses. Everywhere we stepped, or knelt, hundreds of exoskeletons crunched underneath us. If we weren't so panicked about the alarm, it would've been nauseating.

"Check this one," Brent yelled, handing me a stapled packet of invoices and Beekman budget figures. I flipped through the pages, looking at the numbers associated with running the Beekman Mansion on a monthly basis. Holy shit. When figuring out how to afford the Beekman, we'd come up with guesstimates for heating, electric, maintenance, etc. But even quintupling the amounts on utility bills we pay on our Manhattan apartment didn't come close to the numbers I was looking at:

GARDENER: $4,500/YR

POOL: $480/MO

CARETAKER: $24,000/YR
ELECTRICITY: $850/MO
HEATING OIL WINTER AVG: $1,200/MO
NATURAL GAS WINTER AVG: $900/MO
TRASH PICKUP: $400/MO

The list went on for two pages. School taxes. Property taxes. Painter. I mentally began crossing off list items that I knew we'd never be able to afford, starting with "Gardener." Then "House-keeper." Basically everything a boy from Wisconsin would be too embarrassed to have in his life anyway.

Finally I got to the line item I was looking for: "Security." I scanned the address and phone number of the company listed below.

"Give me your cell phone," I shouted to Brent. He tossed it to me and I went back out onto the freezing porch to escape the noise. Shivering, I punched in the numbers.

"Hello, Northeastern Security," the woman's voice answered wearily on the other end of the phone. She sounded tired. Of what, though? I can't imagine that the Schoharie County private security dispatch was generally swamped with emergency calls.

"Um, hello," I began. "I, uh, I mean my partner and I, um, just bought a house here in Sharon Springs, and well, we just arrived for the first time and weren't aware that the alarm had been set."

"What's your name?" she asked.

"Kilmer. Well, it's two names, actually—Kilmer-Purcell. But it won't be in your system. We haven't switched over the billing information."

"So the previous resident would be 'Purcell'?" the unalarmed alarm operator asked.

"No, that's *my* name. Kilmer-hyphen-Purcell. My first name is Josh." I didn't know why I felt compelled to be on a first-name basis with the alarm dispatcher. But people were friendly up here, I assumed. Maybe some neighborly familiarity would speed things along some.

"What's the address?" she asked.

"It's . . . uh, hang on a sec . . . I don't really know . . ." I realized that I was sounding less and less like the homeowner and more and more like a very ill-prepared cat burglar. "We just pulled in, and the key was under the mat . . ."

"But it's your house?"

"Yes, but the name on the account won't be mine." I couldn't help but think that I was making things worse for myself. "Look, I don't know the address, but it's the Beekman Mansion."

"Where are the Beekmans?" she asked, thoroughly confused.

"No, no, the Beekmans are dead."

"Excuse me?"

I quickly realized that this call was going from petty larceny to twenty-to-life.

"Brent!" I shouted through the porch window. *"What's the address here?"* He couldn't hear me through the glass and over the piercing alarm. *"Brent!"* I yelled louder. *"BRENT!"*

"Who's 'Brent'?" the alarm woman asked suspiciously.

"He's my partner," I answered, immediately realizing that the woman now thought we were a team of cold-blooded killers on a cross-country breaking-and-entering spree.

The alarm's wailing was drilling into my head, and I couldn't stop shivering in the chilly early evening air. My voice was beginning to quiver along with my shivering, and I was sure that the dispatcher was simply trying to keep me on the line while she summoned up the local sheriff. I figured I had nothing left to lose . . .

"Look, we just bought this house together but no one gave us the alarm code—or at least we can't find it anywhere—and I'm standing

on the porch freezing my ass off hoping that you'll turn the alarm off so that my boyfriend and I can walk around our house for the first time ever."

"Brent is your boyfriend?" she asked. Sweet Jesus. Now I was going to have to explain homosexuality to this woman.

"Yes, Brent is my partner. My boyfriend."

The other end of the line was silent, except for some rustling of papers. Either she was relaying this new incriminating information to the sheriff or she was busy praying for our souls. I looked at Brent through the window, still frantically looking through the papers for the code.

Suddenly the alarm was silenced.

It echoed in my ears for a few seconds longer before it was completely replaced by the quiet of the country air. I could hear some early crickets or frogs peeping off in the distance.

"Okay, Josh," the woman cheerily returned to the line. "We've got that taken care of for you. But do me a favor, hon, and call me back in the morning to give us all the new information on the account. You'll do that?"

I was confused but relieved.

"Um, yeah. Sure. I'll call first thing. Promise."

"Just ask for Linda. You boys have fun in your new home now," she said sweetly. "Good night."

"Good night, Linda . . . and thank you," I said right before she hung up. I didn't know what I'd said, but somehow I'd convinced her that we weren't deranged, murdering thieves.

I wasn't used to being trusted. Living in the city for so many years had trained me to doubt everyone and bristle with defensiveness at the slightest hint of altercation. Also, after working in advertising, I found myself entering every conversation as if I needed to persuade the other person to either think or act as I wanted him or her to. I spent the vast majority of every day trying to come up with ideas that would convince people to spend money on the things I wanted them to. I had to sell them into buying what I was offering.

But Linda just took my word that I was the new owner of this mansion. I told her the truth, and she bought it. Was everyone like this around here?

This was going to take some getting used to.

Chapter Five

HERE COMES THE BRIDE!

We're woken up by what sounds like someone performing Wagner's wedding march on Model T car horns.

Brent and I had been told that we'd inherit several chickens, rabbits, and one barn cat with the farm. For the time being, we understood, they were still being taken care of by a neighbor.

"Was that a rooster?" I asked Brent.

"You're the one who grew up in Wisconsin," he said sleepily.

"I think it was." But rather than the old standard _COCK-A-DOODLE-DO_, the song stuck in this rooster's head was the classic bridal entrance theme. A few seconds later, he was joined by another rooster greeting the day with "It Had to Be You." They were quickly backed up with choruses of "Papa Don't Preach" and "The Little Drummer Boy." Our farm sounded like a bad cover band.

We jumped out of our temporary sleeping bags gleefully, if not still a little groggy. Having moved into a grand total of eighteen different houses and apartments during the first half of my life, there was still no thrill like waking up the first morning in a new one. I silently hoped that this would be a home I'd wake up in for the rest of my life. While there would always be bigger castles, and more temperate locations, and more expensive addresses, I couldn't imagine a single place more serendipitously perfect for Brent and me to grow old in. The sturdy 205-year-old farmhouse, standing high on a windy hill, represented the sense of permanence and stoicism I've always admired in people. I was waking up in the same exact spot as at least ten generations of people who came before me. In fact, the first morning someone woke up in this spot, America was still composed of only seventeen states, and had only purchased the Louisiana Territory a month earlier. Napoléon was belching his way across France. President Thomas Jefferson was having sex with a slave at Monticello. In fact, someone might have been having sex with a slave right here where I lay.

As we'd learned from our online research, the Beekman Mansion was home to many slaves, and decades later was also a stop on the Underground Railroad to freedom. As a writer, I was thrilled to discover that a young James Fenimore Cooper probably dropped by to play with the Honorable William Beekman's children. We'd also read that a century or so later, during the mansion's descent into abandonment, the Beekman Mansion was a popular squatting place for transients.

Slaves, freed slaves, senators, judges, novelists, and hobos had all passed through the room I'd just woken up in. Though Brent and I had had doubts about whether it made sense for us to buy the Beekman, at least its history proved that we didn't make any *less* sense than someone else.

Since we'd yet to discover any thermostats, the house was extremely chilly. We walked around the house in our underwear with our sleeping bags wrapped tightly around us, trailing the long ends behind us like the lucky kings we felt we were. When we reached the kitchen we discovered that someone—probably the previous caretaker whom we could no longer afford—had arranged all the makings for a fire in the kitchen fireplace.

Even though I'd never officially had one to begin with, I realized that I was going to really miss having a caretaker.

Brent found matches next to the hearth, and in seconds a fire was blazing away, with us huddled in front of it.

"Should we get dressed and drive into town for breakfast?" I asked.

"Don't you want to walk around the property first?" he replied.

"I do, but I'm starving," I answered, realizing that between the train ride, the search for a truck, returning to the station to pick up Brent, and the alarm fiasco, I hadn't eaten a bite since yesterday's breakfast.

"Maybe there's something in the pantry," Brent said.

We rooted around the kitchen, but came up with nothing but a box of Lipton Tea tucked on a back shelf and two well-used, dented saucepans.

"We can go to the Stewart's for a doughnut," Brent offered, referring to the lone convenience store we'd seen on our way in.

"I want something hot, though," I said. "But I can wait. I'll be okay."

Brent knew this wasn't true. He'd been the victim of my hypoglycemia many times. My protestations were merely hallucinatory—like Julia Roberts in *Steel Magnolias* politely declining orange juice while descending into a diabetic coma.

"I have an idea. Come with me," he said.

"Where?"

"Just go get dressed," he answered.

A minute later we were traipsing across the backyard—*our* backyard. I'd never personally owned a backyard. The closest I'd ever gotten was an apartment with a doublewide fire escape. Brent was heading toward the barn—*our* barn. The morning was chilly, but not as cold as the previous night had been. The grass beneath our feet was trampled and brown, having borne the weight of the region's legendarily deep snowfall for the last seven months. The ground itself was solid, still deeply frozen, but when we came upon the part of the yard that had been reached by the morning sun, I could smell it.

Mud.

Dirt + Water. I'm not sure I'd smelled true springtime mud in over a decade. We didn't have real mud in New York City. We had close approximations like Filth + Water. And Grime + Pee.

So this is spring, I thought. I'd nearly forgotten what it felt like. It felt good. The direct sunlight felt warm on the skin, unlike the sunlight reflected off skyscrapers and diffused by thick air. The ground beneath my feet reminded me that the earth's naked surface was porous, not sloped toward the nearest sewer grate. Hearing a robin chirp as it hopped along the driveway reminded me that birds make noises, not just piles of poo on top of window air-conditioning units.

While I stood soaking in the spring all around me, Brent walked ahead and opened the side door on the barn—*our* barn.

"C'mon," he called to me. "Check this out."

By the time I reached the doorway, he was deeper inside. As my eyes adjusted to the dark, I listened to the sounds around me. Cooing. And clucking. And then, suddenly: *HERE COMES THE BRIDE!*

I jumped back toward the door.

"Look!" Brent yelled, startling me even more. In the dim light of the barn, through the swirling haze of floating hay particles, I spotted him. He stood just inside what looked to be a makeshift terrorist holding cell framed into the corner of the barn. He was holding up a small gray ball.

"What's that?" I asked.

"An egg!" he answered. "For breakfast!"

"That's an egg?" I questioned dubiously. "Lemme see that."

"I just figured that where there were roosters, there'd be eggs," he continued. He was so excited that I decided not to point out the obvious flaw in his knowledge of poultry reproduction. He proudly and gently handed over his find. It was more spherical than ovoid. And the surface seemed to give a little in my grasp. Rather than a shell, it appeared to have more of a thick skin. Up close I realized that I'd originally thought it was gray in color not because of the dim light, but because it was semitranslucent.

"Are you sure this is a chicken egg?" I asked.

"Of course it is," Brent answered. "It's in the chicken coop."

It was hard to fault his logic.

Much to the agitation of the chickens and roosters, Brent dug around in the straw-filled cubbyholes mounted to the wall. The longer we stood in the coop, the braver the poultry grew. Within thirty seconds I had four birds pecking at my shins.

"C'mon. Let's get out of here," I said nervously. "Once they get the taste of human blood there's no stopping them."

"There are dozens of eggs," Brent said, continuing to root around in the nests.

"Just grab three," I said. "That's all we need for breakfast. We'll get the rest later."

As we crossed back over the muddy earth toward the house, I turned the eggs over and over in my palms. Our first meal. Entirely provided from our very own farm. This was what it's all about, I thought. Even though I hadn't so much as tossed a handful of grain at these chickens, I had an overwhelming sense of accomplishment. I was feeding myself. I was convinced that soon I'd be creating feasts that were entirely grown and raised on our land—feasts that would be the envy of the greatest New York restaurateurs.

Back in our kitchen, I took down one of the old saucepans,

filled it with water, and placed it on the stove. There was no butter or oil, so I decided to poach the eggs. We stood around the
saucepan waiting for the water to boil.

"What will we eat the eggs on?" Brent asked. "There are no
plates."

"We'll just use our fingers. Like in the olden days."

"They had forks in the olden days." Brent sighed.

As soon as the water began bubbling, I cracked one of the
eggs against the side of the pot. Well, crack might be too strong
a word for it. With its leathery skin, I just sort of pressed it down
against the lip of the pot until it began to tear. The first egg
slipped easily into the water. It swirled around perfectly, cling-
ing together as if it were giving itself a hug.

"Look at how orange that yoke is," Brent observed as I tore
apart the "shell" of the next egg with my fingernails.

"It's orange because the chickens get to eat in the yard," I
explained. I remember my mother teaching me this when we
used to buy our eggs from our Wisconsin neighbor—an ancient
woman who also happened to be the town dogcatcher. When
we'd drop by the woman's house, my mother would push me out
of the passenger-side car door and watch me hopscotch over a
checkerboard of dog droppings that dotted the patchy front lawn
leading to her kitchen door, and then hopscotch back. I think
I developed my talent for dancing in seven-inch heels without
spilling my drink by hopscotching over those dog piles while
carrying two dozen eggs.

The two eggs swirled lazily in the bubbly water, their whites
turning slowly opaque. I reached for the third and final egg. This
egg was the smallest of the three, and probably the least likely to
win an egg beauty pageant. Its shell was on the soft side like the
others, but it was also sort of pockmarked. It seemed less like an
egg and more like what a Hollywood special effects department
might have crafted to portray an alien egg sac.

The skin was a little tougher than the others. I repeatedly poked at it with my thumbnails.

"Go get a pen out of my bag," I said. "Let me see if I can get a hole started . . ." The egg sac tore suddenly and the contents plopped into the pot.

Brent, who had been peering down into the pot just beneath me, reared up quickly, knocking me in the chin with the back of his head.

"What is that?!" he yelled.

Before we could react to the sight of the viscous moss-green blob that had dropped into the pot, the stench hit us. It was completely overwhelming. I retched and backed away from the stove.

Brent, with a stomach trained by years as a doctor, was the first to peer back into the pot, where a swirl of gray-green goo was enveloping the other two perfect eggs.

"What is it?!" I echoed.

"I think it's spoiled," Brent answered, poking at the bits that floated to the surface with his finger.

"Don't touch it," I said, horrified.

It hadn't occurred to us that simply because it was our first day at the farm, it may not have been that particular egg's first morning. Or second morning. It could just as likely have been its fortieth morning. I wasn't poaching eggs; I was performing a partial birth abortion.

"Scoop it out of there," I said, still not quite able to look.

"With what? There are no spoons. Besides, it's all spread out now."

"Are the other eggs done?" I asked.

"I think so, but they're coated in the green stuff."

"We'll just wash the good ones off," I said.

"No way. There's no way I'm eating those other eggs."

I did see his point. As far as contaminants go, that third egg was toxic enough to shut down a Chinese baby formula factory. But that was part of country life, I thought: unpredictable. Food wasn't sorted, and radiated, and sterilized into conformity as it was in the supermarket food chains. These were our very own eggs, and by God, we were going to eat them.

I moved the pot to the sink and used my fingers to pull out the largest bits of green goo. After a quick rinse under the faucet, the two good eggs floated to the top, with their glistening orange yokes. I gently put one in the palm of my hand and offered it to Brent.

"Uh uh," he said. "You first."

I tipped my head back and dropped the blob into my mouth. I rolled it around a bit with my tongue before I bit down on the orange yolk. In an instant my mouth filled with the most vibrant flavors. It was richer and smoother and thicker than any egg I'd ever tasted. It tasted exactly like a newly mowed lawn smelled, and coated my tongue like slowly melting Swiss chocolate.

Brent stared at my face, looking for any signs of a toxic reaction. I smiled and held out the pot with the remaining egg.

"These eggs," I mumbled through the liquid gold in my mouth, "are worth a jumbo mortgage."

Chapter Six

The rest of our first weekend in our new country house was spent exploring the sixty acres surrounding the Beekman, greeting neighbors who stopped by to tell us their stories of the mansion, and sweeping up dead flies. It seemed that the minute we swept a room clean, flies began dropping to the floor again like, well, flies. It was impossible to tell where they were coming from. They just appeared at the windows, carpeting the sills and floor with their slow-motion death throes. We had yet to see a fly that was actually flying. They just kept coming and coming, like a buzzing *Night of the Living Dead*.

Doug, Garth, and Michelle seemed to have prepared the town for our arrival. Nearly everyone who came by to visit already knew that Brent worked for Martha Stewart, and that I had written a couple of books, though no one seemed particularly interested in my literary career. Everyone, however, wanted to talk to Brent about Martha.

I was used to listening to the same old questions and answers about Martha. Ever since Brent began working at Martha Stewart Living Omnimedia, all of our friends and family wanted to know what Martha was *really* like. It was understandable. I remembered how excited I was the first time I'd met her. Brent had been invited to her East Hampton home to discuss some business details regarding a new geriatric center they were creating together at Mount Sinai Hospital. Since it was the Fourth of July weekend, I was invited along to share lunch on her patio.

Martha was only a few months out of prison at the time and was still under house arrest. She was allowed to travel short distances for business reasons, and somehow this weekend luncheon at her beach house qualified. Under her capri pants, her ankle monitoring device, which looked something like a buckled seat belt, was clearly visible. It looked uncomfortable and hot, but she neither drew attention to it nor tried to hide it.

I'd met Martha in her kitchen, which I'd recognized from dozens of photos and television specials. She was making our meal. When we'd been invited to her house for lunch, I hadn't expected her to actually be making it herself. But there she was, making freshly ground tuna and wasabi patties with her bare hands, just like my mother. (If my mother made freshly ground tuna and wasabi patties.)

Given Martha's reputation as a stern taskmaster, I was a little nervous about standing around doing nothing while she cooked.

"Can I help with anything?" I asked.

"Yes, thank you," Martha replied in her adopted Connecticut clipped enunciation. "Would you cut up that celery for the salad?"

I stared at the stalks of celery lying perfectly and crisply prone on the counter before me. I was frozen with fear as the questions started a pileup in my mind.

How big? Diced? Chopped? Do I string it first? Didn't I see her string celery on a Thanksgiving special once? Do I cut straight across? On an angle? Which angle?! Forty-five degrees? Twenty degrees? A slight but decorative slant? Isn't this a paring knife? Don't I need a chef's knife? Can celery be pared? Is this a cutting board or a platter? What if this is the meat cutting board (which must be washed with a

*light bleach solution—Martha Stewart Living, January 1992) and
not the vegetable one (which should be rubbed with a cut lemon to de-
odorize a lingering onion smell—November 1996)? Is the proper way
to slit one's wrist across the veins or along the veins? Can I die without
getting any bloodstains on Martha's spotless kitchen floor?*

I closed my eyes and went for broke.

Chop.

I looked up. Martha hadn't exploded in a rage. So I continued.

"So, Josh, tell me," Martha said, as she began washing freshly
shelled peas in a Martha Stewart green strainer. "What do you
do?"

"Well, I work in advertising," I answered, "and I write."

"Oh. Interesting. What do you write?"

"Um. I, ah, wrote a memoir," I answered, pronouncing "memoir" with an overly pretentious French accent in an attempt to
make a joke out of the fact that I—at only thirty-six years old—
had already written the story of my life. "Mem-MWAAHHE."
The joke fell flat. Apparently French accents aren't all that pre-
tentiously out of place in East Hampton.

"A memoir?" Martha continued. "What did you have to write
a memoir about?"

I looked over at Brent. He furrowed his brow in warning. But
what could I do? She asked me.

"Weeeellll, um, I, uh . . . I was a drag queen for many years
and I worked in nightclubs, but I had a, well, little drinking problem that put me in, ah, rather sordid situations, and then I met
a boyfriend whom I thought was going to help me clean myself
up, but he turned out to be a, um, male escort specializing in, ah,
sadomasochism who I also eventually found out had a massive
crack cocaine addiction, which didn't help my drinking issues.
But it's not all that sad; it's more of a tragicomedy, if you know
what I mean, because, well, I did a lot of funny things and all my

costumes had live goldfish swimming around in my fake tits—
er—breasts, which was really quite creative, Martha. You would
have really appreciated it. Because it was creative. It was like Halloween all year round. A lot of crafting went into my costumes.
Really, it was quite creative. And crafty. Really. Crafts . . ."

For some reason, I thought that if I could successfully reframe
my checkered past as one big craft project, Martha could relate
to it better. She couldn't.

The resulting silence seemed to last forever. Standing there in
the kitchen I'd seen so many times on television, I'd desperately
wished that fate would somehow intervene and cut to a commercial break.

Instead, Martha turned off the faucet, shook the strainer of
wet peas, looked me in the eye and said:

"So. *Are you normal now?*"

I remember biting my tongue to keep from blurting out: "About as
normal as a sixty-five-year-old billionairess wearing a federal penal
system ankle monitor." But I didn't. It was an interesting question.
Looking back, I don't think she was judging, just asking. I think
she would've agreed that she, herself, wasn't all that "normal."

And in fact, at the time she'd asked, I had become far too normal. I'd left behind my drinking, drugs, and drag, and had fallen
into a predictable pattern of work, sleep, and, well, more work
and sleep. And while I might have successfully saved my health,
my life had certainly lost a lot of its entertainment value—not
just for others, but also for myself. I was just another ad guy going into work each day, tossing off a few commercial scripts, and
pretending that I was so much cooler than the accountants, executive assistants, wholesalers, and Wall Street suits riding the
subway car home with me each evening. But it was growing
harder and harder to convince myself.

So purchasing the Beekman was both a step backward and forward at the same time. For good or for bad, buying a farm was just as unexpected a move for an urban gay ad guy as putting on a dress and a wig. Maybe I was well on my way back to abnormal.

Funnily enough, the sheer absurdity of owning a farm felt just as comfortable and wildly unpredictable as my drag gigs in nightclubs. I was excited again for the first time in several years. I had so many new dance steps to learn, so many new costumes to try on. What did I know about owning a farm? My future was suddenly as promising as a roll of free drink tickets once was to me.

By Sunday night, when Brent and I piled into our new truck for the return trip to the train station, we had a to-do list that filled two full pages of a yellow legal pad—both sides. The house needed to be painted. The barn had to be cleaned out of old furniture and equipment. The chicken coop was nearly shin-deep in fossilized manure. Instead of being daunted in the face of all these unfamiliar tasks, I was energized. Finally, I was in unfamiliar territory again without a map.

No, Martha, I wasn't normal yet.

But it had been a close call.

Chapter Seven

Dear Brent and Josh,

I heard about your purchase of the Beekman Mansion from Doug and Garth at the American Hotel. I hope you don't mind me writing to you, but I wanted to see whether you might be looking for a caretaker.

My name is John Hall, and I grew up in Sharon Springs. I have always admired the Beekman, even when it was abandoned and falling apart. It is a beautiful house and farm. If I were caretaker of the Beekman, I would keep it in a condition so that people driving by would want to stop and stare at it.

I am an avid gardener and also own several goats. I always wanted goats as a child. They are very friendly and peaceful. I recently broke up with my partner and am living at my parents' home. If you are interested in having animals, I could bring my goats to the Beekman as well. My ex-partner is letting me keep them at his farm for the time being. I have another month to find them a new home before I have to sell them at auction.

I am including a picture of me in my vegetable garden, and with two of my newest "girls," Darla and Dana. They were born two weeks ago.

Sincerely,

John Hall

Brent looked over my shoulder at the letter and two enclosed photos we found tucked in an unmarked envelope that had been placed in our mailbox. One photo was of a husky balding man who seemed to be about forty-five holding on to a sunflower stalk that must have stood at least twelve feet tall. He was smiling broadly. At his feet were vines and flowers of what appeared to be a lush vegetable garden.

In the other photo, the man was sitting—with the same broad smile—on top of an upturned bucket. On his lap were two small animals . . . either goats or sheep. I couldn't tell. Or more accurately: I didn't know. The goats/sheep were suckling at two bottles he held in either hand. I couldn't tell who seemed more content—the animals or the man. In both pictures the man's smile seemed so honest, guileless. Having lived in New York City for so many years, I wasn't used to seeing a smile that didn't have an agenda behind it.

I was jealous of the man in the pictures. How wonderful it must be to have a job that is instantaneously rewarding. He didn't have to create sixty-page PowerPoint presentations on how to market an aging airline brand to leisure travelers. He didn't have to hold daylong management meetings about year over year growth strategies and merger possibilities. After our first stay in our new second home, the past week in the city had seemed interminably long. All I could think about was returning for our second weekend at the Beekman.

"Don't even think about it," Brent warned.

"But look at how cute they are."

I knew exactly what Brent was concerned about. Being a proud student of Martha's, he was worried about messing up the barn—and the smell. Brent had visited Martha's stables at Bedford. They were spotless and smelled faintly of orange disinfectant. Some people throw around clichés like "so clean that you could eat off of the floor" metaphorically. But Martha actually serves her Thanksgiving dinners each year *in her stable.*

"We can't afford a caretaker," Brent said.

"Maybe he'd work for free. We could give him the empty house and pay for all his utilities." We still hadn't decided what we were going to do with the small modular home where the previous caretaker lived.

"I'm not sure that's fair to him," Brent said. "Besides, we could make some money renting out that house."

"But we can't go on asking the neighbors to feed the chickens during the week."

"It's a fair trade for eggs."

"Look at these baby goats," I said, holding up the picture again. "If he doesn't find a home for them in a month, they're going to have to go to the auction house. And I don't mean Sotheby's."

Brent took a second look at the picture.

"We can't afford it," Brent said again.

"Baaah . . ." I said, in my best imitation of what a homeless baby goat might sound like.

"That's the noise sheep make," Brent said. "And, by the way, the correct name for baby goats is 'kids.'"

"See? You know so much about goats already," I said. "Your mind is a terrible thing to waste."

"Look," Brent said. "We don't need a barn full of animals. We're not real farmers."

"But we wouldn't even have to do any work," I protested. "They're John's goats. All we'd need to do is pet them on the weekends."

"No."

"Okay. You'll think about it."

"No."

"Just get back to me once you've decided."

"No."

"So you'll sleep on it."

"No."

We spent the next forty-eight hours having the same conversation. While we were cleaning out the hayloft:

"You know what eats hay? Baby goats."

"No."

While we were sweeping up the past week's worth of dead zombie flies:

"Goats eat anything. I bet they eat flies."

"No."

While we were arguing about living room paint colors:

"You know what else butts heads?"

"I said *no.*"

Sunday evening rolled around without my being able to get so much as a single "maybe" out of Brent. He argued that we had enough chores on our hands simply trying to keep a 205-year-old house in one piece. I argued that John would actually be helping us. He could keep the lawn mowed and do some other light handiwork.

In Brent's defense, our first two weekends were incredibly full of chores. We worked from sunrise to sunset trying to keep the property in pristine, Martha-worthy condition. Adding yet another element to the farm, especially one that wasn't toilet trained, would probably only complicate our lives even more, which was exactly the opposite of why we'd purchased a weekend home. We wanted a place to relax, to get away from our respective offices with their own peculiar *Animal Farm* style of politics.

I tried one last time on the train back to the city.

"Did you know that goat pupils are actually rectangular?"

"No," Brent replied. "And *no.*"

Much to both of our dismay, Brent was unable to come up to the Beekman the following weekend. He had to travel with Martha to the West Coast for a weeklong string of business meetings ending with a weekend spa retreat in Arizona.

Since it seemed he and I were only able to scratch the surface of chores in our allotted forty-eight-hour visits, I'd decided to surprise Brent while he was away by taking an entire week off of work to check off a wide swath of our Beekman to-do list.

On my first day alone at the Beekman, someone delivered a thin promotional paper to our mailbox called the *Penny Saver*. It was a miraculous publication. I found listings for everything from pool services to house painters to exterminators, and had begun referring to it as "my own personal *Penny Savior.*"

By Tuesday I had a veritable army assembled at the Beekman, and by Wednesday the property was humming with activity. The life was welcome. Without Brent, I'd found the cavernous, empty house to be a little bit lonely at night, and the wide-open windswept fields to be a little desolate by day.

By the time I had to return to the city the following Sunday evening, I'd had the pool opened, new gravel put in the driveway, half of the mansion's east facade painted, the chicken coop cleaned out, the massive flower beds raked, summer screens placed in all of the windows, the gutters gutted, and the lawn mowed.

Brent would be amazed at all I'd accomplished when we returned the following weekend.

Perhaps he'd be so surprised that he wouldn't even mind the eighty-eight goats in the barn.

Chapter Eight

"What was that?" Brent asked as he pulled his heavy briefcase out of the backseat of the pickup truck. A large June bug buzzed past my ear in its kamikaze rush toward the truck's dome light. The evening was surprisingly warm. Our trip to the farm from the train station was slowed by a heavy fog that clung along the roads. My mother used to call this summer nighttime phenomenon a "witches haze."

"What was what?"

"That noise."

"Probably one of the roosters."

"At ten o'clock at night?"

"Maybe he's rehearsing."

"Shh," he said. "Someone's in the barn."

"No one's in the barn," I said, sighing, just as another loud thud echoed across the yard. Shit. I'd hoped that we could make it inside the house, go to bed, and wait until the morning for a tour of all the work that had been accomplished. Winding up, of course, in the barn.

"Oh, whatever," I said. "You're going to find out soon enough. Follow me."

The sliding barn door was heavy, and it took me three heavy pulls before it gave way. Its squeaky protest jolted the barnful of goats into a rousing chorus of "baaahs."

Brent glared at me.

"Just come in and look," I said.

The moment I flicked on the light, eighty-eight goats of all shapes and sizes rose to their feet at once and came running over to the edge of their pens to greet us.

"Oh God," Brent said.

"They're so wonderful," I quickly retorted. "So friendly."

"I can't believe you did this after I clearly said no."

"If after nine years together you still haven't learned that I don't listen to you, then you clearly deserve what you get." I crossed my arms, content with such a logical argument.

Brent sighed.

"What are we going to do with all of them?"

"Nothing. We don't have to do anything with them. Co-farmer John takes care of them."

"You hired him?"

"No, I didn't 'hire' him," I explained. "We don't have to pay anything other than some utilities."

Brent shook his head in disbelief.

"Why didn't you wait until we could talk about this more?"

"Because you would've have said no again. I'm not stupid."

He seemed frozen in place.

"Go on," I said. "Climb in the pen and pet them." The pens were divided by the goats' relative ages. The mothers were in one, the ones born earlier in spring in another, and the very newest ones were in yet another, huddled under heat lamps.

"I have my suit on," Brent said. "I don't want to get dirty."

"Well, go inside and change then," I said.

"Maybe tomorrow," Brent said, turning away. How was he resisting their allure?

On the walk back to the house he kept several steps in front of me.

"Are you mad at me?" I asked his back.

"I'm pissed," he replied without turning around. "We're supposed to be doing this together."

Once we were in the house, he headed straight up to the bedroom. I heard the shower running, then shut off. I'd bought some local cheese to make him an omelet for dinner using our eggs. But he didn't come back downstairs.

By the time I went upstairs to check on him, he was already asleep, having broken our rule of not going to bed angry with each other for the very first time.

The full moon shone across the bed, outlining his curled-up form. Maybe he was right. Maybe my decision had been too rash. What had I been thinking? Wasn't taking care of a 205-year-old mansion enough of a weekend job? Did we really need a herd of goats to complicate matters? I hate when I begin to doubt myself. Especially when it involves things that can't be undone.

I've always been too impetuous . . . and capricious. That's why I used to wake up on the F line at 6 A.M. with stubble growing through my makeup, one high heel missing, and a chorus of tiny empty Absolut bottles rolling across the subway car floor. Last call, my ass.

And this time, I'd started a goat farm, practically overnight. This could potentially be my longest hangover to date.

Being superstitious, I walked over to close the curtains on the far side of the bed. My grandmother used to warn me that sleeping in the light of the moon would bring on madness. And since I might have lost my marbles, I couldn't afford Brent going insane as well.

Brent was already out of bed when I woke up. A quick check of the kitchen showed that he wasn't making me breakfast in bed either. Not really a surprise. I threw on my coat and pulled on my muddy boots and headed outside. Either he was still mad at me and had gone for a walk, or he'd forgiven me and, well, probably not.

Even though it was the beginning of June, the morning air was still chill enough to see my breath. The yard had blossomed in the past few days with millions of dandelions. While I supposed most homeowners would've been perturbed with their omnipresence, to me they were as beautiful as any wildflower. I'd been pleasantly surprised by the waves of different perennials and wildflowers that had been springing up in the backyard's formal flower garden. The Beekman grew more beautiful each passing week.

I slipped quietly through the barn's side door. The only sound from inside was the rhythmic munching of goats chewing. John must have just finished his morning chores, the last of which was filling the feeders with hay. I'd asked him just after he arrived why the goats didn't go graze in the fields like the storybook pictures of my youth, and he'd answered that they were still a little too timid. It would take a month or so for the skittish herd to grow adventuresome enough to go exploring.

"Brent?"

I heard a whisper from the far end of the barn.

"Over here. Shhh."

My eyes adjusted to the speckled darkness. Bits of hay chaff floated through the air, catching what little light streamed in from the dusty windows.

"What's going on?" I asked, approaching him slowly. He was peering intently over the edge of one of the pens.

"Shh. Come look."

"What? I don't see anything."

"Look at that goat in the corner."

On the far side of the pen, against the wall, a brown-and-white goat was contentedly munching on a mouthful of hay. She was a Nubian goat, I believe. Farmer John had explained the different breeds to me on their first day here. Her ears were long and floppy, and her nose broader and more pronounced than the Alpines and Saanens.

"What's going on?" I asked.

"Just watch a second."

The goat held our eye contact for a few seconds longer, then turned to walk back to the feeder for more hay.

"Holy God!" I said. "What the hell is that?"

An immense bubble, probably about ten inches in diameter, was protruding from her hindquarters, just beneath her tail. She seemed completely unaware of it as she nudged her fellow goats aside to reach the feeder.

"It's the birth sac, I would assume," Brent said.

"That thing? It's huge! Does she even know what's happening?"

Just then she raised her head and let out a long, anguished bleat. The bubble pulsed a little and grew larger.

"I'm pretty sure she knows something's up," Brent said.

"Shouldn't we go get John?"

"I already went and knocked on his door, but he must be out," Brent said. "There's no truck in the driveway."

"Should we call nine-one-one? Is she breathing correctly?" I was remembering the many stories of our pregnant New York City friends who underwent months of Lamaze training and practiced simulated childbirth in family-size hospital hot tubs. None of them ever described a giant bubble being blown out of their hoo-has.

Brent rolled his eyes. The mother goat raised her head and bleated again, retreating as she did, back toward the corner of the pen.

"It sounds like she's in pain," I said. The translucent bubble bounced as she walked past us. "What's that stick in there?" I

said, noticing a pointy dark protrusion in the shadowy depths of
the birth sac.

"Probably a snout or a leg."

"Shouldn't we *do* something?" I said, growing far more anxious than the mother appeared to be.

"She's just giving birth. It's totally normal."

"Normal? She has a foot-wide bubble coming out of her ass.
If I'd figured out that trick when I was a drag queen, I could've
retired on tips."

"Goats give birth all the time," Brent explained. "There's no
way that Farmer John could be here for every one."

We stood and watched in silence for several more minutes as
the mother alternated between eating, bleating, walking around,
and reclining. While she was lying down a third time, she let out
the loudest bleat thus far, and then craned her neck around to
inspect her hindquarters.

"Can you see anything?" I asked Brent. Her back end was facing away from us.

"She's licking something," he answered excitedly. "I think it
was born. Let's go in and check."

"Go in? Is that allowed?"

"Why not?" Brent said. "I don't see visiting hours posted anywhere."

We slowly climbed over the top rung of the pen and hopped
down onto the soft hay-covered floor. Several of the other
mother goats were startled and stampeded to the other end of
the enclosure. But they slowly wandered back a moment later to
sniff at our pant legs and sleeves. The youngest kids were bolder,
crowding around our feet and nibbling at our shoelaces. The
new mother remained reclining, licking at the small glistening
jelly-covered shape behind her, which was struggling to stand up
on its spindly legs.

"It's like Bambi!" I whispered excitedly.

"Except not a deer," Brent clarified.

"Right. Not a deer."

We crept closer to inspect the newborn. Its coat looked to be mostly shiny black with several patches of white. Suddenly the mother stood, which severed the umbilical cord and assorted other birth detritus that hung from her hind end. She walked to the far side of the pen, leaving the newborn behind, steaming on the hay.

"We startled her," I said. "Maybe we should go."

"It's okay," Brent said, crouching down next to the newborn. It was roughly a foot and a half long, and in between futile, wobbly efforts to stand, it laid on its side, flanks heaving with its first chilly breaths.

"It's beautiful," I remarked. "Is it a he or a she?"

"How would I know?" Brent asked.

"Well, that seems a topic that would've been covered sometime during med school."

Brent lifted up one of the kid's hind legs.

"I believe it's a boy," he said, reaching down to pet the slick baby kid. Two other kids, probably not more than a week or so old, came over to greet their new cousin. Not counting a heavily censored sex-ed video in sixth grade, it was the first time I'd actually witnessed something being born. I was shocked at how easy—and messy—it all seemed. The clumps of bloody goo surrounding the new kid looked a little superfluous to me. Was all that glop really necessary? If human beings could engineer a spotless McDonald's take-out window, couldn't God have done the same?

Our perfectly pastoral moment was interrupted by another loud bleat across the pen. It was the same mother again.

"What's she doing now?" I asked. "Maybe she wants us to leave her kid alone."

As I spoke, another package of slimy goop fell from her back end and landed with a thud on the pen's floor. The other goats continued with their munching, oblivious.

"She's had another," Brent said, rising from his squatting position.

"Just like that?" I asked, incredulous. "I thought labor lasted for hours."

"Well, I think she's been in labor at least since I came out this morning."

"No, I mean 'labor.' As in 'laborious.'"

"Giving birth really isn't that big a deal," Brent said. "It's been happening without much fanfare forever, you know."

"Not with our friends," I say. "Most of them schedule C-sections to fit in with their yoga schedules."

The mother was attending to her second born. She first licked gently around its snout, removing whatever bits of birth Jell-O might have been impeding the kid's first breaths. The second baby was more fawn in color, punctuated with black spots around its head and neck.

Having grown completely acclimated to our presence in only a few minutes, all of the goats, except the mother, were now crowding around us. They nudged at our thighs trying to get our attention. For what, I'm not sure. Food? Petting? Maybe it didn't even matter. They were just happy for the company, it appeared. They even looked to be smiling. Having come out to the barn dressed only in my thin sweatpants and T-shirt, I was grateful for the crowded warmth. Brent seemed to be too, as he scratched two goats under their beards. They craned their necks toward him in sheer bliss. The other baby kids, crowded out by their mothers, retreated en masse to a corner where they began a tiny head-butting Olympics.

It would've been harder for me to feel any further away from the city than I did at this moment. The soft hay under my feet, the earthy smells, the furry textures . . . there was absolutely nothing remotely similar to it within miles of our Sixty-third Street apartment. I crouched down to envelop myself even more in this living goat group hug, and was immediately tousled and toppled by a surge of curious goat snouts. They licked my ears and hair. I squinched my eyes shut, feeling their hot breaths about my head and neck. I couldn't help but begin giggling. Brent joined in, tickled at the sight of me being stampeded by a herd of goats.

Our bliss was again interrupted by a piercing bleat. I struggled to stand to my feet again amidst my adoring fans.

"My God. She's dropped another one," I said. Our prolific mother was already busy licking the coat of her third kid, which had landed smack dab on top of the second. "How many is she going to have?"

"I've got no idea," Brent said. "Maybe if I knew we had goats before I got here, I could've done some research."

"She's not a goat," I said. "She's a clown car."

We stayed and played with the goats for another hour or so. Eventually, the firstborn kid miraculously managed to half walk, half drag himself over to his two new siblings. The mother finished cleaning them off, as they writhed and struggled in an instinctive urge to stretch tall enough to reach her udder. Before climbing out of the pen, Brent walked slowly over to the mother, who was patiently standing still while her brood lunged for her teats. Brent reached out his hand, and she extended her nose to sniff it. Her demeanor seemed no different from any of the other goats in the pen, as if she was completely unaware of her accomplishments during the previous hour.

"Good girl," Brent said softly. "Good mom." She ducked her head for Brent to scratch around her floppy ears. "Good job."

Good job, I agreed silently in my head. In less than an hour, this mother had completely erased any grudges Brent may have held against me this morning. Good job.

Chapter Nine

In the course of only a month we'd turned the Beekman back into a living, breathing farm. With goats now grazing in the fields, John had excess milk to feed to a newborn calf he'd bought down the road, whom we immediately named Cow.

Cow was a Holstein bull calf. John explained to us how dairy farmers often sold off their male calves to their neighbors for very little money, to raise for their own beef. While it seems obvious, we hadn't realized that on a dairy farm, females rule. With the exception of a stud or two, males of any animal on a dairy farm just take up space and feed. (And since the invention of frozen semen by mail, sometimes not even that.)

When John explained this fact of dairy life to me, it made perfect sense. Until I looked around and realized that the barn was full of adorable baby kids and roughly half of them, by sheer odds, were male, including one we'd seen born less than one month ago. I swallowed hard.

"What happens to male kids?" I asked.

"They go to auction," he answered. There was that auction word again. "The early ones go for Russian Orthodox Easter, and the later ones for Ramadan."

Though I wanted to believe that Russian Orthodox Christians put colorful bonnets on the kids and herded them down the street in a festive Easter parade, I had a sinking feeling that the only parade they'd be attending went from the oven to the table.

"How much money do you get for them?" I asked.

"Depends on the day," John answered. "Sometimes forty dollars. Sometimes fifteen."

Fifteen dollars? That was it? I wanted to run into the house and bring out cash to buy up the whole lot of male newborns. But I also knew that that wasn't how things worked. If this was going to be a working farm, I'd have to play by the rules.

Another one of those rules was that a farm should grow its own food. It seemed as if the only amenity the Beekman didn't have when we bought it was a vegetable garden. I'd grown up in a family that ate for most of the year from what was harvested and preserved from our quarter-acre vegetable garden.

And what we couldn't grow on our own, we picked by the pound at local farms. From the period of 1978 to 1985, my mother pickled, froze, canned, and preserved metric tons of foodstuffs.

At the time I hated all of it.

My friends all ate brown-bag lunches consisting of whatever was the most current prepared snack food being advertised on Saturday-morning television. I, on the other hand, ate raw snap peas and plain jelly sandwiches made from strawberries that I'd picked, washed, and stirred in five-gallon stock pots over a hot stove in the middle of July. I still have a slight hunchback from spending the daylight hours of every summer vacation hunched over, pulling up the crabgrass and stinging nettle growing between the endless rows of green bean plants. When McDonald's first came to Oconomowoc—which was an unattainable luxury for us—I remember my mother baking breaded zucchini sticks and trying to convince me that they were "just like" the French fries we couldn't afford.

They weren't.

Once I moved to New York City—the epicenter of gourmet food markets—I saw that my mother could have made a killing with her elderberry jellies and raw fermented sauerkrauts if she'd only had access to the buyer for Balducci's. I too had come to belatedly appreciate my indentured green-thumbed upbringing. Maybe it was the first time I forked over seventy-six dollars for a dozen heirloom tomatoes at the Union Square Greenmarket that I finally realized the gifts my parents had given me with our garden.

The garden seemed like so much work as a kid. But now it seemed quaint in comparison to the daily stresses I faced with my job, Brent's job, and New York City in general. At least at the end of a long row of green beans, I used to have a basket of something to show for my work. What did I have to show for myself now? A reel of television commercials and a tiny two-room apartment that would have fit in the garage of our modest Wisconsin ranch house.

I'd decided that we needed to have a vegetable garden at the Beekman in order for it to be a true farm. It was getting fairly late in the season to put one in. If I wanted to have any kind of harvest this fall, I'd have to start now. Luckily I had the four-day Memorial Day weekend ahead of me to get it accomplished.

"I think I'm going to put in a garden this weekend," I told John.

"That's good," John replied.

I'd learned that John was a man of remarkably few words. Part was due to shyness, but another part was that brevity seemed to be the official local dialect. I am the sort of person who could chat on and on about everything from the war in Afghanistan to the latest in spring menswear. In Sharon Springs, however, I was learning that the art of conversation was less like the rapid volleying of bon mots, and more like playing volleyball with balloons. It was almost as if there was a daily quota of words assigned to the county, so each response was measured and meted out as carefully as candy to a child.

"Can I borrow the rototiller?" I asked.

Part of John's initial letter to us listed every piece of farming equipment he would be bringing with him. Pretty much the only piece of machinery I recognized was the rototiller. It was certainly the only one I had any hope of successfully operating.

"Sure. I gassed it up yesterday," John answered.

"I think the best spot is out on the other side of the old silo foundation, out past the raspberry patch."

"Um-hm," John responded, sounding neither overly affirmative nor pessimistic.

"Do you think the soil will be good there?'

"Could be."

"I got some pea seeds down at the Agway."

"Might be a little late for peas."

"Do you think so? I was reading online that they could be planted up until the end of May."

If John were the chuckling sort, I'm sure he was stifling one. I doubted many people in Sharon Springs got their gardening information from any source ending in ".com."

"If it stays cool enough, maybe," John said doubtfully.

"It's been a cool spring," I said, repeating a tidbit I'd picked up at Agway along with the peas.

"It has."

"And there was a surprise frost last night." Another Agway sound bite.

"Yep."

I could see that John's daily noun/verb ration was running out, so I wandered over to the tiller, gave it a grunting push, and rolled it out into the sunlight. It was heavy . . . and stubborn. It took me five minutes to push it a mere twenty yards.

I was halfway across the barnyard, alternating between pushing and tugging the reluctant machine toward the prospective garden patch, when John took a break from his own chores. He walked over to me and gave the starter cord on the tiller a mighty pull. It turned over with a roar. He put the machine into gear and the wheels sprang into action. He quickly squeezed the clutch on the handle to keep the tiller from sprinting across the yard. Over the noise, he motioned for me to grab hold where his hand was, and proceeded to wordlessly show me which gears moved the machine forward or reverse, and which activated the tines.

I steered the tiller toward the small twenty-by-thirty-foot patch of grass that I envisioned would supply our multitude of summer dinner parties. Though there still was a spring chill in the air, I was sweating profusely by the time I reached my destination. I tugged at the lever that I thought activated the tines. It did. They began spinning, slowly and determinedly, tugging at the long weeds. At first the tines simply scraped at the surface of the ground as I walked back and forth over my plot of dreams. The grasses wrapped themselves around the axle of the tiller's blades. By the third pass I'd accomplished nothing more than collecting what looked like a large knotted spool of raffia ribbon.

Just when I convinced myself that I was going to harvest nothing more than hay, one of the tines sank into the hard, clumpy dirt . . . and immediately kicked up a baseball-size rock that rocketed with great force directly into my shin.

"Fuck! Ow!"

But there, in the concave hole where the rock had just been, was a bare spot of dirt as black and rich as any I'd seen in my Wisconsin youth. I wiped my sweaty forehead with my sweatshirt sleeve and pushed onward, forward, back and forth, up and down what would eventually be the rows of my heirloom vegetable Eden. Each pass across the plot drew new bruises on both shins as rocks, chunks of old fenceposts, and random rusty machine parts shot up out of the earth, as if it kept its own artillery down below.

Strangely, the most common pieces of detritus were bones. Ranging from the size of a thumb to a shin (literally), the ground was coughing up as many gray and stained skeletal pieces as rocks. I hadn't thought about it, but the number of dead animals that must have been buried this close to the barn over the course of 205 years must have been staggering. And I hoped they were animals. For all I knew, I could just as easily be desecrating an old slave burial plot. If that was the case, I prayed they were gaining some comfort in watching the plantation master sweat his own ass off with bleeding shins.

For the next six hours I shoved, and grinded, and clawed at the muddy ground. Occasionally I'd spot Brent around the barnyard, but I had no idea what he was doing. I was completely focused. I didn't feel a minute of chill as the sun set behind the hills of Cherry Valley off to the west. By the time I noticed John shutting off the light inside the barn after the evening milking, the purple cloudless evening sky was just barely light enough to keep me from chopping my own feet off. When John appeared in the barn's doorway, I could see him squinting out into the darkness toward me and the sound of the tiller's engine. Having been inside with the goats all afternoon, he'd surely forgotten that I'd been steadily hacking away. He stood and watched me for a minute. I'd like to think he was impressed that this city boy had been sweating at his chores for as long a time as he had been.

As he crossed the yard to the small "co-farmer's" cottage, he avoided making eye contact.

He was probably still thinking that it was far too late in the season to plant peas.

My next three days were consumed with the alchemy of turning my six-hundred-square-foot neglected pasture into an oasis of silken chocolate earth. I arose at the first *HERE COMES THE BRIDE!* and brought my morning cup of coffee out to the "garden" where the tiller waited for me, coated in dew. I'd come to learn its most intimate secrets, from the barely audible squeaking when one of the tines needed readjustment to the complaining flatulence when the gas tank ran low.

Brent came to check on me occasionally, but he'd been with me long enough to know that when I become obsessed with a task, it's best to stay out of my way—especially if I'm wielding a piece of heavy machinery outfitted with rotating claws.

My only real company was Bubby the Barn Cat. Bubby sat on the fencepost by the garden-in-progress and watched me toil through most of the day. Occasionally he jumped down to glide between my feet as I tilled my rows, defying the spinning tines of death in an effort to get me to pick him up and carry him on my shoulder.

Bubby was another of the animals we'd inherited with the farm. Most of the barn cats I'd known in my youth subscribed to the "good mousers should be neither seen nor heard" philosophy. Perhaps having escaped the weighted-burlap-bag-tossed-in-cow-pond fate of most barn kittens, they felt it best not to tempt further human contact.

But Bubby was different. When he was introduced to us by the previous caretaker's wife, she'd explained that from the day he mysteriously showed up at the Beekman he'd always been the number-one mouser at the farm. His large size attested to his skills. Back then he wasn't any friendlier than most barn cats, she told us, but he was the best at his job. He didn't tolerate anything smaller than a foot long within a hundred-yard vicinity of the barn. He was known to sit high in the hayloft door, watching for approaching intruders in the surrounding fields. Within a split second, he'd run down the hay conveyor belt, leap onto the split rail fence, and race down the pasture, reaching his victim before it even knew it was in a war zone. We were pretty sure it was Bubby's remarkably bright goldenrod-yellow eyes that gave him his super-feline x-ray vision.

Then one evening a few years ago Bubby was struck by a car on the road in front of the house. He survived till morning. The caretaker and his wife spotted him at sunrise dragging himself toward the barn on his front paws. Even with his back legs mangled, Bubby was not going to miss a day of work. They called the Selzners, the Beekman's previous owners, who instructed them to bring their chief mouser to the vet and to spare no expense in his treatment and recovery.

Which is how Bubby wound up being perhaps the only barn cat in the world with his hip held together with an intricate patchwork of titanium rods. His nickname was "Bionic Bubby."

And, as if he knew how fortunate he was, he also returned home from the animal hospital as the world's most grateful and loving barn cat.

By the time the sun had reached its highest point in the sky on Memorial Day, I'd spent three full days working the rough patch of dirt. It probably wasn't ready for a *Martha Stewart Living* photo spread yet, but at least I had workable dirt that could sustain life.

"What do you think, Bubs?"

Bubby, perched on my shoulder, carefully surveyed the new garden with me, making sure that I hadn't unearthed anything mammalian. Along the side of the garden, I'd made one pile for the rocks I raked through and another pile of all the bones. The bone pile was easily three times as large. I picked up a shovel and scooped them into the wheelbarrow, filling it almost to the point of overflowing. I wheeled it through a broken section of the split rail fence and halfway up the eastern pasture. When I reached a spot fifty yards or so from the garden, I tilted the wheelbarrow sideways, letting the various bones slide out into the deep weeds.

I didn't know if there was an appropriate catchall, reburial service for two hundred years' worth of mixed remains of Native Americans, slaves, childhood victims of scarlet fever/consumption/measles/etc., cows, chickens, and horses. But as I took my hands and spread the bone pile more evenly across the springtime pasture, I hoped that the past spirits took some solace in my efforts to revive, even on a small scale, a part of what they contributed their lives to years ago.

Now we were a real farm.

Again.

Chapter Ten

———

"What do I do with this?" Jason, one of the summer interns at my ad agency, asked me. He was holding his mug of coffee in one hand and staring quizzically at the produce dangling tentatively from his other.

"You eat it," I answered, sweeping up the scattered dirt that had fallen onto the counter in the agency's kitchen area. A crowd had gathered around the basket filled with the earliest bounty from the Beekman garden. One of the account executives, Julie, was holding an egg with the same perplexed look on her face.

"Don't you have to *do* something to eggs before you can eat them?" she asked.

"Well," I answered, "You can fry them or boil them—"

"No," she interrupted. "I mean, are they *safe*? Do we have to sterilize them somehow?"

It would've been easy to make fun of my colleagues' lack of knowledge about where food comes from, but I was actually quite pleased at the number of them checking out the array of dirty and misshapen produce I'd arranged under a sign with the handwritten words: BEEKMAN FREE FARMERS MARKET. Most New Yorkers barely grocery shopped, let alone knew the details of the journey their food took before it reached the store.

"Rinse it off and take a bite," I instructed Jason. "Go on."

He held it under the running faucet for a moment, as tentatively as if it were going to wrap around his wrist and climb up his arm. He shook off the excess water drops and took a minuscule nibble with his front teeth.

"What *is* it," he asked, obviously not quite sure if he liked it.

"It's a radish," I answered. He immediately broke out into a wide grin.

"Oh *yeah*! It *is*!" he responded, as if he was finally able to reconcile the sharp taste in his mouth with his memory of a salad. "I've never seen a *whole* one!"

Within minutes the basket was empty of the Cimarron lettuce, French breakfast radishes, Freezonia pea shoots, baby Bloomsdale spinach leaves, and the few tiny Scarlet Nantes Half-Long carrots I'd picked early because I was too excited to let them mature. By the time I returned to my desk, I had a dozen e-mails asking me for more details about the garden. What else was I growing? What was I holding out from them? Did I have beans? Potatoes?

I'd grown to relish my role in the office as a sort of rural conquistador. It was like I'd opened up a trade route to far-off mysterious lands. Excursions for many of my colleagues meant weekends in the Hamptons, shopping at the same high-end stores and eating at restaurants manned by the same chefs as in Manhattan. By comparison, my three-hour weekly trek to Scoharie County was practically the Silk Road. I'd already advised one colleague about how to plant tomato plants on her Brooklyn fire escape, and another one was considering buying a couple of chickens for her Bronx backyard.

Over at Martha Stewart Living Omnimedia, Brent too was enjoying his role as gentleman farmer. On rainy weekdays, he'd taken to wearing the shiny black rubber barn-mucking boots he bought at Walmart to his work. The fashionistas there loved them, and he'd already had to bring back several pairs in women's sizes.

The only downside of our new nomadic life was how long the week seemed in between the weekends. I hadn't expected to feel so at home at the Beekman as quickly as I had. We'd purchased it as a second home, but it was already easily winning our affections over our home in the city.

We'd also made many more new friends in Sharon Springs than we'd expected. The sudden rash made me realize how many of my friends in New York City were colleagues. All of them, really—just another indication of how my career was beginning to completely define me. In Sharon Springs, our new friends seemed to have no real interest in the advertising and marketing world. The Stewart's Shops convenience store at the village's only stoplight didn't carry *Adweek* magazine or *PR News*. It was surprisingly much more rewarding to spend five minutes talking about the weather in the Agway parking lot than at a three-day seminar about the future of digital direct marketing. Okay, maybe it was just surprising to me.

An additional bonus of having a new social circle in Sharon Springs was that they never made me feel uncool. New York City sometimes seems like one large competitive cocktail party. From the moment I chose an outfit to wear each morning to the moment I chose which new restaurant to eat at in the evening, I felt as if every choice I made was being evaluated by my friends and colleagues. Was the new belt I was wearing stylish? Or at the very least, ironic? Should I risk eating at that new Indonesian take-out place that had just opened in a warehouse basement near my office? It was recommended by a popular blogger, but there was clearly a rat's nest behind the stairway leading down to the entrance.

Like most advertising agencies, the average age of the employees at mine seemed to hover around twenty-four. Most of the people I worked with were born just around the time I was busy being uncool in high school. It felt as if I'd had a brief moment

of inexplicable popularity sometime in my twenties, mostly at-
tributed to my drag queen escapades, and ever since I'd been slipping back toward geekdom or worse—complete irrelevance. I
only knew a handful of successful advertising colleagues who
managed to be gainfully employed past forty-five. The rest, I was
convinced, were shipped away to the Midwest after they showed
up to work one day wearing the wrong shade of denim. Hell, I
didn't know if "denim" was a word anymore.

But none of that mattered in Sharon Springs. I could show up
at the Agway wearing my high school prom tux and the person
behind me in line would still just bitch about the rain.

To celebrate all of our new "uncool" friends, and to thank
them for all their help in getting the Beekman back up and running, we decided to throw our very first party a few months after
we'd moved in. Brent had planned for it to be an old-fashioned
Fourth of July picnic, Martha-style, with bunting on the porch,
grass-fed hamburgers, sparklers, and, to top it all off, a cherry pie
from the cherries of our very own tree.

We'd watched all spring as the old cherry tree in the backyard
grew heavier and heavier with ripening fruit. Two weekends before the Fourth, I followed the advice of someone I'd met in line
at Agway (of course, where else?) and purchased a large roll of
black plastic bird netting. It wasn't easy to cover the twenty-foot
tree, but Brent and I finished it late the previous Sunday evening.
We knew that by the time the holiday came around, the tree
would be laden with jewel-red fruit, unscathed by the flocks of
birds that called the Beekman their home.

"I think we should crank our own ice cream to put on the
cherry pie," Brent mused on the train trip up to the Beekman
that long holiday weekend.

"I don't think we're going to have time to make our own ice
cream," I said. "The cherry tree is loaded. Most of the weekend
will be spent picking, pitting, and freezing them."

"Oh, that can't take more than a couple of hours," Brent said.

"Look at my palms," I said, holding them out for his inspection. "See how white they are?"

Brent, not knowing exactly where this was heading but equally certain that I was about to make a pointless point, rolled his eyes.

"They were permanently bleached from pitting sour cherries, day after day after day, when I was a child. One tree will give buckets and buckets of cherries."

"Your hands were not permanently bleached," he sighed.

"They're awfully white, aren't they?"

"Yes, you're suffering from a very rare case of reverse melanoma." In his capacity as house doctor, Brent frequently diagnosed me with terminal cancer just to get me to quit complaining. When I do finally die, I plan to do so writhing in pain and bleeding from all orifices, simply to spite him.

"Plus this is the weekend we said we'd clean out the hayloft, weed the flower garden, and trellis the beans," I said. "By the time the party rolls around, we'll be exhausted. Let's just buy ice cream."

"That's not very Martha Stewart Entertaining," he said.

"I think two gay city boys trying to light a grill will be entertaining enough for them."

First thing Saturday morning, having been awoken to the usual Wagner/Madonna/Sinatra rooster medley, we grabbed two buckets from the barn and headed out to the cherry tree.

"Wow. It's loaded," Brent said. The branches were bent to the ground, weighted down with the most beautiful sprays of ruby red globes. Brent reached through the netting, picked a cherry, and popped it in his mouth, then quickly spit it out. "They're not ripe yet," he said. "They're still really sour."

"They're supposed to be," I explained. Having grown up in the South, Brent was used to sweet cherries. Where I lived, only sour cherry trees would survive the winter. "They're sour cherries. For pies. And jellies. You can't eat them raw."

"Blech." He spit out the remaining unchewed pieces.

"I read online that they're one of Martha's favorite pie varieties," I said, completely lying. "Now help me get this netting off."

He walked to the other side of the tree and began tugging at the black netting. We struggled for a good half hour before the netting finally landed in a tangled heap of snagged leaves and branches on the ground next to the base of the tree.

And then it began to move.

Random corners of the billowy netting were flapping and fluttering at our feet. I lifted up one of the moving corners to investigate.

"There's a bird caught in the net," I said.

"I know. There's one over on this end too."

I dropped to my knees and began trying to unravel the terrified sparrow. Each time I managed to free so much as a tail feather, it spasmed and flapped and became even further entangled. I shifted my position to get a better angle, and wound up kneeling on something soft. Moving my knee I found a corpse of another bird, this one long dead. It must have become tangled earlier in the week and starved.

"There are dozens of dead birds!" I called out. Brent realized the same thing at his end. *"Go get me some scissors."*

The rest of the morning was spent creating a sort of triage on the yard. The dead birds were put in one pile, the mostly dead birds were wrapped tightly in kitchen towels so as not to further injure themselves, and the healthiest freed birds were set underneath the nearby mock orange shrubs with a saucer of water where they would hopefully recuperate from their shock.

Bubby, of course, had to be continually shooed away. He and the other barn cats circled the scene like leopards at a watering hole.

We finally extricated the last bird around noon. The few of them that had survived limped and flapped their way to their own private hiding spaces in the flower garden.

Bubby, perhaps sensing our crestfallen exhaustion, moved in closer and rubbed against my shins while eyeing the bounty of the fallen battleground all around us.

"Go on," I tell him. "Just make it quick."

As Brent and I gathered up the netting to carry to the Dumpster, I realized that in pursuit of perfectly unblemished, Martha-worthy cherries, I'd murdered at least a dozen songbirds. This fact probably wouldn't have bothered most farmers—like the one at Agway who'd originally given me the netting tip. I wasn't naïve enough not to realize that death and farms go hand in hand. But what bothered me was that I would've been perfectly happy with a few pockmarked or missing cherries. I'd only been planning on using them in pies anyway.

I'd been selfish. I hadn't yet realized that the true goal of organic farming wasn't harvesting crops in *spite* of bugs, pests, and predators. It was about harvesting crops *alongside* of them. It was about planting more than the amount we need. And it was about making sure there was enough extra to go around for everything that made its home on the farm. For every sparrow I'd killed, there would be millions of fewer seeds spread over the fields from their droppings and millions of uneaten bugs, which would in turn attack our vegetable garden. We'd be paying for our unblemished cherries in some way or another for the rest of the season. Sure, we hadn't sprayed chemicals all over the cherries. But we'd been just as deadly.

It took Brent and me the entire rest of the day to pick all of the fruit off the tree. We ultimately wound up with twenty-two full baskets. It was gratifying to know that after pitting and freezing our haul, we'd have our own fruit to eat all winter. But I cannot tell a lie. They tasted more bitter than sour.

We spent much of the rest of the weekend pitting cherries and preparing for our picnic. My preference was still to host something similar to the Fourth of July parties of my youth, when someone in the neighborhood set up a buffet on a picnic table in the garage, and others would bring all manner of red, white, and blue–themed foods, generally involving Jell-O. But Brent was insisting on a Martha-style holiday with hand-cranked ice cream, meticulously "informal" floral arrangements, and three different varieties of lemonade. If we had an extra day to prepare, I was sure he'd have us taking trombone lessons for a parade in front of the house.

Even though we had a long five-day holiday break to prepare for the party, we'd barely put a dent in the list of chores Brent had wanted to accomplish. The evening before the Fourth found us frantically weeding the formal flower garden well after the sun went down.

"It's too dark to see. I'm going inside," I said, brushing a mosquito off my forearm. I couldn't help but think that I wouldn't have needed to if I hadn't killed so many birds in the netting. "I can't tell the difference anymore between the crabgrass and the stinging nettles. My hands are on fire."

"Just put your gloves back on," Brent answered. "All there is to do inside is read or go to sleep."

"Precisely. It's a holiday. That's the definition of *time off*."

"There are no holidays for farmers."

"I'd hardly call manicuring peonies 'farming.'"

"You would if you were a peony farmer."

While I too wanted to make a good impression on our new neighbors, I had a higher tolerance for imperfection than Brent did. Even though I worked to make sure that my ad clients always put their most seductive foot forward, Brent's job took things a step further. Being surrounded by perfectionist Marthabots all day gave one a warped sense of reality—or perhaps a perfectly smooth sense of a warped reality.

"Okay. That's it," I said ten minutes later. "I'm going to bed."

Brent stayed crouched over in front of me, his butt crack gleaming in the moonlight.

"Okay. You can always get up early tomorrow to finish," he said.

It took all the willpower I had not to shove a stinging nettle down his pants.

"Happy Overt Nationalism Day!" came a booming voice from the driveway. It was Doug and Garth from the hotel, and Michelle, our realtor. The three of them were best friends, and we'd rarely seen them when they weren't all together. We'd learned that Michelle also resides in the village, next door to Doug and Garth. She lived alone—except for her two giant Bouvier dogs—in an incredibly huge stone mansion at the top of a hill overlooking the valley. She'd come dressed in a stunningly stylish outfit—a polka-dotted vintage dress that flared out just above the knees.

"We brought you some wine," Doug said, and then gestured toward Michelle. "And also the spinster on the hill."

"And I brought some beer and the fags from the dell," Michelle responded. She looked around the yard. "Martha isn't here yet?"

We laughed, assuming she was joking. But by the confused look on the trio's faces, we realized she wasn't.

"No, Martha's not coming," Brent said. "Did someone tell you she was?"

"Oh, everyone in town thinks she's coming," Doug answered. "They've been gossiping about it for weeks now."

Our party was going to be a disappointment before it even started. I felt like Marcia Brady when she told everyone that she was going to get Davy Jones to appear at the school dance. Except that we hadn't told anyone anything. Who would seriously think that Martha would make a three-and-a-half-hour drive to the middle of nowhere on the Fourth of July?

Soon after Doug, Garth, and Michelle's arrival, Farmer John walked over across his driveway accompanied by an older couple.

"These are my parents, Harold and Barbara Hall," John said. They extended their hands.

"I didn't know what you might need for your new house, so I sewed up some potholders for you," Barbara said softly. "Everybody can use potholders."

Inside the tissue she handed me were three beautifully handsewn potholders, made with fabric depicting the same perennials found in our flower garden.

"These are beautiful," I said, marveling at their craftsmanship. In the city they could've sold at a folk art fair for at least fifty dollars.

"You boys are certainly doing a good job with the farm," she said.

"It's mostly John," I said. "I don't know what we'd do without him." Gay men know that the way to a woman's heart is through her son.

"Well, he says you two are some of the hardest-working people he's seen," she added. I nearly blushed at the compliment. John was so naturally quiet that I had no idea what he thought of us. I figured he was adhering to the adage that if you don't have anything nice to say, don't make fun of the person paying the mortgage.

The rest of the guests arrived within fifteen minutes. We figured that no one wanted to miss a minute of partying with Martha Stewart. But even without her, everyone seemed to be having an idyllic time. Some people were feasting on hot dogs and hamburgers, another group went for a hike in the fields, another played bocce ball on the lawn, and yet another went skinny dipping in the pool. It was practically iconic. The Beekman had been around to celebrate nearly every single Independence Day in our country's history, and I hoped ours was as festive as any of William Beekman's.

From the history I'd read, the first Independence Day at the Beekman Mansion probably found the Beekman family heading off to the white steeple church, which we could see from on top of Lookout Hill on the southwestern corner of the property. It's the same church that caught our eye last fall when we happened upon the Beekman. Judge Beekman and the other men from the area probably would have started the day with gun and cannon salutes in the churchyard before spending the rest of the morning singing hymns, offering prayers of thanks, and giving patriotic speeches about the new "Universal Yankee Nation." In the afternoon, Joanna Beekman and her neighbors would have served picnic lunches and desserts in the churchyard. And in the evening there would have been one final round of gun and cannon explosions before bed.

We might not have had cannons, but as soon as the sun dipped below the horizon we brought out the sparklers. We gathered everyone on the long back porch and handed them out. One by one our partygoers lit their sparklers from the glowing tip of their neighbor's. Soon the porch was aglow in sparkles. People were waving them about trying to spell letters in the growing darkness.

When the final one had extinguished, we realized that the flower garden beneath us was sparkling all on its own. It seemed as if every peony, mock orange blossom, and lupine stem had Christmas lights strung around it. Lightning bugs. They were fervently flashing their answer to our sparkling signals on the porch. It was breathtakingly beautiful.

I thought back to that previous Fourth of July that we'd spent on Martha's patio in East Hampton and wondered what she was doing this year. Even though our peony bed had thistles and I had no wasabi mayo for our burgers, even she wouldn't be immune to the charms of a full firefly chorus. Would she?

After people left, Brent and I walked around the moonlit yard picking up paper plates and cups.

"Do you think people had a good time?" he asked, handing me one.

"Seemed to. Did you?"

"I had a great time."

"Even though we bought the ice cream at the gas station?"

"Don't be silly," he said. "Nobody cared about where the ice cream came from." It sounded to me a little like a Declaration of Independence from Martha World.

Chapter Eleven

By the end of summer it seemed as if we had been farmers for years. At least to us. The garden had been producing bushels of produce, John had met a soap maker who was buying at least a portion of the milk his goats produced, and we cut the fields enough times to fill up the hayloft for the winter ahead.

It also seemed as if we'd become full-fledged members of the community. We'd exchanged zucchini bread with our neighbors and been to chicken-and-biscuit fund-raisers at the local church. Each Friday on our drive from the train station, we stopped off for a drink at the American Hotel, where half of the entire village could be found. The other half enjoyed soft serve at the Dairy Carnival on Route 20. Brent and I usually hit them both and I invariably wound up going to bed with a stomachache and waking up with a headache.

The last week in August had been grueling at the office, and I found myself working late each night on a new client pitch. Consequently, we'd had to take a much later train than usual on that Friday night. By the time we reached the American, the dinner rush was over and Doug and Garth were eating their own dinners at the bar.

While the hotel restaurant's food is excellent, we've come to learn that perhaps the greatest reason for the American's success lied with Doug and Garth themselves. The summer tourists who came to visit nearby Cooperstown made the drive to Sharon Springs year after year just for the two of them. Garth played the role of the straight man, sincerely asking patrons how their years went, remembering the names of their grandchildren, and making sure their dinners reached their tables hot and in a timely fashion. Doug was the showman. His collection of kilts was legendary. I laughed to think of the reaction he must have received the first few times he wore them after arriving in Sharon Springs in the early 1990s. Since I also once made a living wearing skirts, I knew just how off-putting it could be to some people at first. But I also know how it can also stun everyone into letting their guard down enough to let loose and have one of the most memorable nights of their lives. It's impossible for anyone to feel uptight and self-conscious when there's a man in the room with a hemline above his knees.

"Well, look who's here," Doug called out loudly as we entered. "How nice that you brought your grandfather out for a nightcap," he said to Brent, nodding at me. I'd come to learn during these first few months of friendship that Doug believed that the strongest sign of endearment was a constant stream of insults. As it happens, a well-aimed barb was the quickest way to my own heart.

"I guess it's true," I said, pointing at Doug in his kilt. "They say even the best hotels can't avoid prostitution."

"A *real* lady never ridicules another woman's ensemble," Doug fired back.

"A *real* lady never leaves home without nylons," I volleyed.

"And a lady like you never comes home in them."

Brent and Garth rolled their eyes as they hugged each other in greeting. Behind us, the hotel's door opened again, letting in a gust of cool evening air. It was John, coming in for a drink after his late night of milking and chores.

"Hi, John," Brent said. "Can we buy you a drink?" He ordered a beer from the bartender, George, who also happened to run the village's mortuary.

"What's new?" I ask John.

"Well, I've got good news and bad news," he answered, and then sat quietly.

"Okay," I responded. Knowing that John metes out his words like a prisoner shares cigarettes, I debated which news to ask for first, just in case he ran out. "I'll take the good news," I finally volunteered.

"Well, it's about the turkeys . . ."

We'd been bugging John for several weeks to find some turkeys for the farm. Ever the perfectionist, Brent had started planning our first holiday season at the Beekman back in June. While most people might find such proactivity a bit compulsive, it was par for the course in Brent's world. The offices of Martha Stewart Living Omnimedia were abuzz with holiday activity beginning in July. There were holiday magazines that needed to be laid out, gingerbread cookie recipes that needed to be updated, and television specials to be conceived. What the public doesn't understand is that the true spirit of Christmas doesn't come from the heart; it comes from the ad sales.

In the course of his research, Brent had learned that Martha used to raise her own turkeys at her home called, appropriately (or maybe morbidly), Turkey Hill. Martha's daughter, Alexis, once told Brent a story about how on Thanksgiving mornings, some of the house staff would bring the turkeys into the basement kitchen, give them shots of tequila to calm them, and then slaughter them. After hearing the story, I wondered whether the tequila wasn't actually used to calm the staff. Alexis said she had to leave the house every Thanksgiving morning while the deed was being done, and rarely ate any of the recently deceased bird come dinnertime. As an adult, she'd become a vegetarian very active in PETA.

Since hearing about Martha's ritual, Brent had become convinced that we too needed to raise our own turkeys. I agreed with him, not because of the Martha mimicry, but because ever since buying and cooking a fresh heritage breed turkey from Balducci's several years ago, I vowed never to cook a bland frozen turkey again.

Once we'd decided we needed to bring our very own turkey home to roost, we didn't realize that most farmers buy their poultry stock in the springtime as chicks. Locating someone willing to part with half-grown birds in the middle of summer was a miracle even my *Penny Savior* couldn't perform. So we gave John the task of procuring us some live turkeys.

"The good news," John said, continuing his report, "is that I've found four turkeys. Three hens and a tom."

"What's the bad news?" Doug interjects. "I love bad news. When it happens to others, of course," he adds, sipping his martini and taking a spoonful of lobster chowder.

John took a swallow of beer before proceeding. Clearly whatever it was had been weighing on his mind.

"Well," he said, hesitating momentarily before finally blurting out the awful truth: "They cost five dollars apiece."

George winced and let out a low whistle.

I realized that any reaction might work against me. If I was honest and proclaimed that I found that price for my own homegrown Thanksgiving dinner quite reasonable—if not cheap—I risked coming off like a pretentious urban snob.

On the other hand, if I pretended to be as outraged as they were, they'd wonder at the sanity of someone who was paying the mortgage on a mansion but wouldn't pony up a couple of five-spots for a few measly turkeys.

I decided to take the middle ground.

"I'll think about it," I said. The turkeys were cheap for us. But at the same time they were wildly cost ineffective given that we could've purchased a dozen chicks this past spring for less than the round of drinks we just bought.

"What's to think about?" Doug asked. "If you want the turkeys, get the turkeys. It's not brain surgery. Unless you're really good with a hatchet."

"It's just . . ." I said haltingly. "I'm still not sure I could kill my own dinner," I finally answered.

"Why not? With a face like yours, you've already killed mine," Doug said, pushing away his bowl.

Saturday morning I awoke with a slight hangover from the previous evening's imbibing, but I had no time to indulge it. As the summer was drawing to an end, the garden was producing far more harvest than we could ever eat fresh. There was a large chest freezer in the basement, but I'd decided that the more environmentally conscious and historically appropriate approach to preserving food was to can it. The basement of the Beekman had a separate bricked-off root cellar with the date 1876 carved in the bricks, and I was determined to fill it just as the original Beekmans had. It was what Martha would do.

One of the earliest *Martha Stewart* shows I remember watching was dedicated to the art of canning. It aired sometime back during my nightclubbing drag queen days. It was the mid-1990s, and her half-hour show aired on PBS on Saturday afternoons— roughly about the same time I was waking up from the evening before or, sometimes, just as I was arriving home. It served as a sort of hangover cure for me.

While my stomach's stability was far too questionable at that hour to actually eat anything, for some reason it was very soothing to watch Martha—with her calm, almost monotone voice— as she methodically went from sink to stove to counter in her immaculate kitchen studio. Little did I know that it was the very kitchen in which I would enjoy a Fourth of July lunch of wasabi tuna burgers a decade later. Watching her prepare a meal was a sort of virtual sustenance—the only kind I could keep down with the gut-wrenching hangovers I used to cultivate.

I remember the canning episode in particular because the science and aesthetics fascinated me. Baskets of colorful, ripe, healthy produce were reduced to rows of sparkling glass jars on a shelf right in front of my eyes. At that point in my life, I didn't know where I was going to wake up the next morning—*and this woman was preparing for a dinner six months from now.* It was mind-boggling.

Which was why, that first summer on our farm, I'd decided that I was going to "put up" bushel after bushel of garden produce. I wanted to prove that I too had gained some sort of foresight with age. As opposed to my reckless youth when I wasn't sure I would survive past any given Sunday, I now felt a sort of middle-aged urge to make gestures toward my immortality—or at least six to nine months hence. And I felt the best way to do that was to be able to open a jar of my own canned tomatoes in January.

So it was appropriate that my first attempt at canning would be accompanied by a hangover.

Brent and I headed out to the garden to gather our harvest for canning. Because of work, we'd both missed coming up the previous weekend, and we were shocked at the sheer quantity of cucumbers, tomatoes, and green beans hanging from the plants. The last two weeks of August had been like steroids for the garden.

"This is amazing. It's a jungle. Can you believe all this food from one tiny plot of dirt?" I asked, smiling. Bubby joined us and nudged at my shin. I picked him up and threw him over my shoulder. "Look at all this, Bubs. You and me did this. Told ya it would work." He fixed his gold eyes on mine then nuzzled my neck.

"What are we going to do with everything?" Brent asked.

"Well, we'll pickle the cucumbers. And some of the beans. We'll make sauce out of some of the tomatoes using the herbs. Then we'll can some whole tomatoes plain. Oh, and some salsa . . . we'll use the peppers and cilantro to can with them. And we'll juice the ugliest tomatoes for Bloody Marys come the holidays."

"Bloody Marys don't seem particularly holiday-ish," Brent noted.

"Hey, you celebrate your way. I'll celebrate mine."

We quickly ran out of baskets to carry the tomatoes, and took turns ferrying them into the kitchen, unloading them of their produce, and returning to fill them again. By noon, we'd barely made a dent in the harvest.

"You'll never get all this done," Brent said.

"If Martha can do it, I can do it," I replied confidently.

I'd done much of my canning research online, but quickly found that in the world of home canning, there was no one right way to do things. But however different the various instructions were, each claimed that if its directions weren't followed meticulously, the dreaded *Clostridium botulinum* spores would take up residence in my pickle spears. One of the sites even took the trouble to illustrate the spore, giving it a sickly green-mottled coloring, hairy arms and legs, and a nose shaped like a barbed javelin. It was obvious one shouldn't mess with *Clostridium botulinum* or it might poke you. Hard.

Working systematically, Brent and I ran load after load of jars through the dishwasher to sterilize them, and methodically dipped each Mason jar lid in hot—"but not boiling"—water.

Finally, the counters were lined with sparkling clean jars and lids. We could begin.

According to Martha's Web site, our first task in canning the tomatoes would be to skin them. Brent filled every pot we owned with water and brought them to a boil. We started by patiently dipping them in the roiling water one by one, watching their skins split, and then immediately transferring them to the sink full of icy water, which was supposed to "shock" them right out of their skins.

At this point, according to the video I found on Martha's Web site, the skins were supposed to slip right off. Of course the tomatoes she used for her demonstration were perfectly smooth and orblike. Our heirloom tomatoes came in all shapes and sizes, with bulbous protrusions and deep crevices that bordered on pornographic. While Martha's skins fell off her tomatoes like a silk slip off a supermodel, our skins got caught in the deep folds and stuck stubbornly. It was like trying to peel leather pants off of a sweaty, hairy, fat guy.

Our patience wore thin within the first couple of hours. We never got the skins to peel off cleanly, and we wound up ripping each tomato to shreds. Two piles started to form: one of clumpy seeds and pulp, and the other with clumpy skins and meat. The kitchen looked like a wartime operating room.

"Should we eat dinner?" Brent asked as the sun started casting long shadows across the room.

"Just grab a handful of green beans," I answered, wiping the sweat off my brow. "We're going to be up all night at this rate."

We pressed on. We cut twenty pounds of cucumbers into spears for pickling. I minced armfuls of cilantro for salsa, while Brent chopped up the habanero peppers. I warned him to wear gloves while cutting, since habaneros have ten times the amount of natural capsaicin as a cayenne pepper, or so I learned online. One swipe across his eyes or nose would unleash a furious burn.

Brent, who had the natural God complex that comes with being a doctor, shunned gloves.

Finally around midnight Brent snuck off to bed while I was setting up the pressure cooker. I didn't even realize he was gone till I heard a yelp from upstairs.

"What's the matter?" I yelled into the darkness of the hallway.

"The peppers!" he yelled back.

"Just rinse your eyes under the faucet."

"It's not my eyes!"

"What is it?"

I heard the shower come on full blast.

"I PEED BEFORE WASHING MY HANDS!"

I spent the rest of the night trying to make a dent in our harvest. Since our time is so limited at the Beekman, I knew that whatever food I hadn't sealed in jars by 5:45 on Sunday night when we left for the train would have to be composted. The thought of taking even a single tomato out to the compost pile filled me with dread. It seemed like such a waste after all of the tilling, and planting, and weeding, and watering that I'd sweated through this summer. To then take the fruits of my labor and simply turn them back into dirt again was out of the question. If it meant I needed to stay up for thirty-six hours straight to add a speed bump into this circle of life, then I would.

By the time Brent came down in the morning, I'd managed to work my way through about half of the tomatoes. I'd given up skinning the most stubborn ones and instead decided that a few peels would add a certain "rusticity" to our sauces. The windows in the kitchen were so steamed over from the constant boiling that I couldn't even tell what the weather was like outside. In fact I barely knew dawn had snuck up until I heard the familiar choruses of *HERE COMES THE BRIDE, IT HAD TO BE YOU, and PAPA DON'T PREACH* over the hissing pressure canners.

"Man. What a mess." Brent said, entering the kitchen in his robe. "What's for breakfast?"

"Breakfast? I've been up all night. Why don't you make me something."

Brent looked around the messy kitchen. Even if he wanted to cook, he'd have to spend an hour clearing space.

"How about I go get a doughnut for you down at Stewart's."

"Whatever. Just hurry back and help. There's still a lot to do before we head back."

While Brent purposefully wasted the next hour getting coffee and doughnuts, most likely trying to avoid me, I finished the third big batch of tomato sauce. The filtered sunlight from the steamy windows made the finished jars lined up on the counter glow like a photo in a magazine. Like a photo in Martha's magazine.

By 7 P.M. I'd barely processed half of our week's tomato harvest.

Brent wisely avoided the kitchen all day. With only thirty minutes left to make the last train back into the city, he was outside sitting in the truck, repeatedly honking the horn for me to join him. I'd decided to carry the remaining bushels of tomatoes into the basement and was stuffing them as fast as I could into the chest freezer—whole, unpeeled, complete with leaves and bits of stem.

I would not waste this food.

I couldn't.

I'd worked too hard. I dug up *bones* for that garden. People *died* for these tomatoes.

I was clearly delirious from lack of sleep and food. All I'd eaten the entire weekend was one doughnut, scraps of tomato skins, and habanero pickles so hot that my tongue had blistered.

Brent continued honking the damn horn.

Didn't he understand? I couldn't leave while there was a single tomato left on the battlefield. I would win this war. We would have tomatoes in January. We would be immortal. Martha had promised me as much in a vision many years ago.

"I'm coming! I'm coming!" I screamed, squishing tomatoes into every available space in the freezer.

He couldn't hear me. I knew that.

But the tomatoes could.

And they knew that they'd been vanquished.

Chapter Twelve

The first frost fell like a guillotine at the Beekman.

While people in the city were still wearing shorts and shirt-sleeves, Sharon Springs ushered in its annual flannel fashion season almost overnight. Down at Stewart's, the talk around the registers was all about the upcoming hunting season and new snow plows. In the fields, some crafty farmers painted the ends of their rolled-up hay bales to look like jack-o-lantern faces. I bet Martha never thought of that.

The sky had lost all of its summer milkiness, and the row of ancient sugar maples in the front yard glowed so brightly orange that all the rooms in the front of the house looked to be on fire. After endless weekends of weeding, mowing, harvesting, canning, and freezing, October brought a lull so deep it was almost disconcerting.

In the vegetable garden, the frost had broken down the cells of nearly all of the various stalks and stems, so our once tall tomato, bean, squash, cucumber, and melon plants had drooped over, lying prone on the ground, ready to be smothered under months of snow. Bright orange pumpkins and great gray-green winter squash lay exposed to the sky, dotting the ground like deflating water balloons. Other than picking a few fall raspberries and leafy greens, our garden chores had ended for the year.

I felt as bittersweet as I was relieved. The only activity we had planned for this weekend—our one-year anniversary of stumbling on the Beekman—was our ritual chore of sweeping up piles of dead flies.

Against all logic, our zombie flies seemed to be growing in number once it turned cold outside and the windows were shut. We realized that they must be coming from somewhere *inside* the house.

"There's got to be something we can do about these flies," Brent said, running the Dustbuster along the bedroom windowsill for the second time since we'd arrived three hours ago.

"Just come to bed and don't fret about them," I said.

After a long week of work, Brent tended to fall asleep the moment he crawled under the covers. I usually wound up reading all hours into the night, trying to clear away the spiderwebs of client conference calls and failed advertising concepts from my mind. Brent had been asleep for only about ten minutes this particular night when the noises started.

"Do you hear that?" I asked Brent, nudging him awake. He rolled over and propped himself up on his elbows. After having had to respond to hospital beepers for years, he'd developed the skill of being perfectly alert from the very moment he opened his eyes.

"Yeah. What is it?"

"I dunno."

The noise was coming from downstairs, maybe the kitchen. It was intermittent and sounded like a wooden spoon clanging on the side of a pot. Sometimes there was a noise like plates being set on a wooden table. And, though incredibly faint, I thought I heard sounds of a woman laughing.

Brent and I lay motionless in bed, listening for several minutes. At one point I heard a floorboard creaking that I recognized as the one that divided the kitchen from the dining room. It was unmistakable.

"Someone's broken in," I whispered.

"Why? To make themselves a midnight snack?" Brent answered.

"You should go check it out," I finally told Brent.

"Why?"

"We can't just lay here and do nothing," I said.

"Actually, I think it's generally best to do nothing about nothing."

He had a good point. The amount of noise our visitor was making ruled out the possibility that he or she might be a cat burglar. It was clearly something otherworldly. And if it wasn't real, what was the point of investigating?

Even more than the supernatural noises, the moment was surreal. I'd never been the type to tell ghost stories, let alone be in one. But I'd always assumed that if I were to have an otherworldly experience one day, it would be fleeting and frightening. In reality, this was neither. The noises continued for at least five minutes as we calmly listened in. We found ourselves in the strange predicament of either going to check out thin air or going back to sleep, which we finally did.

The next morning I reminded Brent of our midnight visitation.

"It was probably just a mouse or something," he said.

"Banging on pots and laughing?" I asked.

The truth was that up until that night we'd been sort of disappointed at our lack of firsthand paranormal experiences. Nearly everyone in town had at least one ghost story to tell about the Beekman. Some people claimed that lights moved from window to window during the years it had been abandoned. The renovation contractor told us he'd seen a small girl giggling at him one night when he was working late by himself. Earlier in the summer, the woman who made the soap from John's goat milk, Deb, brought her friend by the Beekman to "read its spirits."

I'd always pictured psychics and paranormal experts to look something like Stevie Nicks circa Fleetwood Mac. But the woman accompanying Deb was wearing a beige sweater and faded jeans. Her hair was cut short and neat, and she was wearing conservative wire-frame glasses. She reminded me of a woman you'd meet at a Lutheran church's basement potluck supper.

"Hi, I'm Gwen," she'd said, holding out her nicely manicured hand.

"Gwen is an energy reader," Deb had explained. "She's been wanting to come by the Beekman for many years. I hope you don't mind that I brought her by."

"Of course not," I'd answered. "Just keep the really scary bits to yourself."

As we walked toward the house, Gwen told us the story of how for many years she'd spotted the spirit of a black man limping down the road in front of the Beekman. When she pulled over her car to "talk" to him, he asked if she knew "where the lady of the house is." Apparently whichever Beekman woman he was searching for had a healing balm for the bruises and welts covering his legs. Gwen assumed that he may have been a runaway slave who was seeking shelter at the Beekman—a theory that would make some sense given the mansion's history as a stop on the Underground Railroad.

Once inside we asked Gwen if we should be quiet or wait in another room while she did her work. I pictured her walking from room to room speaking in guttural tongues. Perhaps levitating every once in a while.

"No, you guys can just keep talking with each other," she answered. "Just do whatever you'd normally do. I'll just wander around and see what hits me."

A few minutes later, as Deb, Brent, and I chatted about soap making, Gwen wandered into the dining room from the kitchen.

"So sorry for interrupting," Gwen said, "but I'm picking up a spirit in here. A man. He's dressed in buckskin and is very angry about something. It looks like he's shouting."

"What's he saying?" Brent asked.

"I'm not sure," Gwen answered. "Sometimes I'll just get one or two senses. A smell. A picture. Sounds. With this man I can only see him."

She returned to her wandering and the rest of us continued our small talk about the weather. She began climbing the stairs.

"Oh look!" she said at the top, as if we too had a window into the great beyond. "There's a woman, very tiny and dark. West Indian, I feel. She's walking back and forth, across the hall, from that room to that room." She was pointing between the master bedroom and the guest room. "She has a fireplace poker. I think she's checking both of the fires. Perhaps she's a char maid."

Gwen continued to roam. She seemed disappointed by the attic. Apparently she'd heard many stories over the years about a teenage girl who'd been scalped on the stairway while fleeing from attacking Indians. But all she was able to pick up was the faint sound of a woman humming distractedly. She turned to head back down the attic stairs.

"I guess that's it. I thought I would pick up more. I apologize," she said, as if taking personal responsibility for the paltry haunting of our house.

But as we began to say our good-byes by the back porch door, Gwen stopped. She looked down the wide center hallway toward the front of the house and let out a small laugh.

"I *knew* someone was following us," she said, staring in the direction of the front door. "I see you," she said, smiling.

"Who?" I asked.

"There's been a little girl, following us everywhere," Gwen began. "She seems small for her age—maybe four or five years old. Maybe six. I kept spotting her out of the corner of my eye in the doorways. She's wearing a little bonnet and standing on her tiptoes. She giggles. And she seems to be pointing at you and Brent." I got a little chill. "I think that you guys are her imaginary friends."

"We're *her* imaginary friends?" Brent asked.

"Something like that," Gwen replied. "I find that most spirits aren't aware that there is another plane going on around them. They just go about their business. But some, like this one, can see us just as we feel them."

"Is she looking at us now?" I asked.

"Yes," Gwen answered. "She keeps poking her head around the dining room door."

"Can you tell what her name is?" Brent asked.

"Hmm," Gwen said, closing her eyes. "I don't know. I'm sort of feeling an 'M' sound." She paused, as if listening, then shook her head. "No. That's all. Just an 'M' sound."

As she spoke I remembered the conversation I had two months ago with the contractor who'd seen the little girl ghost. After he told me the story he took me on a tour of the house, helpfully pointing out different structural elements of the house that we should be aware of. Toward the end of his visit he showed me a carving someone had made in the wooden floor of the center hallway. It was in the crude penmanship of a young child. It read: MARY.

After hearing the ghostly kitchen noises that night, Brent and I spent the rest of the weekend picking the apples from our trees. It seemed like a fitting way to celebrate the anniversary of finding the Beekman on our annual apple-picking excursion. After we'd picked all of the fruit from the trees that had been planted by the house, we walked up into the far field to pick the tiny sour apples from the few ancient trees that stood in the corner of the property. They'd be good to add to cider if nothing else.

Standing under the gnarly black branches of the overgrown

hillside trees, we could look out over the brilliant orange-and-yellow blanket of the valley. Who knew when these trees were planted, and how many generations had picked their fruit? Were they around when Mary was a girl? Was the woman in the kitchen last night making a pie from apple harvests long past?

Maybe it wasn't just a coincidence that we'd been visited by former Beekman inhabitants on our first-year anniversary. Maybe they were just waiting until we were enough of a permanent part of the Beekman's story to include us in their midst.

It felt nice to be acknowledged.

Chapter Thirteen

In the advertising world, Thanksgiving no longer exists. If you were a bedridden invalid with television as your only link to the outside world, you'd hardly even know it came and went. (Of course if you were a bedridden invalid with television as your only link to the outside world, perhaps you wouldn't feel very thankful anyways.)

It's not that surprising that advertisers no longer acknowledge the holiday. It was always nothing more than an annoyance to retailers—a day when Americans took a break from shopping to celebrate their good fortune. But to American businesses, what good is good fortune if you aren't spending it?

Brent and I were resolute in celebrating our first Thanksgiving at the Beekman in the most authentic, least commercial manner possible—namely, by being thankful. As the chickens began laying fewer and fewer eggs in the waning light, and we harvested the final tough, frosty leaves of kale, we finally had time to take stock of the previous year. It would have been hard for us to have been any fuller of thanks. We had a root cellar brimming with harvest, substantial year-end bonuses, all sorts of new friends and neighbors, and, of course, each other. I was actually beginning to feel nervous about all we did have to be thankful for. This was more than a boy from Wisconsin was ever supposed to have.

Maybe that was why, that first frigid Thanksgiving morning at the Beekman, I had a peculiar sense of dread.

"Don't wear that coat," Brent said when I entered the kitchen in my favorite corduroy winter jacket.

"Why not?"

"You don't want to get blood all over it."

I headed back upstairs and threw on an old flannel barn coat. Thanksgiving morning used to be one of my favorite times of the year. As a child I used to come downstairs and watch the Macy's Thanksgiving Day Parade in my pajamas while my mother and father wrestled the stuffing into the turkey. But at the farm we didn't have a television. And we didn't have a Butterball. What we did have were three turkey hens and a tom contentedly clucking away out in the barn, pecking at their morning grain. What one of them didn't know was that it was having its last meal.

"Do you have the Absolut?" Brent asked me. I opened up my jacket to show him the bottle tucked in the inside pocket. We were following Martha's tradition of boozing up the bird before slaughtering it. Supposedly squeezing a baster full of alcohol down the bird's throat before decapitating it would lesson the resulting flailing and flapping of the headless torso. And the less the beheaded fowl flopped, the less bruising there was supposed to be in the meat.

As Brent walked ahead of me to fetch the hatchet from the barn, I quickly unscrewed the bottle's lid and snuck a large swallow. The all-too-familiar burn reminded me of a Thanksgiving that fell somewhere in between those idyllic childhood ones and now, specifically the Thanksgiving I hosted in the penthouse of my first New York boyfriend—a crack-addicted, high-end male escort who warned me against using his turkey baster for its intended purpose. It apparently had been employed in various orifices completely unrelated to poultry.

Back then I was more concerned with internally marinating

myself with Absolut. Unlike a turkey, however, it didn't numb me. It gave me the courage to lose my head, flail about wildly, and bruise myself. Part of me couldn't believe how far I'd traveled from a child watching parades in pajamas, to a drunken drag queen stepping over crack pipe shards on the kitchen floor, to a middle-aged gentleman farmer about to slaughter his own dinner. Maybe it was the sip of vodka, but I was suddenly and intensely thankful for all my Thanksgivings.

I was standing next to the chicken coop when Brent returned with the hatchet, joined by John.

"Which one are you gonna take?" John asked. I stared at the four birds, pecking the ground and cooing.

"I dunno," I said. "It'll come to me."

I didn't realize how literal I was being until Brent opened the door to the pen. One of the turkey hens waddled right over to me, perhaps mistaking me for John, who entered the very same door every morning to scatter grain. She chirped impatiently at my feet, no doubt pissed that I wasn't tossing flakes of feed onto the ground. Their daily ration had been increasing exponentially over the past few weeks in advance of this very day.

The tom, behind her, spread his tail feathers to appear more intimidating. His neck waddle turned from a mottled blue and white to scarlet red in warning. As is the case in most of the animal kingdom other than humans, he was far more decoratively beautiful than the three comparatively plain females. It was his looks that would save him from the ax. It definitely paid to be a flamboyantly good-looking turkey on a farm where Martha Stewart-style matters.

I suddenly felt very tired. I'd slept fitfully the night before, as I'd had many conflicting emotions about the deed I was about to do—some obvious, some personal, and some simply silly and vain.

I'd proudly told all of my friends and colleagues of my turkey-slaughter plans, just as I had when I quit smoking after my drag days. I somehow felt that the more people who knew of my goal, the less likely I would shirk from accomplishing it. Even so, I still had doubts about my own motivation and resolve.

As I stared at the hen at my feet, the doubts rushed in manifold. Why was I doing this? Some answers were easy: I liked good food. I know from experience that this heritage breed turkey we'd raised ourselves would taste infinitely better than a frozen Butterball from the supermarket.

It was also a comfort to know that although I may be killing one bird today, it will at least have had a relatively quick death after a happy life—unlike the vast majority of factory-farmed birds brought to American Thanksgiving tables.

Still, some of my motivations were more difficult to explain. Why didn't I just have Farmer John or a neighbor slaughter our bird? There were plenty of good reasons for me to consume a bird that had been healthily and happily raised on my own farm. But there didn't seem to be one logical reason for me to actually kill it myself. I pay money for people to handle services for me all the time. We have a cleaning woman who comes once a week in the city. We pay the Laundromat on the corner to wash and press our dress shirts. I pay taxi drivers to drive me around the city. These are all tasks that I can do myself but have no particular qualm paying someone else to do for me. And as far as I can tell, they have no particular difficulties accepting my money. Why, then, don't I just pay John or another experienced farmer to take care of this unpleasant task?

Part of the answer was curiosity. While I paid others to help me clean, cook, and drive, those were also all tasks that I've done myself many times and have simply chosen to delegate. If I'd been born into privilege and had all my chores done for me since birth, I probably would be just as curious to give a washing machine a whirl simply to see what I'd been missing. Just as I was curious to put seeds in the ground to see how much produce I could bring to my own table, I was also curious to see whether I could take the same journey with my meat.

But as I stood there staring at my victim, I realized that the biggest motivator for what I was about to do was honor. The simple truth was that these particular birds don't exist for any other reason than to be killed and eaten. And, as it was, I stood to be the biggest beneficiary of that fact. Not my dinner guests. Not the farmer who sold them to us. Not Farmer John. Not the Price Chopper supermarket. Me. The Moi Chopper.

It was I who would have the satisfaction of being nourished and of nourishing my friends and family with this bird. The very least I could do was take care of the unpleasantness in getting to that point myself—mano-a-poultry.

The hen that had run up to me when I entered the coop hadn't left my feet. I supposed that meant that she would be the one. I bent over to pick her up and she cuddled into the crook of my elbow with no resistance. She chirped and cooed exactly as she had done every day since arriving at the farm.

Brent, Farmer John, and I headed to the opposite side of the barn where we'd set up a thick stump from the woodpile. As we walked by the chicken coop, only one of the roosters was outside futilely pecking the frost-covered ground for bugs. As I passed with the hapless turkey in my arms, he looked up to the sky and crowed IT HAD TO BE YOU.

Once at the chopping block station, Brent unscrewed the top from the bottle of Absolut and inserted the turkey baster. I gently held the hen's head back and she opened her beak slightly. Brent squeezed the contents down her throat. She didn't resist at all, other than a slight sneeze after swallowing. In fact she seemed quite eager for more, pecking at the baster like I used to tap on my empty glass at a bar. Brent obligingly gave her one more baster-full. I'm not sure if it was just wishful thinking, but she seemed to relax into my arms even more.

Farmer John cleared the light dusting of snow off the chopping block, and I laid the hen down sideways. She didn't squirm or try to right herself. Perhaps the vodka was working as intended. John used both of his hands to hold her body in place while I used my left hand to gently hold her head. I was sure to cover the one eye that was looking up at me. Even though I knew that her prehistoric brain was unable to add two and two together to understand that she was about to undergo division, I didn't want the swinging hatchet to be the last thing she saw.

Brent handed me the hatchet.

There was no more delaying.

Whack.

Goddammit. I'd practiced for two days chopping kindling until I could finally sever a three-inch-diameter branch with one swoop. But unlike a dead branch, the turkey's neck was soft and kind of bouncy. My worst fear was realized: I hadn't made a clean cut.

Whack. Whack.

I swung the hatchet two more times in rapid succession. The bird did struggle after the first unsuccessful chop and, surprisingly, even more so after the last. John held the thrashing body down with his hands, and I was left clutching the hatchet in one hand and the head in the other.

John quickly grabbed the headless bird by her feet and carried her upside down into the garage, wings still flapping. He expertly wrapped a pre-tied slipknot around her talons and hung her from a beam over a trash barrel. The blood first flowed out in a steady stream, but quickly subsided into a steady dripping.

I stared at the dangling bird, wings akimbo, as it emptied. With the drama over, I noticed that the glove on my left hand was torn between the thumb and the forefinger, and that my own hand was throbbing in pain. Taking the glove off, I realized that the reason the first swing of the hatchet didn't sever the bird's head was because I'd hit my own hand. I sliced through the glove and rather deeply into my flesh. Brent took a look and, like most of my illnesses and injuries, declared it minor.

John quickly moved on to begin his morning chores, and Brent and I went inside to clean the wound and fix breakfast while we waited for the turkey to drain completely of blood.

When I'd explained to my colleagues at work that I planned on killing my own turkey, most of them were less grossed out by the killing part than the dressing details. "You're going to pluck it yourself?! What about the guts?!" To me, this was far less daunting than the executioner's task. We all have blood and guts. And like anyone careening toward forty, I was growing acutely more aware of them as my body began adding its various aches and ailments to its permanent collection.

But also, like anyone smack dab in midlife territory, I was beginning to truly realize that there was some point in time, either just about to happen or just past, when there would be fewer Thanksgiving Days left for me rather than more. Sometime down the line, Brent (who is four years younger than I and far healthier) would probably be sitting down at a Thanksgiving table at which the turkey had been alive more recently than I had.

As the magnitude of dying starts to sink in (or, perhaps more frighteningly, the "minitude"), the plucking and gutting part of dying begins to seem fairly insignificant. It's the irreversibility of what comes before. I was starting to really understand the existential comfort behind my mother's explanation for most any unpleasantness in life: what's done is done.

After breakfast I returned to the garage with several buckets of scalding water to finish what I'd started. It was important, I'd read, to remove the intestines and fecal matter as quickly and cleanly as possible so as not to contaminate the meat. So first I plucked the feathers near the bird's anus, which was not hard to find considering that she had (like most of us will) made good use of it during her final moments.

Then using a hunting knife borrowed from John, I carved a small hole into her flesh just wide enough for me to insert my clenched fist. Pulling out the viscera proved easier than I thought. Most of it fell out in a clean clump onto the gravel of the driveway. Removing the hen's internal organs seemed no more stubborn than gutting the fish I used to catch as a boy. Part of me was a little disturbed at the thought of how unattached everyone's insides must be to our outsides.

Bubby showed up at my side and carefully sniffed around the turkey's internal organs, deciding which to devour first. At least it would make the cleanup easier.

Once hollow, I dipped the carcass into the hot water to loosen its feathers slightly, and began the arduous and monotonous task of plucking. The repetitive act of finding and pulling each feather was sort of meditative—along the same lines as plucking petals from a daisy. "He'll taste good . . . He'll taste good not . . ." Soon the turkey began looking less like it did just an hour or so ago, and more like the familiar pale pimply flesh of a supermarket turkey.

Except it seemed smaller than a Butterball.

Much smaller.

More like the size of a small chicken. A very small, very flat-chested chicken.

Brent came out to check on my progress.

"That's *it*?" he asked, inspecting the denuded hen.

"A bit wee, isn't it," I said, holding it up with my fist firmly jammed up its ass.

"How many pounds is it?"

Together we found the hanging scale that John used to weigh buckets of milk.

"That can't be right," I said, looking at the dial. John came and looked over our shoulders.

"Nope. That looks about right," he said, chuckling.

We had seven people arriving from the city for an old-fashioned Thanksgiving dinner. I did some quick calculations in my head.

"That means we're going to have less than a quarter pound of turkey apiece," I said.

Our prize turkey, for which we had paid the exorbitant sum of five dollars earlier in the summer—about three times what a Butterball turkey would have cost us, even more if we factored in feed—weighed only four and a half pounds.

"Why don't you kill another one?" Brent asked.

I held up my bloody hand in reply.

"Well, maybe some Indians will come by and share their bounty," Brent joked.

Eight hours later we were clearing the dishes off of the Thanksgiving table. Other than the flour and sugar used in the recipes, every dish served on our Thanksgiving table came completely from the farm. The turkey, mashed potatoes, green beans, corn casserole, squash, pickles, sour cherry sauce, apple cider, homemade cornbread stuffing, and pumpkin pie were all provided courtesy of the ground underneath the Beekman. It probably wasn't much different from the Thanksgivings that the early Beekmans shared. Our guests were amazed at the bounty. I doubt even Martha could have put together a better spread. Well . . .

The turkey carcass had been picked clean, of course. Everyone got about two bites, which made up for in flavor what they lacked in size. The meat wasn't as tender as the flavorless supermarket turkeys, and the breasts were far smaller and leaner, but our turkey had a delicious flavor—almost like roasted grain and nuts, with a hint of yellow apples.

All of our guests enjoyed the running commentary on each dish—the history of the garden and seeds, how everything was harvested, the process of canning and preserving it all. It was different from most Thanksgivings I'd been a part of. It was less about stuffing ourselves to excess, and more about how miraculous it was that there was a full table of food in the first place. I couldn't help but think that was supposed to be the point of the holiday all along. I also couldn't help but think that my role as an advertiser contributed to the misperception of food as a commodity whose value was distinguished mainly by calorie count and serving size. Boasting about the size of one's holiday turkey is really only genuine when one had something to do with feeding it.

After dinner I took the scrap pail out and emptied it onto the compost heap. The still warm scraps that had been scraped from the plates and the small turkey carcass steamed in the chilly late-afternoon air. Even though it was only 4:30 the sun was already beginning to set, and the remaining three turkeys cast long shadows across the barnyard. I noticed that the wishbone was still attached to the carcass. I reached into the compost pile and pulled it free, planning to share a wish duel with Brent later that evening. The bone was tiny of course, and with one hand bandaged it was difficult to get a good grip on it.

Just when I thought I had loosened it enough to break free, it broke. I was left holding the smallest prong.

The turkey won.

But it didn't matter. This boy from Wisconsin already had most of his wishes come true.

Chapter Fourteen

I'd been dreading the weeks between Thanksgiving and Christmas ever since I first learned that I'd have to spend most of them in Chicago working on the same damn health insurance project that had been dragging on for almost two years with no progress. Ever since we'd purchased the Beekman I'd had holiday season wet dreams. Ice skating. Hot chocolate. Snow angels. The Beekman Mansion's fourteen-foot-wide center halls were practically designed for maximum boughs-of-holly decking.

Instead I was stuck in what I'd long considered the most banal big city in the Western Hemisphere. There'd been a sweeping change in marketing management at the health insurance company, and I'd been sent out to help reassure the new executives that I remained just as committed to doing nothing as I had been before. This would involve many expense account dinners and rounds of cocktails paid for by the sicknesses of the company's membership. "To their health!"

I had a couple of down days between scheduled meetings and the resulting focus groups, and one of my clients had offered me a pair of tickets to an *Oprah* taping. At first I declined. I'd been nursing a slight Oprah grudge for several years, ever since my first book had been released and I'd learned through a friend who worked for Harpo Productions that several of *Oprah's*

producers were reading it and enjoying it. Even though the drag
and drug topic seemed a little dark for your average housewife, I
believed that maybe it could be the perfect, if unconventional, fit
for Oprah's Book Club—troubled young man struggling to find
himself, overcoming obstacles, blah blah blah.

If Oprah had picked my book, I could be on easy street instead of toiling away on Madison Avenue. She was the most powerful force in publishing and an endorsement by her would sell
millions. It seemed like a sure thing. I started to believe it was
going to happen, especially after my friend forwarded me an e-
mail in which her *Oprah* producer friend had described my book
as a "good read."

Instead, Oprah's next pick was Sidney Poitier's autobiogra-
phy. Sure he was an Oscar-winning actor, but had he ever tried
performing drunk in seven-inch heels and with live goldfish in
his tits?

But even given Oprah's obviously dubious taste in literature,
a few days into my business trip I changed my mind and accepted the tickets. I realized that attending an *Oprah* show taping
was still more appealing than sitting in my hotel room watching
Judge Judy.

Sitting in the audience before the taping began, I was fascinated by the crowd. The studio was packed with women who'd
traveled from all over. I knew this because there was a contest
led by the audience warm-up host for who traveled the longest
distance to come to the show. The winner came from Norway,
but the woman next to me (from Indiana) claimed the contest
had been unfair. The Norwegian was merely in town visiting
family who happened to have an extra *Oprah* ticket. This Scandi-
navian scoundrel was clearly not a dev-O-tee like the rest of the
eager audience.

During the twenty-minute warm-up, the excitement in the
air reached a fever pitch. Looking around I realized I was the

sole male in my audience section. Each woman seemed to be wearing some bright color or accessory that she believed would surely capture Oprah's attention. They shouted out messages to the crew members, hoping that someone would pass on the information to Oprah herself. One woman had gone to the same high school as Oprah. Another was married to someone who used to cut Oprah's hair. Yet another had brought along a copy of her own self-published diet book to pass along to the famous host.

By the time the warm-up host was wrapping up, the entire crowd was shrieking in anticipatory excitement. I was actually a bit frightened by the pack mentality. It was like a rock concert. Oprah was imminent. The lights dimmed, and the director began the countdown . . .

As the lights flashed on again, the crowd of women rose simultaneously and turned into one giant, screaming, clapping entity of jumping flesh and brightly colored accessories.

Oprah appeared at the studio entrance to my left and waited a moment until the director motioned for her to make her entrance—which she did, immersing herself in the outstretched worship of the audience like one of John's goats facing into a welcome stiff spring breeze.

I have to admit I wasn't immune. During the hour-long taping, we were treated to several guests who'd transformed their lives into what Oprah called their "Best Lives." It seemed to be a mantra of sorts. One woman left her boring corporate job to work with handicapped animals. Another started a small confectionary business that had hit the big time. The audience oohed and aahed at a young man who fled his abusive parents and spent three years helping African tribes dig wells for freshwater.

By the end of the hour of taping, I too had been magically transformed from a cynical ad guy into a full-fledged Oprah banshee. I clapped when the director mimed for us to. I frowned in concerned empathy whenever an audience camera zoomed by my head. I clapped with wild abandon until my palms hurt each time we went into a commercial break.

The stories of personal transformation and triumph of Oprah's guests buzzed through me the way vodka used to. It was addictive. And no matter how hard I fought it, it was inspiring.

There I was, stuck in Chicago on a business trip while Brent was making goat milk hot chocolate and pulling Christmas ornaments down from the attic. Was *this* my Best Life? I was boring myself to tears watching the same hotel pay-per-view movies each night after spending all day shilling taglines and thirty-second commercials to clients who were more concerned with not making a wrong decision than making any decision at all.

I was nearing forty years old—six years removed from the eighteen- to thirty-four-year-olds that advertisers lusted after. The clients who paid me to come up with ad ideas weren't even interested in advertising to *me*. I didn't know of many people who lasted in advertising past forty-five or fifty, no matter how talented they were at doing nothing.

I needed to get back to the Beekman.

I wasn't exactly sure what my Best Life was supposed to be, but I was pretty sure it had something to do with cooking Thanksgiving dinner with food from the garden, canning enough tomatoes to last through the winter, sweeping up zombie flies, picking apples, and baking cherry pies for a Fourth of July picnic.

I needed to make some Best Life changes before it was too late.

Oprah told me to.

Chapter Fifteen

———

For true Martha-philes, the real spirit of Christmas is giving or, more specifically, giving up every moment between Thanksgiving and New Year's in pursuit of beating baby Jesus at his own game.

The stakes are even higher if one happens to work at Martha Stewart Living Omnimedia. While most of us merely have to deal with the ten-dollar Secret Santa swap at our offices, MSLO employees find themselves having to put to practice the crafts they've been preaching on television and in glossy print for the last twelve months. Exchanging Isotoner gloves and Starbucks gift cards aren't going to put anyone on the fast track to the MSLO boardroom.

Brent had been fretting since Halloween, trying to come up with a handmade gift worthy of bestowing on his colleagues— and Martha herself. The previous year he'd scored a hit with gingerbread cookies decorated with an elaborate white-and-Tiffany-blue snowflake design, accented with silver dragées. We'd spent an entire weekend baking and decorating, and by that Sunday night I was lying on my stomach on the floor, squeezing royal icing from the pastry bag onto the nude cookies. My back had given out from bending over the kitchen counter, but Brent wouldn't let me stop until the final gingerbread fellow was properly dressed. Worse yet, he acted as quality control, quickly weeding out unacceptable ginger-dudes for transgressions such as cracked limbs and lopsided torsos. It had been pastry eugenics of the most sinister sort.

But they had been a hit. Martha dutifully gave her gracious approval on receipt, which only meant that the bar had been raised for the next year's effort.

"Why don't we just do the cookies again," I asked Brent as we drove to the cut-your-own-Christmas-tree farm in Cherry Valley. This December morning was the coldest morning of the year so far. The thermometer on the truck's visor read 6 degrees. Plus there was a steady wind blowing up the valley. Since we hadn't visited Sharon Springs in the months between last fall's discovery of the Beekman and the springtime closing on it, we had no idea how harsh the winter could be.

"You can't give the same thing twice."

"Why not? It'll be your 'thing.' A tradition."

"At Martha we don't *have* traditions, we *make* traditions," Brent recited. "I'd rather give something from the farm."

"How about the apple butter we made?"

Brent scoffed.

"Pickles?" I offered.

"Not something that any old farm could make," Brent explained. "Think more Martha-ish."

"Hand-knitted scarves made from molted goat fur dyed with turkey blood."

"Something from the goats *would* be cool," Brent said, perhaps not realizing that I was joking.

The wind had caused a four-foot snowdrift across the driveway leading up to the Christmas tree farm. So we parked the truck on the side of the road and hiked toward the small cabin with a picturesque puff of smoke coming from its stovepipe chimney. Our plan for the day was to bring home our tree, decorate it, string some homemade garlands for the front of the house, and go to bed with sugar plum faeries dancing, etc., etc.

"It's really freezing," Brent said.

"Yep." I forced myself to bite my tongue. It's a particular pet peeve of mine that Brent doesn't dress for the weather. Sometimes I think he dresses as if he's going to a photo shoot of whatever occasion we're attending rather than the actual event. It's especially maddening in the winter, and was even more so at the Beekman than in the city. I have to remind myself, however, that he's a southern boy at heart. In his head he really doesn't understand the difference between 32 degrees and -15 degrees. To him there is simply "hot," "warm," and "I should put on a jacket or something." The concept of windchill is completely beyond his imagination.

Brent knocked on the door of the little shack, and a man opened it just enough to stick his head out. He seemed surprised that we were there.

"We'd like to cut down a tree," Brent said.

"Today?" he asked, as if the thought of someone visiting a Christmas tree farm in early December was somehow not part of his business plan. "Kinda cold, don't you think?" he elaborated, giving Brent's light flannel jacket and baseball cap the once-over.

I looked across the hills and fields scattered with evergreens.

"Which direction should we head?" I asked.

"Depends. Whacha lookin' for?" the man asked. Didn't we just go over this? A Christmas tree. What did he think we're looking for—the lido deck?

"Well, up over there I've got your blue spruce, and on that other hill are the white pines. And those are Douglas firs down by the creek." Except he pronounced "creek" like "crick." Clearly our years of buying stumpy trees from New York City sidewalk stands hadn't educated us on the intricacies of Christmas tree selection. It was too confusing. And everywhere he was pointing seemed miles away.

"Great, thanks. We'll find something, " I said.

"Good luck! Twenty-five bucks apiece, no matter the size," he explained. "Pay on your way out." Before closing the door he pointed out a pile of rusty saws leaning against the doorframe for our use.

We began trudging through the snow up a hill toward a distant stand of white pines . . . or maybe Douglas firs. It didn't matter. We were overjoyed to be there, traipsing through the snow to pick our very first Christmas tree for the Beekman. Later in the day we'd string up the garlands, come back inside, and decorate the tree while drinking cups of homemade goat milk hot chocolate. We loved Christmas. We didn't even pretend to hide it. We were one of those cliché couples who purchased Christmas ornaments from every place we visited together, so decorating the tree each year was like reliving all of our fondest memories.

"*Oh tannenbaum, oh tannenbaum . . . !*" I hollered against the wind at the top of my lungs.

"*How lovely are thy branches!!!*" Brent sang back. We sang our way up the hill, starring in our own perfect little Christmas variety hour, until twenty minutes later we reached the most windblown, barren, and gnarled stand of trees I'd ever seen. Each one we came upon was sparser than the last.

"These are hideous!" Brent yelled above the wind.

"Let's try down there." I pointed down the hill toward the stream. We began trekking even farther away from the cabin and truck. The snow whirled around my face, creating almost whiteout conditions. I tried to remember my Cub Scout training on how to survive outdoors in a snowstorm, but quickly remembered that the only badge I earned was the "Showman Badge" for writing, directing, and starring in a finger puppet show about playground safety. ("Don't stand too close to a swing set in use . . . LOOK OUT!!!")

Chunks of ice were forming on my knit scarf from my breath. I couldn't imagine how Brent was tolerating the bone-chilling cold in his light jacket. I thought that we really should've turned back, but Brent was too far ahead of me to shout to.

The next stand of trees turned out to be no better than the first. But there was no way we were going to move on to another. We must've covered three miles already. The trees in this stand were all about two stories tall, and mostly bare of branches the first ten feet up from the ground.

"Let's just chop down a tall one and use the top," I suggested.

We circled through the trees with our necks craned upward, looking for one that was fullest at its peak. Around and around we went, deeper into the woods. I was about to point out a possible contender when I heard Brent yell from about twenty feet in front of me.

"*Fuck!*"

Brent doesn't swear. Ever. He doesn't even use the word "swear." Some parts of his southern Holy-Roller background cannot be shaken. I rushed over to him to find him shaking his left leg as if it were on fire.

"What happened?"

He pointed downward toward a rushing stream of water under the snow. We didn't even realize that we were walking around staring upward at the "Douglas firs down by the crick."

"You're not even wearing boots!" I scolded as Brent sat in the snow taking off his thin athletic socks to wring them out. "Why the heck would you wear Crocs in the middle of a snowstorm?"

"Let's just pick a fucking tree and get out of here." His feet were almost a translucent white as he struggled to get the wet socks back on.

It took us fifteen more minutes to saw, chop, and hack one of the monsters to the ground. This one's top looked much fuller when it was two stories above our heads. On the ground it looked more like a giant toilet brush with half of its bristles missing. I wasn't going to point this out to Brent, however, since he was jumping back and forth from one foot to the other trying to keep blood flowing into his wet appendages.

"Grab that side," he said. I did as he instructed, and we began to drag the behemoth back toward where we believed the cabin and truck to be. It must've weighed two hundred pounds. Soon I was wheezing. My heart was racing and throbbing so loudly that it was all I could hear under my ski cap. Ten years ago—hell, even *five*—this sort of task might've tired me out, but it wouldn't stop me in my tracks. I couldn't believe how badly my body was rebelling against me. I started thinking about all the stories I've heard about friends of friends who've dropped dead of heart attacks at forty years old.

"I . . . can't . . . make . . . it . . ." I wheezed to Brent. "It's . . . too . . . heavy." I dropped my end and bent over with my hands on my knees trying to catch my breath.

"C'mon. Don't be a drama queen."

"No. REALLY, I can't." I wondered how long Brent would be able to administer CPR on me before his feet froze solid.

Brent muttered something I couldn't hear above the wind and began yanking and tugging the tree all by himself. He was really pissed. We made our way back slowly, in fits and spurts. I joined in the pulling when I could, and collapsed into the snow whenever I ran out of breath again.

When we finally reached the driveway, the old man stuck his head out of the cabin again.

"Saw ya draggin' that thing all the way up the hill! That's a monster!" he yelled. "That'll be thirty-five."

Brent, ignoring him, continued to drag the tree toward the truck while I walked over to pay.

"I thought . . . *wheeze* . . . you said . . . *wheeze* . . . they were twenty-five dollars . . . *wheeze* . . . no matter the size."

"Yeah. But that's a big one."

I was too utterly spent and freezing to argue, so I pulled two twenty-dollar bills out of my wallet and pushed them into his hands.

"Keep the . . . *wheeze* . . . change."

"Merry Christmas! Keep warm!" he shouted after us, before quickly disappearing back into the cozy cabin.

The rest of our perfect holiday Saturday didn't go much more smoothly. We gave up on our garland-making attempt after we'd laid out hundreds of boughs down the center aisle of the barn, carefully wired them together, and then watched them fall back to pieces the moment we tried to lift and carry them outside.

Then we turned our attention back to our tree. After wrestling it inside, it became apparent just how spindly and sparse the top ten feet of our giant tree was. There weren't nearly enough branches on which to hang our 'round-the-world collection of ornaments. This tree couldn't hold an ornament collection of an agoraphobe.

There was no silver or gold lining to this tree. It was ugly. Even Cindy Lou Hoo wouldn't have missed this one. While I probably could've lived with it, Brent, with his Martha Stewart mind-set, would have grown to hate it more and more each day. By Christmas morning he probably would have set it on fire.

"Brent?"

"What." His demeanor was utterly deflated.

"Get your jacket."

"I don't want to go anywhere."

After ten years together, I knew exactly how he was feeling. About the only time Brent gets in a real funk is when he feels as if he's wasted his time. The day was nearly over and we had nothing to show for it. No tree. No garlands. No goat milk hot chocolate memories.

"Just let's go," I said, pulling warm jackets for both of us out of the hallway closet. "And wear real boots this time."

An hour later, Brent and I were chewing Quarter Pounders and sipping hot chocolate in the McDonald's parking lot with a perfectly proportioned, unnaturally green, lush Walmart Christmas tree tied to the roof of the truck.

"Merry Christmas, Grinch," I said.

He leaned over and kissed me with French fry–salty lips.

I've always thought that one of the signs of true adulthood is when you realize that you spend each Christmas trying to relive childhood memories that never really happened in the first place.

But that first Christmas at the Beekman taught me otherwise. It lived up to every sappy holiday commercial ever produced. Both Brent and I had two full weeks off of work, and we spent each day as if we were living in a Macy's holiday display window. We bought ice skates for our pond, toboggans for the steepest hay field, and made snow forts in the glacier-size drifts by the far woods. We cooked pies and cookies with fruit from our cellar, and made snow cream from the new snow that seemed to tumble down fresh every night. We drove around the village to look at Christmas light displays, and lay down in the hay with the goats to take naps whenever we felt like it. In short, we had everything and nothing to do, and we did all and none of it.

While we're both close to our families, it also felt wonderful not to have to travel during the holidays. We decided that we deserved to start some of our own Christmas traditions. We were growing bored in our roles of eccentric gay uncles who swooped in from the big city with exotic presents that nobody really wanted, and who complained about having to go to church.

Luckily for us, Sharon Springs readily embraced us in its own traditions. For a town that looks long dead to people who quickly pass through it, it had a social calendar that rivaled the Upper East Side's. Doug and Garth invited us to their annual Christmas Eve buffet, complete with silver chafing dishes and hired waiters. Garth's mother comes into town each year for the sole purpose of making guests the most potent margaritas north of Tijuana. Margaritas may not be the first drink one thinks of when listing holiday cocktails, but Garth's mom makes sure it's the last thought running through everyone's brain on Christmas Eve.

It seemed as if everyone in the village turned out for Doug and Garth's party, and they all treated us as if we'd lived in the village forever. With the winter so brutal, the village used every possible communal occasion to catch up on local gossip. It was always entertaining to hear about Brent's and my life from outside sources. It had been rumored that we were buying up land all over town. And that we were going to buy all of Main Street and turn it into something called "Marthaville." Naturally we had to squelch new rumors that Martha would be joining us at the Beekman for Christmas.

At midnight, as he did every year, Doug donned a pair of footie pajamas and recited " 'Twas the night before Christmas" to all of the guests before everyone stumbled home, full of holiday margarita spirits.

The next morning, Michelle hosted her annual extravagant Christmas Day brunch. The exact same group of villagers, except this time hungover, drove up the long icy driveway to her stone mansion at the top of a hill overlooking the valley. We'd been especially excited about Michelle's party, since we'd been hearing about her legendary Christmas punch concoction since we'd arrived in town. It was called, simply, "pink stuff." No one quite knew exactly what was in it, but it was assumed to be some sort of 7Up, sherbet, and marshmallow concoction. The legend goes that no matter how much of the pink glob was served up, the mass regenerated itself in the punch bowl so that it always appeared full. Some people have even theorized that it is simply put in the freezer and reused each year.

Holiday traditions like those explained exactly why Sharon Springs seemed to be the perfect island for misfit toys and eccentric gay uncles.

By New Year's Eve, both Brent and I had practically forgotten all about our parallel lives in the city. We decided to stay at the Beekman by ourselves and celebrate by opening the first bottle of hard apple cider made from our own apples. It had been brewing in the basement since we picked the apples on our one-year anniversary of finding Sharon Springs.

As we waited for midnight, Brent remembered to go online to check the holiday train schedule. We both needed to be back early to prepare for 9 A.M. meetings on the second.

"Let's open some champagne," I suggested, while he searched the timetable.

"It's not midnight yet."

"So what? I've always been a trendsetter."

While he was busy entering our credit card information on the Amtrak site, I poured us two glasses. Except that we didn't have any wineglasses at the Beekman yet, so I improvised with two small jelly jars left over from our canning adventures.

"Here's to my favorite year so far," I said handing him his glass.

"To William Beekman," he added.

"And Farmer John."

"And Sharon Springs."

"And the goats, turkeys, and cabaret roosters."

"And the full root cellar."

"Mary and all the ghosts."

"And the zombie flies."

"Really?" Brent said. "The flies?"

"Hey, as a wise woman once said: you take the good, you take the bad, you take them both, and there you have the facts of life."

"To the facts of life!" Brent echoed. We *ching* our jars and take a sip.

"Do you want to hear my New Year's resolution?" I asked Brent over his shoulder.

"It's not midnight yet."

"So what? I've always been a trendsetter."

"Go on."

"My New Year's resolution is to be in this exact same place next New Year's," I said.

"Well of course," Brent said, clicking the BUY NOW button for the 4:35 Empire express train for the following afternoon. "Where else would we be?"

"No, I mean I want to be here permanently." Brent didn't say anything, so I continued. "If next year is just as good as this year, I want to take our Christmas bonuses, quit advertising, sell the city apartment, pay off this mortgage, and move here full time. I want to become a farmer."

"You already are a farmer."

"I mean a *real* farmer."

"That's a pretty major resolution."

"I know, I know," I said. "It's Oprah's fault."

"Of course," Brent answered facetiously.

"Look, I didn't even realize what was missing from my life until we bought this place. But this last year has been one of the best years of my life. It's been unpredictably, exhaustingly, satisfyingly my Best Life. I just can't face spending the rest of my life behind a desk selling dish soap to Middle America. Hell, I want to *be* Middle America."

Brent was quiet again. I wondered if the same thought had ever even occurred to him.

"I think that's probably something we should decide together," he finally said.

"We already did," I said. "You just haven't realized it yet."

Chapter Sixteen

"Guess what?" Brent asked, calling me in my office from his. "Martha really liked it."

"She did?" I had no idea what he was talking about. I had just sold a rebranding campaign to the agency's newest and largest account—an airline that was about to emerge from bankruptcy with nothing much going for it but a new logo and uniforms. I'd been so busy during my first week back in the city that I couldn't even remember if there was something I was supposed to remember.

"She especially loved that it didn't smell," he continued.

I wracked my brain trying to remember something about Martha that didn't smell.

"And she loved the packaging . . . the logo you designed." It finally came to me: the soap.

In a moment of last-minute holiday inspiration, we'd decided that our Christmas gift to Martha this past holiday would be homemade soap, made from the milk of the Beekman goats. We'd contacted John's buyer, Deb, and asked her to teach us how to make some. She helped us pour and cure dozens of small guest bars, which we handed out to our friends and associates—each one stamped with a new logo we'd created for the Beekman.

Although I was dubious at first, I have to admit I was surprised at how well the soap had turned out. Having failed chemistry both in high school and college, I didn't have much confidence that I could combine the milk, lye, and hot oils into anything other than a raging fireball.

"That's great," I said proudly. I knew our present probably blew away any other homemade gifts she had gotten. Between landing the airline account and getting on Martha's good graces, we already had a good start on what were sure to be record-setting bonuses for next Christmas. We were one step closer to a life of pastoral bliss.

"So," Brent continued, "can you make the 4:45 train this afternoon?"

"Probably," I said.

"Bring your laptop," Brent said. "I have an idea I want to run by you."

"What is it?"

"Nothing much," Brent said. "Just your New Year's resolution come true."

"Really? *How?*"

"Well, don't get too excited," Brent said, tempering my enthusiasm. "It's just an idea. And it'll be a lot of work."

"As a closet farmer," I said, "I'm not afraid of work."

"Just bring your computer."

"Do farmers use computers?"

"Well, we will."

As we settled into our seats on the train, I could tell that Brent was eager to download his brainstorm. Since he's usually so composed, even the slightest bit of excitement reads on his face like the sun shining on new snowfall.

"So what's the big idea?" I asked.

"It's just a thought," Brent said. "We still need to really think it through."

"I can't start thinking till you start talking."

"Well, you know how you said you wanted to become a real farmer?"

"Yeah."

"We both know that most farms don't make enough money to break even."

It was true. Small farms all around us were going out of business each month. The *Penny Savior* was full of classified ads for farm equipment auctions. Small farmers simply couldn't compete with the huge factory farms of the Midwest.

"We'll be different," I said, not having the first idea why.

"Right," Brent said. "That's where Martha comes in."

"She's going to back us?"

"No," Brent said. "Well, yes. Sort of. Martha liked the soap so much that she thought I should do a segment on the show about the benefits of milk soap on the skin. And she wants us to make some more to give away to the studio audience."

"Oprah gives away cars, and Martha gives away soap," I said. "She's cheaper than I thought."

Brent frowned. He hated when I made fun of Martha, even in jest.

"Martha also thought it would be cute to bring in a few baby goats," Brent continued, ignoring me.

"Okay," I said, not sure where he was heading.

"Most companies pay tens of thousands of dollars for product placement on Martha's show. I get to go on for free."

"But you're on the show all the time."

"Not with something to sell," Brent said.

"We're going to sell baby goats on TV?" I asked. "That seems a little sordid."

"No." Brent sighed. "We're going to start a line of artisanal beauty products."

"We're going to become a soap farm!" I said excitedly, finally getting it.

"Exactly," Brent said.

It was a brilliant idea. And it just might work. Farmer John had been mentioning that he might have to send some goats to auction if he couldn't find an additional buyer for his milk. *And* soap maker Deb wanted to move into a larger store on the village Main Street, but was worried whether she could afford the rent. *And* Doug and Garth could use official Martha-approved soap in the hotel. *And* we'd heard the Sharon Springs post office was in danger of being shut down for lack of volume. Suddenly I realized that if we started a mail-order company, we wouldn't just be selling a few bars of soap; we'd be helping to put Sharon Springs back on the map. (Almost literally—many of our houseguests had had trouble finding us since Sharon Springs wasn't in their GPS systems.)

"This is how I'm going to get out of advertising!" I announced.

"Well, let's not get ahead of ourselves," Brent cautioned. "It's just a start. Not many people get rich off of soap."

"Try telling that to Mr. Unilever."

Brent rolled his eyes. "It takes a lot of soap to make up for a six-figure salary. We'd have to build it into a larger brand. It's still a long shot."

I knew he was just testing me. He wanted to make sure that I really meant what I'd said about becoming a full-time farmer. I did, wholeheartedly. I could go from selling soap commercials to selling *actual soap*. Finally I'd be doing something real. No more endless business meetings about target demographics and brand attributes. No more filling in time sheets and arguing over font sizes.

I'd be free.

My Best Life seemed right around the corner.

But I also wanted to be sure that he too had the same level of conviction. I decided to play my own trump card.

"Well, you know, if you don't think you can pull it off . . ."

It was the Donald Trump card, actually. With Brent's dual degrees, Martha Stewart perfectionism, and—to be frank—outsize ego, Brent couldn't stand when his skills were doubted.

"Oh, I can make it happen," Brent said, defensively. "Just get out your laptop."

By the time we reached Albany, Brent already had the beginnings of a business plan sketched out. The company would be more than just an online mail-order catalog. We'd model ourselves after Martha in a way. We'd have a Web site, but it wouldn't just sell soap; we'd also have articles, slideshows, and videos sharing all of the lessons we'd learned during our first year in the country. There'd be sections on gardening and on raising animals, and recipes using our produce. We'd help people rediscover lost arts like canning and making hard apple cider. We'd met and admired so many regional craftspeople who had no market for items that we knew urban dwellers would pay through the nose for. We could help them sell their creations through our site.

Just as my office colleagues were intrigued to hear stories about my shadow life as a farmer, maybe there were people all over the world who were looking for someone to show them the path toward the simple life.

We were forced to stay inside for the duration of the weekend; a massive snowstorm squalled outside for forty-eight hours. But it didn't bother us at all. We huddled over the kitchen table with the fireplace roaring, and brainstormed business ideas and brand concepts. By Sunday evening, just about the only thing we lacked was a name.

"Maybe something with the word 'goat' in it," I suggested as we continued our discussion on the Sunday-night train trip back into the city.

"Nah," Brent said. "As the brand grows, we'll have to sell things that don't use goat milk."

"We could name it after ourselves, like Martha," I said.

"There are two of us," Brent said. "How would that work?"

"I don't know. A combination of our names? *Brosh? Jent?*"

We went back and forth for the entire ride home, tossing out bad puns and turns of phrase. It wasn't until we were pulling into Penn Station when the obvious occurred to us.

"What about 'Beekman'?" I asked.

"Makes sense," Brent said. "But it's a little vague."

"Beekman Farm? Beekman Mansion?" I offered.

"Too boring," Brent said. "We need something kinda stylish, otherwise we'll seem like any other homespun mom-and-pop company."

He was right. We'd be a pop-and-pop enterprise. People would expect us to be a little chic.

"What are some other fashion-y names?" Brent asked.

I went through every fashion brand I could think of. Most of them were people's names: Tommy Hilfiger, Dolce & Gabanna, Vera Wang. Some were foreign sounding: Anthropologie, Adidas, Oilily. I moved on to perfumes: Poison, Envy, White Diamonds, Chanel No. 5.

"Hey," I said, perking up in the backseat of the cab as we were pulling up outside our apartment building. "How about 'Beekman 1802'?"

The farm and mansion were built in 1802.

Brent mulled it over a moment.

"Not bad," he said. "I think we just started a soap farm."

Book 2

Chapter Seventeen

"And welcome back."

As the studio audience applause dies down, Martha continues reading off the cue card. "Up in the Mohawk Valley of upstate New York is a beautiful nineteenth-century farm called the Beekman Mansion where our own Dr. Brent Ridge relaxes on his weekends, growing vegetables and flowers and raising his own herd of dairy goats . . ."

Martha and Brent are sitting side by side on small milking stools under the bright television lights. The art department has made a small pen from birch branches and covered the floor with artfully strewn straw. At their feet lie Trent, Terrence, Troy, Tammy, and Thandy, all peacefully nodding off in a pile, with their heads resting on one another's backs. They're glowingly snow white again, thanks to my furious wet-nap wiping out on the sidewalk. When Martha reaches down to pick up a sleepy Troy, the studio audience, on cue, sighs *"Awwwwwwww."*

The *Martha* audience isn't much dissimilar from the *Oprah* audience I'd experienced just a few months ago. Viewers flew in from all over the world to get a glimpse of their hero. Perhaps they were a bit more mannered and neutrally dressed, but still they rose to their feet, shrieking with glee, the moment Dear Leader took the stage.

What was different this time was that I was the guest. Well, not me specifically—I was watching from just offstage ready to chase any runaway goats. But Brent's and my life was the main guest. The B-roll footage (filmed earlier at the Beekman) that played on the giant video screens above the stage looked impossibly perfect, and perfectly Martha-esque. There were no photos of our messy canning adventure, or our spindly hand-cut Christmas tree, or the sulfurous rotten egg breakfast of our very first morning. Instead the montage included impressive architectural shots, shiny and clean goats in the pasture, and non-weedy close-ups of the flower garden. Yes, our life was the guest on stage—but only the most picturesque bits. I looked at the audience members as they took in the montage. They were at the edge of their seats, smiling . . . rabidly. This is what they came to see. Oprah teased her fans with their impossible-to-achieve Best Lives while Martha tormented hers with Photoshopped fantasies of Good Things.

No one, of course, noticed the middle-aged ad exec smelling of goat shit standing in the wings, wet naps at the ready.

Naturally, like everything in Martha Land, the segment comes off without a hitch. Martha and Brent spend the first eight minutes chatting about the farm and the secrets of healthy country living, and the second segment after a commercial break making a flawless batch of homemade goat milk soap.

Thankfully Martha also takes a moment to acknowledge our soap mentor, Deb, who is seated in the audience. The Sharon Springs gossip network has practically blown a circuit during the past few weeks passing along word about the goats' big-city television appearance. Even John seemed a little impressed. A little.

As in most small towns across America, everybody in Sharon Springs has his or her own unique set of skills to share with neighbors. Those who can cook bring food to those who are hungry. Those who can repair help those who are broken. Those who have extra money hire those who need work. There is no safety net in a small town like there is in larger cities. If your neighbor doesn't have it, you won't either. But if your neighbor does have something, you'll probably be able to share.

Perhaps Brent and I don't have the years of rural skills that our friends and neighbors do. We're not around during the week to whip up a casserole for a grieving family. We're not knowledgeable enough to fix a broken tractor. We don't even have a snowplow to help a widow clear out her driveway.

But what we do have are connections; lifelines to the world outside of troubled Sharon Springs. By launching Beekman 1802 on Martha's show, we've made the first formal introduction between Sharon Springs and the rest of the country. Who knows how well they're going to get along. But at least we've done the polite thing.

After the credits roll and the studio lights are switched off, Martha walks over with Brent to say hello.

"These little guys are adorable, Josh," she says, still cradling Troy in her arms. "Thanks so much from bringing them in this morning."

I thank Martha for inviting them on the show.

"Of course," she says. "I'll have to come up to see you guys some weekend."

"You're welcome anytime," Brent says. I want to nudge him with my elbow. Anytime? Really? I'm pretty sure I would need a few weeks' notice before Martha Stewart just dropped by—months, actually.

When she walks away I finally have a chance to check the steadily vibrating BlackBerry in my pocket.

Beekman 1802 New Order Notice.

Beekman 1802 New Order Notice.

Beekman 1802 New Order Notice.

Beekman 1802 New Order Notice . . .

Chapter Eighteen

Before the show had finished airing on the West Coast, our lives had changed completely. Martha's influence exceeded even my expectations. I'd always admired her for the effect she'd had on America's homemaking aesthetic. I grew up in an era where the vast majority of people bought their furniture and housewares from places like the Sears catalog and local hardware stores. Martha almost singlehandedly turned America's housewives into eager design students, with the television show and magazines as her classroom.

Even though I recognized her wide-ranging influence, I hadn't experienced the power behind it firsthand until the soap segment on her show. We'd been anointed. Or rather, our soap was. Her followers were rabid to get a piece of the same soap that Martha used. The soap touched her body, and now vicariously, they could too. The resulting enthusiasm was orgiastic.

We'd had tens of thousands of hits to our new Web site, and it showed no signs of slowing. Beekman 1802 had become a living, breathing business. And like every other living, breathing thing on the farm, it needed to be constantly fed.

We'd spent the weekend immediately after the *Martha* show wrapping and mailing more than eight hundred orders of soap. The first flush of orders had abated slightly the following week, so Deb was able to have most of them mailed off before we arrived for the weekend, which meant we had time to begin on our other springtime chores, which took on an even greater importance than last year now that more than a thousand people tuned in daily to Beekman1802.com. They'd be watching our every move.

After the goats' Martha appearance, the Beekman went from being a weekend getaway to a flagship HQ. No longer were we satisfied making our own yogurt; now we had to photograph every step of the process and write a blog entry about it. We didn't merely make another batch of soap; we created a whole beauty line inspired by the different seasons at the farm. Scratch that— at Beekman 1802.

Even though the ground was still frozen solid, it would soon be time to put in the garden again. But we'd decided that a replica of last season's garden wasn't good enough. If we were going to include a garden section on our Web site, we'd have to create something worthy enough to blog about, something more impressive than a regular backyard garden.

Something like the Beekman 1802 Historical Heirloom Kitchen Garden.

Luckily, we'd recently met a new set of neighbors who lived over the hill from us—Peter and Barbara. They were a semiretired couple who'd decided on a whim to buy one of the country's oldest seed companies, D. Landreth Seeds. Once the largest seed company in America, Landreth had recently fallen on hard times and was rapidly sinking into oblivion. Single-handedly, the couple was reviving its historic catalog collection of heirloom vegetable and flower seed. The company was getting ready to celebrate its 225th anniversary, which would make it the fifth-oldest company in America. Its historical achievements included being the first to sell tomato seeds to Americans, introducing the zinnia from Mexico, and selling seeds to every U.S. president from George Washington to FDR. By the mid-nineteenth century the company was so large that it was sending a seed catalog and almanac to every single home in America.

I'd asked Barb if William Beekman would have sold Landreth seeds in his mercantile, and she assured me that he wouldn't have had many other options. They were the perfect corporate partners for the new Beekman 1802 garden.

Now we simply had to build one.

Brent and I huddled over the kitchen table with the fire roaring against our backs. We'd been poring over the pages of the Landreth seed catalog for hours, referencing and cross-referencing all of the historical varieties.

"Ooh . . . look at *this* one," I said, pointing out yet another listing to Brent. "It's a *white* cucumber from the eighteen-forties!"

Brent started to pen a star next to it and then realized that we'd already starred five other varieties of cucumbers so far.

"We have to thin out this list a little," he said.

"But all of these seeds are so interesting. They have stories."

Many of the heirloom vegetables' stories are as interesting as the history of actual people. They *are* the history of America, in some sense. Many of the seeds immigrated to America in the holds of ships, tucked into the pockets of the men and women who wanted to find a better home, but couldn't bear to part with their favorite foods. Others were brought back from exotic continents by horticultural and culinary explorers. Some were on the brink of extinction before the modern movement to save our heirloom horticultural history discovered them growing in the backyards of Appalachian mountain homes and old midwestern farm gardens.

With the exception of heirloom tomatoes, most heirloom

vegetables haven't yet rooted into the consciousness of American grocery shoppers. Because they haven't been genetically hybridized to be shipped across the country or to ward off common pests and diseases, they aren't grown commercially on a scale that would allow them to be sold in the local A&P. Which is a shame, really. How fun would grocery shopping be if instead of simply grabbing a plastic bag of carrots, we could choose between the Chantenay long variety (developed in France in the 1830s) or the Belgium White carrot (a snow-white carrot that was one of the most popular varieties sold in 1863)?

"We don't have room for all their stories," Brent said.

"Maybe we need to make the garden bigger," I said.

"We were hardly able to keep up with all we grew last year."

"Yeah, but think of the Web site," I said. "The more varieties we have, the more recipes and canning we can blog about. It'll give us new content to keep up our hits."

"And you're going to take care of this new huge garden?" Brent asked, dubiously enough for me to take slight offense.

"Of course," I answered. "I'll design it so that it practically takes care of itself."

I spent most of the rest of the Saturday indoors, plotting out a new, expanded garden on my laptop. On Sunday, when the meager winter sun was at its highest point, I grabbed Brent and we went to survey my proposed locale for the new garden. We paced across the frozen tundra of the barnyard, occasionally consulting the laptop, stringing twine along the outline of where we wanted our new garden to be.

Bubby watched from his perch in the hayloft as we tramped across his most fertile hunting ground.

"I designed the plan so that we can plant the pumpkins here, along the edges," I explained to Brent. "That way the vines can grow out into the field as far as they want. And over here will be a row of blueberry bushes. On that side will be the corn, which should grow tall enough to shade the lettuces from the after-noon sun."

Watching us march across the frozen barnyard with our lap-top, Farmer John's curiosity finally got the best of him. He came out of his house and joined us.

"What's going on?"

"We're thinking of expanding the garden this year," I an-swered.

"How big?"

Brent pointed toward the stake we pounded into the hard earth at the far corner of our plot. John raised his eyebrows ever so slightly. For a moment I worried he was upset about our plans. After all, when we were in the city for the week, it fell on John to water and keep an eye on the "crops." John looked at the staked outline, glanced down at my computer screen, then looked up again, trying to visualize the space. The proposed new garden was easily eight or so times larger than the old one. He squinted, then smiled.

"Cool."

I'd forgotten how, when John had sent us that very first letter introducing himself, he'd extolled his skills and passions as a gar-dener. As our first summer together went by, he'd been mostly preoccupied with moving his herd over, building new pens, get-ting hay in for the winter, and generally turning the Beekman into a working farm. This year he'd have more time to help with the gardening.

"Are these all raised beds?" John asked, pointing at the com-puter screen with his gloved finger.

"Fifty-two of them," I answered. "Each one is four foot by six foot, twelve inches deep."

"Maybe we should make them eighteen inches deep. It'll be easier to weed," John said. For the rest of the afternoon we staked out where each of the beds would go. By the time the

sun began to set in the late afternoon, the barnyard was covered with stakes. When I squinted my eyes I could almost see
the rows of bean trellises and tomato cages. Our feet and fingers
were numb in the cold, but we'd all worked up a sweat building
our imaginary garden.

Before we left for the train the next day, we'd divvied up
what the account executives in my office would call "next steps."
John would contact someone about building the beds and see if
he could borrow a bulldozer to completely level the area. Brent
would finalize the seed list and place the order. I'd research and
buy the growing lights, seed pots, and warming trays to start the
various tomato, melon, and pepper seeds.

As we climbed back into the truck to leave for the station,
Brent turned to me and asked if I really thought we could build
and install such an ambitious garden in just a few weeks.

"Well, it's too late now," I said, patting my bag containing my
laptop. "I've already announced it to our readers."

Chapter Nineteen

A rusty light brown sedan of early-1990s origin pulled into the Beekman driveway and around to the side of the barnyard where John, Dan (the neighbor helping us construct the beds), and I were working. The driver, a woman who looked to be about sixty, dressed in church clothes, leaned over the front seat to manually roll down the passenger-side window.

"What in God's name are you doing?" she asked. I couldn't tell if she was actually pissed or simply kidding.

"We're putting in our garden."

"Oh," she said, puzzled. "I thought you were turning the place into a cemetery." Then, without another word, she rolled the window back up, reversed out of the driveway, and roared back down Route 10 from the direction she came from.

The three of us had to chuckle at the absurd interaction, but quickly got back to work piecing together the collection of fifty-two four-by-six-foot plain wood boxes that would soon become the Beekman 1802 Historic Heirloom Kitchen Garden.

Drop-in visits by strangers were becoming almost commonplace. The previous weekend, Brent and I walked into the barn to find a middle-aged couple chatting happily away with John. We joined the conversation, and it wasn't until they'd departed that the three of us realized that we had no idea who the couple was. "They called me Farmer John," John explained, "but I'd never met them."

We figured out that they knew his name from Brent's mention of it on the *Martha* show and from our weekly blog entries on the Beekman 1802 Web site. They simply looked up our address on the Web site and drove on over. From where, we had no idea. Along with the Beekman, Farmer John was becoming famous. While he might have been a little surprised at his new celebrity, he didn't seem to have a problem with it.

Starting with the *Martha* show, we'd begun referring to him publicly as "Farmer John." We'd never asked him if that was okay. It just seemed colloquial. I'd learned after publishing my first book that in the media, all introductions are reduced to their simplest form: Farmer John, Former Drag Queen, Martha Stewart's Dr. Brent. There is never any time to go into further detail. A lot has to be crammed in between commercial breaks.

So, without asking or desiring, John had become the famous Farmer John. Even his goats were celebrities. People dropped by specifically to see the ones we'd brought to the show. Normally, Trent, Terrence, and Troy—the males of the bunch—would have gone off to "finishing school" by this time of year. But because of their newfound fame, John wound up selling the three male kids to a hobby farmer who wanted to attract visitors with the "goats who'd been on *Martha.*" They'd become a tourist attraction. As seen on TV.

As soon as we finished installing our massive historical garden, I planned to put the map of it online. It would probably become a tourist attraction as well. But even without the constant interruptions, the garden was turning out to be an almost overwhelming undertaking, just as Brent had predicted. In addition to leveling the ground with the 'dozer, we had to lay the boxes out in a precise grid, with weed-preventing landscape fabric underneath every aisleway between them. John sat by on the tractor, scooping up dirt to fill each one as we laid them out. Then we planned on carting in wheelbarrows full of gravel to line the paths.

Barb, our neighbor and seed proprietress, had come up with the ingenious idea of dividing our garden up into three different "eras." We'd have seed varieties that would have been planted in the original Beekman garden (1802–1850), seeds that would have been grown in a midlife Beekman garden (1850–1900), and finally, varieties that would have been planted from the turn of the twentieth century to the present day. From the comments on our Web site, people seemed to love the idea of such a historical garden.

The progress had been slowed a little because Brent was needed elsewhere. The soap orders were still coming in steadily, so Brent was spending nearly every waking hour of the weekends with Deb. Together they were making batch after batch of soap, wrapping them individually in brown tissue paper, tying them with string, and packaging them for mailing. The publicity we received after the show brought additional editorial coverage on everything from individual blogs to radio shows to e-mail shopping newsletters.

We were swamped and tired. The Beekman 1802 beast needed to be fed constantly. Brent and I blogged about every move we made, and followed each other around with cameras to record every minor accomplishment during the weekend.

But we were also thrilled. Beekman 1802 had become a reality, and my plan to retire early to the country was falling into place quicker than I'd ever imagined. Oprah would be proud of me. Which reminded me, I needed to follow through on a PR contact about an article about the soap with O magazine.

"Should we lay out the last row, or do you want to call it a day?" Dan asked me. I must have looked as exhausted as I felt. I'd been working at least sixty hours a week at the ad agency.

The relaunching of the airline account had worked even better than expected, so we were getting inquiries from several potential new clients each week. Between advertising, the farm, my magazine columns, and the new business, there wasn't a moment left for beauty sleep.

"Let's finish it up," I said. "Gotta get the peas in."

We worked another hour and a half laying the final eight beds into place. After Dan went home for supper, and John left to start his evening chores, I stayed behind to cart in the final loads of gravel. As I was raking level the last pile of rocks, Brent pulled in the driveway. He parked over by the house and was heading up the porch when I shouted for him to come over to inspect all that we'd accomplished.

"Look!" I said excitedly. "Just about done!"

He looked even more tired than I did. At least I'd been out in the springtime sun all day. He'd been hunched over indoors wrapping and filling soap orders.

"You're done?" he said. "This is it?"

I wasn't sure what he meant. All of the boxes were in place and filled with soil, and the aisles were covered with neatly raked gravel.

"Yeah," I answered tentatively. "All put together."

"You're not going to level the boxes anymore?" he asked, nudging one with his knee.

"What do you mean?"

"They're not all the same height." He squatted down and peered over the edge of one like a surveyor.

"Well, they *are* sitting on the ground," I replied, getting defensive. "The earth isn't completely flat, Columbus."

"I think you mean Magellan."

"I think you mean 'Great job, Josh. Good work.'"

"No, it's fine. It looks . . . *fine*," Brent said, wearily turning to head back toward the house.

I looked back over the 7,500 square feet that I'd spent four weeks planning, building, and laying into place. "Fine."

I knew what he really meant: "It doesn't look like something Martha would put in her magazine."

Ever since Martha mentioned that she'd like to visit the farm, Brent had been seeing everything through her eyes. And when one peers through Martha glasses, the world isn't rose colored. It's a great big collection of disappointing imperfections.

I'd thought the garden beds looked more than fine—pretty great, actually. Dan, John, and I had put the entire garden together in an amazingly short time period. But now that Brent had pointed out its imperfections, I too couldn't help viewing it as a ragtag collection of wooden boxes laid out in rows, just like the woman driving by who mistook it for a cemetery.

And if *I* thought it looked like a cemetery, I could only imagine what Martha would think of it. Martha had recently asked Brent again about visiting the farm during an editorial meeting. Her assistant followed up with Brent to schedule two possible free summer weekends for Martha to come. Martha was curious how we traveled to the Beekman, and she'd decided that she'd probably take the train up with us on a Friday and return with a driver on Saturday evening. The thought of driving Martha from the Albany Amtrak station to the farm in the backseat of our pickup seemed like a scene from a Samuel Beckett adaptation of *Driving Miss Daisy.*

And even though we hadn't mentioned the possibility to anyone in Sharon Springs, the buzz about a possible Martha visit had grown exponentially since the spot on her show. We'd even had to enlist Doug, Garth, and George to squelch any rumors they overheard at the hotel bar—the epicenter of the town's gossip orbit. They'd become our own personal Homeland Security team, monitoring "chatter levels" about possible Martha attacks.

A visit from Martha would probably mean another round of

publicity for Beekman 1802. She would no doubt blog about it, and her words and pictures about us would reach another million or so readers. What if we could get another appearance on her show? Maybe a summer gardening segment? Now that I too had basked in the glow of Martha's approval, I could feel my own addiction to perfection setting in.

But the cost of perfection is steep, and can only be paid for in elbow grease.

I grabbed my shovel.

Those garden beds weren't going to level themselves.

Chapter Twenty

"Where are all these orders coming from?" I finally reached Brent in his office on a Friday. Lately it felt like if I didn't make an appointment to get on to his calendar, we'd never speak during the week. As if our day jobs weren't busy enough, we found ourselves staying in our offices, working late into the evening catching up with Beekman 1802 business. Whoever came home to the apartment last quietly slipped into bed trying not to wake the other.

"DailyCandy picked up the soap," Brent answered.

"We're getting, like, five orders every minute," I said. "I can't even set my BlackBerry down or it vibrates off my desk."

"I know. Terrific, right?"

It *was* terrific. Beekman 1802 continued to explode. At this rate it was looking like we'd have to leave our jobs sooner than either of us expected just to keep up with it.

"When are we going to get all these orders out?"

"We'll have to do it this weekend, I guess," Brent said.

"But I'm three weeks behind on the gardening."

"Soon to be four," Brent said. "Oh, and on your way home from work tonight, I need you to transfer 10K into the Beekman account."

"Ten thousand dollars?"

"Yeah. We need to order more packaging, and Deb wants us to get another five hundred soap molds. She can't keep up production with the few she has. And we have to pay Deb's mother-in-law for all the wrapping she's been doing."

"Ten thousand dollars is a lot of money," I said. "Can't we just pay Rose at the end of the month after we've got the cash from these orders?"

"You want to give an IOU to a ninety-year-old woman?"

"Seems like a shrewd business gamble to me," I said. "Okay, gotta go. Someone's at my door. See you at the train?"

"Four forty-five. Be on time," Brent answered.

Jess, the head account person on the airline account, came in and sat in the chair next to my desk.

"You're not going to like this," she said.

"I already don't."

"We have to come up with a national fare sale ad to run on Monday."

"Monday?!"

"They just called."

"Why didn't you tell them it was impossible?" I already knew the answer, of course. If our largest client asked us to clean the bathrooms on every one of its planes, we'd print up celebratory T-shirts and use our own toothbrushes. It was the element of advertising that I'd miss the least. As a farmer, I'd be beholden to things like weather and goat whims—no more jumping through hoops for marketing departments to earn my paycheck.

"We have to have eight variations for twelve different papers," Jess said. "They'll look at them Saturday night, and we can make revisions overnight to send to the printers on Sunday morning."

"I've got a lot to do at the farm this weekend."

"So write a few headlines in between mucking or whatever. Just don't let on that you're not slaving away in the office."

I wasn't sure how I was going to manage getting out all of the orders coming in from DailyCandy, plus update the Web site, plus do the regular spring chores, *and* crank out dozens of headlines.

I couldn't wait until the day I never again had to write a line like: "You Toucan Save on Flights to the Caribbean."

The 4:45 was packed, and Brent and I had to take aisle seats across from each other. We hated when that happened as it made it harder to catch up on all the Beekman tasks we saved to discuss on the train ride.

As soon as we sat down, I began complaining about all the work that needed to be done over the weekend—including the airline ads.

"Remember," Brent reminded me for the hundredth time since January, "this was your resolution."

"I know, I know."

"And also remember—"

"*Stop lecturing me,*" I said, interrupting.

"I just wanted to remind you that we have that photo shoot you arranged this weekend."

"Oh Christ," I said. "I forgot all about that."

We'd become so busy that I was no longer forgetting things as simple as car keys and phone numbers. I was forgetting high-fashion photo shoots in our backyard. A month or so ago I'd agreed to let *Out* magazine use the Beekman as a location for a shoot by a famous photographer.

No matter how busy we were becoming, however, I refused to give up our Friday-night ritual of stopping in at the American for a drink on our way home from the train station to the Beekman.

"I'm sorry," Doug said as we entered. "We're a respectable establishment. We don't allow prostitution at the bar."

"You're just afraid of competition," I rebutted.

"Well, it is tough to compete when you're just givin' it away. *Slut.*"

"*Whore.*"

Garth stepped in to give both Brent and me a hug. George the bartender/mortician began making my drink.

After we'd exchanged pleasantries, Garth turned a little serious.

"So . . . how is John doing?" he asked.

For a moment I was worried that he was going to reveal that John had an incurable disease or a secret drug problem. Garth was not the type of person to spread gossip, so his even bringing up the subject meant that whatever the issue was must have great importance.

"He's doing great," we said. "We love him."

"He hasn't complained about anything to you guys?" Garth asked.

Immediately, our concern turned toward ourselves. We knew that even the slightest bit of information about us usually streaked its way through the village, being twisted and turned as it was repeated.

"Why. What did we do?" Brent asked.

"Well, it's more of what you didn't do," Garth said. "John was in the other night and he seemed kinda down. So we asked him what was wrong and, after two beers, he told us that when he'd moved into the Beekman, he'd thought that you and Brent would be, well, that you'd be . . ."

Garth struggled getting out the truth. We'd be more *what*? Generous? Were we underpaying him? Not friendly enough? Too New York City abrupt?

"Well, he thought you guys would be . . . *gayer.*"

"Gayer?"

"Apparently, he read your first book about your days as a drag queen. And he just thought that you'd be a little, I dunno, sassier."

I couldn't imagine what John could have possibly meant by that. Did he expect us to have giant rave parties in the backyard? That we'd fill the pool with skinny-dipping hired hustlers? Sure, we had some gay couples come to visit us occasionally, but like us, they were more popcorn-and-pay-per-view-movie gays than poppers-and-pay-by-the-hour gays.

Then again, his timing couldn't have been more perfect. In a matter of hours the farm would be swarming with male models, fashionistas, and designer labels. The farm would be less about goat herding than animal magnetism, and more about photo cropping than crops.

John wasn't merely going to get a little more gay this weekend, he was going to be at the epicenter of a gayquake measuring seven on the hipster scale.

"Just come downstairs," I prodded Brent, who was lying across the bed the next morning paying Beekman bills on his laptop. "For Christ's sake. There are male models changing clothes in our dining room and you won't come down to watch?"

"They're scratching the floor," he said. "I don't want to see it."

"They're not scratching the floor," I said, sighing. "The wardrobe racks all have rubber tires."

"Then they're getting black scuff marks on the floor."

Brent had been torn about the prospect of the photo shoot ever since I'd arranged it. It brings into direct conflict his two most prevailing neuroses. His control issues usually mean that we don't invite more than a couple of guests up at one time. He can't handle any sort of domestic chaos. Everything in the house always has to look like it's ready for a magazine shoot.

But today, faced with an *actual* magazine shoot, he was on the verge of a panic attack with all of the crew and models roaming around the house and grounds.

We'd been told that the photo shoot's "story" was "Depression-era farming" and "dust bowls." Even after so many years in advertising, I was still just barely fluent in the language of high fashion. Photos aren't pictures; they're "narratives." Models aren't models; they're "talent." On my best days I'm lucky to choose pairs of pants and shirts that have somewhat similar colors. But on fashion shoots, the clothing has "textures," "shadows," and "lines," and can be "derivative" and "expository."

I went back downstairs alone and found a short, slight, middle-aged Asian man standing in our front hallway.

"Hello, I'm the photographer," he said, holding his hand out. He's a very well-known fashion photographer whose work has appeared in nearly every magazine on any newsstand around the world. "This place is beautiful. Amazing. Such historic textures!" Apparently textures exist in time as well as in space.

Two of the models emerged from the dining room for the photographer to inspect. Marcus and Jaithan. They were stunningly beautiful. Marcus had perfectly curled jet-black hair and a jawline sharp enough to cut firewood. Jaithan had close-cropped hair and soft blue-gray eyes that made him seem more vulnerable than his wide shoulders and impossibly broad chest suggested. Both seemed almost not quite human, more like creatures that mustn't be approached directly for fear of marring their physical perfection with the accidental grit of day-to-day existence. While the crew bustled around setting up its stations, the models waited patiently on the sidelines, waiting to be called into non-action. Jaithan went to lean against the wall and put his hand down on a small collection of zombie flies on the windowsill. He winced and withdrew his hand quicker than last season's line from a Barneys window.

In addition to turning the dining room into the wardrobe room, the kitchen was taken over as the makeup and hair station, and the center hallway served as the staging area. I turned around to see Brent leaning over the second-floor banister. Curiosity had gotten the better of him, but I could tell from the look on his face that he was not happy with all the activity.

"C'mon," I said. "Let's at least get a little time in the garden while they're setting up."

"There are so many of them," he whispered as we headed out the side door.

"Well, it's a lot of work," I said. "The Depression didn't just *happen*. A lot of work went into plunging the nation into glossy sepia-toned narrative textures."

We'd at least gotten the garden bed weeded by the time the photographer, crew, and models came out on the porch. They followed the photographer around the yard en masse as he scouted possible locations and angles for the first shot. Finally settling on a spot by the pond, he instructed the models to recline on the grass in their meticulously styled designer "work clothes."

Brent went down to watch while I continued my war on stinging nettles. He returned in less than fifteen minutes, with John in tow.

"Wow. That's boring," Brent remarked. Having once spent two days filming a caramel pull for a candy bar television commercial, their progress seemed almost nimble to me.

"They just take the same picture over and over again," John said.

"But the models are cute, aren't they?" I asked John.

"I guess. If you like 'em skinny."

John joined us with the weeding. He knew how incredibly busy we'd been over the last couple of months, and how busy he'd been trying to pick up our slack.

An hour later, the photographer, the models, and crew moved

on to their next location—by the woodpile. We watched from
a distance as one of the models carried logs to the other one,
who was resting his foot seductively on the large mechanical log
splitter.

"Look at the huge log on that model," I joked.

"Did they even have power log splitters in the Depression?"
Brent asked.

"You're *sooo* literal," I sighed. "It's supposed to be derivative."

I wondered what the Beekman actually did look like during
the Depression. We knew the Beekman family no longer lived
in the house by then. From the history we'd read, the mansion
in the 1930s was only a decade or so away from being completely
abandoned. It certainly didn't look like how it was going to be
portrayed in these shots. Whoever the farmer's wife was at the
time wasn't spending her days weeding a vast formal flower garden. The closest she probably came to makeup and designer labels were soot smudges and hand-me-down aprons.

Eventually either she or someone who came right after her
failed in her quest to keep the Beekman alive and productive.
From the late 1940s until the day the Selzners purchased it, it
disintegrated into a rickety shell. Though we can't quite piece together the lineage exactly, we knew that it was by turns a board-
inghouse, then a camp for migrant laborers, and then, for long
stretches, it was simply nothing. We had a photo hanging in the
living room of the grand center hallway, given to us by a local,
taken sometime in the mid-1970s. Scrap lumber leaned against
the peeling plaster walls. A dented birdcage rested on a pile of
debris. And someone had spray-painted the name THEO in large
letters on top of the ripped wallpaper.

I wondered what the Depression-era cross section of Beekman ghosts thought about the re-creation of their time happening around us.

As the fashion mob wandered the grounds finding new shots,

I thought about the hundreds of various tableaus the house had staged over the last two centuries. Brent and I would eventually take our place as nothing more than another scene in a very long play. I still wasn't entirely certain how our scene would eventually play out. Would we be lifetime residents who'd be buried in the crypt? Or will local history remember us as the earnest city folk who dreamed of rebuilding the farm—but didn't quite make it.

"Jump on the hay pile! Good! Good! Throw some hay at each other."

The shouted instructions were coming from the other side of the barn. At first Brent, John, and I didn't even notice them. Lost in our battle against the weeds, we'd tuned out the constant chorus of directives the photographer shouted at the models.

"Okay, now roll around in the hay pile a little!"

Both John and Brent looked at me. I could tell they were thinking exactly what I was thinking: We don't have a hay pile. We listened a little more until curiosity finally got the better of us.

We cut through the barn to see what was happening on the other side. When we spotted the bunch in the distance, John busted out laughing

Out beyond the garden, the models were indeed rolling in what they believed to be a hay pile. Except it wasn't. All winter long, when the goats are penned up in the barn due to the freezing weather, John layers fresh straw underneath them each day. By the year's first thaw, the bedding is allowed to build up to almost four feet deep underneath the goats for two reasons: because it's impossible to scoop out into the barnyard through the deep and drifting snow, and as the manure builds up in the straw beneath them, its decomposition helps keep the barn a few degrees warmer and more comfortable for the goats. When the snow finally melts, John uses the tractor to scoop up five months' worth of collected straw and manure, and dumps it in a large pile in the barnyard, to be spread over the hayfields over the course of the summer.

"More rolling! Roll around more!" the photographer continued to shout, focusing his lens.

Our "Depression-era" models, in their $1,600 pants and $2,300 jackets, were rolling around in a two-story-tall pile of winter manure.

"Shouldn't we tell them?" Brent asked.

"Nah." I giggled. "Let's wait to see if the shot makes it in the magazine."

We watched them frolic unaware in the goat shit for a few more minutes before I turned to John.

"So . . . is this gay enough for you?"

He looked surprised that I'd heard about his complaint. But then he chuckled.

"Plenty," he answered. "Gayer than a goat in clover."

As the crew members were packing up their gear and loading up their vans to drive back into the city, I picked up my BlackBerry to find that I had missed twelve phone calls from the same 212 area code number. Three seconds into the first voice mail I realized what I'd done. Or rather, not done.

"Josh, hey, it's Jess. Just checking in to go over those headlines before the call tonight."

I didn't bother listening to the next ten messages and skipped to the final one.

"Where the fuck are you? The call is in ten minutes, and you haven't sent anything to anyone."

Shit shit shit. I checked my watch. The client conference call had started five minutes ago. I frantically scrolled through my e-mails looking for the call-in conference number.

Right before I was patched into the conference, I took a deep breath and grabbed a pen and paper off of the counter next to me.

"Josh Kilmer-Purcell has joined the call," said the robot operator.

"Oh good! You're here," I heard Jess say in her best calm account executive manner. "I was just telling everyone that you were probably having difficulty printing out the headlines." Despite her professional demeanor, I knew that she was actually hoping that I'd died in a plane crash—on a competing airline, of course.

"Yes, exactly," I said. "Boy, how does the toner always know to run out just before a big call," I joked. Everyone on the line laughed politely. In advertising, everyone always laughs politely at the Creatives. They're afraid not to be in on the joke—even when there's not one.

"Let me take you quickly through—" Jess said. She was interrupted by:

HERE COMES THE BRIDE!!!

Jesus. Really? It was six in the evening. The sun hadn't even gone down yet.

"What was that?" one of the lower-level clients asked.

"Sounded like an air raid siren," someone on the call remarked.

"Or a broken car horn," someone else suggested.

"Oh that's just on my end," I said. "I have the office window open. Lots of traffic on the street."

"Let me take you quickly through the strategy," Jess quickly repeated. She knew damn well what it was, and she didn't want the client to find out.

At least by going over the strategy deck she'd bought me a little time. When she finally finished droning on about the habits of business travelers and the key insights into their behavior,

I had half a dozen lines scribbled on the back of an Agway receipt.

"Okay," I said. "Everyone ready for some thought-starters?" I'd learned to always call creative ideas "thought-starters." That way no one had to feel pressured into approving them, and they could also take credit for "finishing" them down the line.

"Fire away," said the main client impatiently.

I began reading the half dozen I had on my list:

> BEEF UP YOUR PASSPORT WITHOUT LIGHTENING YOUR
>   WALLET.
> SEE MORE LONDON. SEE MORE FRANCE. PACK ENOUGH
>   UNDERPANTS.
> MORE ¡HOLA! FOR LESS MOOLA.
> TO RUSSIA WITH LOVE. FROM RUSSIA WITH CHANGE.
> MUCHO SOMBREROS FOR MINI DINEROS.
> NAAN-STOP BARGAINS TO INDIA.

There was a pause on the other end of the line. I couldn't tell if the call had dropped due to the spotty reception at the farm, or if Jess had just cut off the entire call in a rage.

And then the main client spoke up.

"I love 'em. Pick whichever you want. Good work."

"Thanks," I said. "We had a bunch but really tried to winnow down to the most effective ones."

As soon as I hung up I went to wash my hands. I felt like I was covered in more bullshit than the models.

Chapter Twenty-One

_____

"You're cute. Take this train often?"

Brent was waiting for me at our usual Friday meeting spot on the lower level of Penn Station. He was furiously tapping away at his BlackBerry. As soon as he spotted me he turned and headed toward the stairway that led down to our regular train.

"You in a bad mood?" I said, catching up to him.

"You're late," he said.

"The train's still here."

"We'll never get seats together now."

"With that reception, I don't even want to sit in the same car."

He ignored me, still tapping away as we boarded the Albany car. There were two adjacent seats left, but they were near the bathrooms, which I knew would piss him off even more, so to speak.

"You hungry?" I ask. "I'm going to go get a beer from the dining car."

"Nope."

He didn't look up from his BlackBerry until we were almost at Poughkeepsie.

"So should we try this again?" I ask.

"Try what?"

"Starting the weekend."

"Sure. Okay. How was your week?"

"I'll start. My Thursday flight was three hours late, I missed a new business pitch, my assistant quit, and eighteen focus groups in six different cities all hate my new campaign equally."

"Where were you Thursday?"

"I was in Cleveland from Tuesday through Thursday," I said. "You didn't notice?"

Brent squints one eye, trying to remember.

"I knew you were gone. I just didn't know where."

"What would you have done if my plane had crashed?"

"I assume someone would have contacted me."

"Hopefully my obituary wouldn't have gone into your spam folder."

"What's that supposed to mean?"

I turned and looked at the landscape rushing by. The tracks run directly along the Hudson River all the way from Manhattan to Albany. William Beekman himself probably took this same trip several times—by boat, of course. It's a stunning vista in May. It was the first trip of the year when all of the trees had fully leafed out. They were so fresh and new that it was almost startling. I took a deep breath and tried to restart our first real conversation of the weekend with a similarly fresh outlook.

"I can't wait to get to the garden this week," I said. "I can't believe I'm channeling my dad, but I need to putter."

"We also have to get that big West Coast wholesale order together," Brent said.

"Right."

"And do that blog about the new baby goats. I think you should put together a video for YouTube."

"Sure."

"And on Sunday we're meeting with Doug and Garth."

"Brunch?"

"No, I e-mailed them about creating a bunch of heirloom veg-etable recipes for the restaurant. We're going to brainstorm."

"So when can I hang out in the garden?" I asked.

"There might not be time," Brent said. "John might have to plant whatever you need done during the week."

"But that's pretty much all I've been looking forward to all week."

Brent's BlackBerry vibrated on the armrest between us. Saved by the buzz. Brent's weekend chore lists were beginning to re-ally bug me. It wasn't that I wasn't aware of how much we had to do. It was just that I didn't want to be reminded of it in a "to-do" form. We'd had several arguments about this fact in the past few weeks, and each one ended with him reminding me that it was my decision to try to find a way to make a living off of the farm. Brent had an uncanny way of passing the buck for any problems back to me. I think they taught that in his MBA program.

"I think," I said while Brent was sending off his latest volley of e-mails, "that I'll take next Friday off so that I can spend a little time in the garden."

He winced. "You can't."

"How could you possibly have something planned for me to do already? Two seconds ago I was free."

"Next Friday night is Martha's Peony Party."

"A Peony Party? What the hell is a Peony Party?"

"It's a celebration of the first blooming of her new peony patch at her Bedford farm."

I'm torn. I really wanted to spend a little time in our new gar-den. But on the other hand, Martha's throwing a party. A Peony Party. As far as deathbed regrets go, missing Martha Stewart's Peony Party would certainly rank near the top, I'm certain. Be-sides, now that I'm consumed with making our own farm pic-ture perfect, seeing Martha's farm will no doubt inspire me even more.

"So what does one bring to a Peony Party?" I ask. "Probably not deli carnations, I bet."

"Just be on your best behavior," Brent says. "And no stories about your drag days."

"So I can't walk around with my fly unzipped claiming that I thought the invitation was for a Penis Party?"

Brent sighs.

"You're such a Peony Party pooper," I say.

"Don't go stealing ideas!" Martha hollered playfully to Brent from across her Bedford lawn. "I don't want to visit and find the exact same varieties on your farm!"

Brent and I looked up startled. No matter how playfully she meant her admonishment, when Martha Stewart yells "don't" at you, you pretty much freeze in your tracks.

As if prearranged, the morning had brought a cleansing rainstorm to Bedford, so each blossom cradled hundreds of clear rain droplets—seemingly magnifying both their colors and fragrance. It wasn't a peony "patch," as Brent had described. It was a peony panoramic. It seemed almost as large as a football field, or at least that large to someone who had no idea how large a football field actually is.

The blossoms stretched out in neat rows, organized by variety. Each plant was staked perfectly. The mulch in between was immaculately mounded, without a single weed poking through. It didn't seem physically possible. The entire farm looked like a painted movie set.

When Brent and I had finally reached the last row we came upon a label that read: PEONY MARTHA STEWART. She has her own peony named after her. Of course she did. And of course it was one of the most unique and beautiful ones in the entire collection.

We walked over to the catering station where Martha was chatting with a man on the board of directors for MSLO.

"So nice to see you," Martha said, extending her hand to both Brent and me. I took it firmly and leaned in to kiss her on the cheek. For whatever reason, it's always been my natural reaction to greet people—especially women—with a kiss. Martha accepted, perhaps a little awkwardly, but friendly nonetheless. She is a beautiful woman, and in person it was easy to see why she worked briefly as a model in her younger days. Her broad Eastern European face showed few signs of her sixty-eight years. The evening light made her look almost girlish.

"Do you guys have any peonies at your farm?" Martha asked, making polite cocktail party conversation. I thought of the smattering of peony bushes in our flower garden, which by most people's standards seemed formal and gorgeous, but in comparison to the floral show in Bedford seemed straggly and self-loathing.

"Yes, a few," Brent said.

"But nothing like this," I added. "I've never seen a variegated peony before in real life."

"There are some great examples here," she went on. "It's been a perfect year for them. Here, try a radish," she added, gesturing toward an artfully arranged platter on the table.

"Oh, they look fantastic. Ours have just started coming in," I said. "We grew some black Spanish radishes this year that really stand out. Very peppery."

"I've never tried those," Martha said.

"Oh, Brent will bring some into the office for you," I said, secretly thrilled to have added something to Martha's encyclopedic knowledge. "You know I just read that radishes weren't initially grown for their roots at all."

"Really? I'd never heard that." Many people have found Martha easy to lampoon for her seemingly supercilious attitude in her writing and on television. But what few people realize is that unlike most "lifestyle experts," Martha actually knows what she is talking about. She doesn't rely on teams of writers and producers to make her look supremely knowledgeable. Sure, she has hundreds of creative folk working for her, but at the end of the day, she has a nearly photographic memory for all the facts she learns.

And she *enjoys* learning new things. She actively seeks out experiences to broaden her knowledge. I once heard an interviewer ask her how she would describe her "job." "I'm a teacher," she answered. It was an answer that surprised me in its simplicity at first, but later made perfect sense. And, like all expert teachers, she's also an expert learner. She's supremely curious. And while she and I might have had no other personality traits in common, we share an eagerness to soak up practical knowledge, no matter the source.

"Yes, originally radishes were grown for their seed pods," I continued. "We let some of our radishes bolt last year, and used the pods in salads. They were fantastic. Hopefully there will be some ready by the time you visit."

"I'd love to try them. I'm going give that a try myself this year," she said. And I completely believed her.

As thrilling as it was to have a conversation with Martha, there was also the constant fear of saying something wrong—at least for me. I have a habit of crossing lines of tact that, even as I approach middle age, are still completely invisible to me. So after having successfully exchanged several dozen words that didn't seem to have jeopardized Brent's job, I turned back toward the radish platter to let Martha continue her conversation with the business executive. I doubted he was similarly inspired by my radish pod stories.

Many more guests had arrived by then, and Brent and I walked up toward the main house to check out the banquet table set up there. On the way Brent stopped to chat with his colleagues. Many of them have worked with Martha for over a decade, and there seemed to be a sort of hierarchy of seniority that completely transcended titles. There also seemed to be a covert weariness and cynicism that came from working in Martha World as well.

Nearly every conversation that I dipped in and out of revolved around a work-related complaint or gossip. I wished I was better at remembering names, since I was sure that the person whom group B was calling "spiteful" and "conniving" was probably one of the people I just finished chatting with in group A—who was similarly griping about "backstabbing" and "favoritism." About the only thing that every single group had in common was that no one was truly enjoying the beautiful summer evening. To some, the amazing ceviche salad served in individual scallop shells was too bland. To others, the sour cherry juleps were too weak. As someone who once made his living making parties fun and lively, I doubted that I could have turned a party like this around, even in my tallest wig and highest heels.

What surprised me was that no one seemed to *want* to have a better time. They were all seemingly content being discontent. In my partying days, if we didn't like an event or venue, we would simply reapply our sparkliest lipsticks, double cinch our corsets, and get out there and try harder. We'd dance harder, drink more, and shoot off bon mots like automatic fire aimed at ennui.

But maybe there was good reason for the negativity. This was, essentially, a work party. Members of Martha's board of directors were here, along with editors, stylists, writers, and photographers. It wasn't very much different than a company-wide meeting. And, if the financial media could be believed, things could be much better company-wide. Brent had come home lately complaining about budget cutbacks and restructuring. Other than a brief revitalization immediately after Martha's release from prison three years ago, the company had been stuck in a seemingly irreversible slump. And if work was a drag for these people, then it stood to reason that a work party would be a drag. And not in the good drag way.

While Brent was talking to a clump of other disaffected MSLO employees, I took the chance to explore a little. The early summer evening was too beautiful to stand around discussing stock prices and ad revenues. Martha's farm, which she had named Katonah after the town's Native American name, was once nothing more than a run-of-the-mill rural homestead that had the good fortune to be located within commuter distance to New York City. As the years went by, Katonah, eventually to be known as Bedford, became home to some of the richest businessmen in the world. And now it was home to one of the richest businesswomen in the world. The old family farms were torn down and replaced with bankers' mansions, and the fields plowed under for more formal gardens and swimming pools.

I gave Martha a great deal of credit for trying to return her multimillion-dollar grounds, surrounded by mansions and formal estates, to its farming roots. Of course she was taking it to an extreme that no aspiring farmer could ever replicate, including ourselves. But hopefully she was teaching her wealthy neighbors as much about the value of simple fresh chicken eggs and hand-dug potatoes as she was teaching her television audience about the value of white truffles and clementine aspic.

I walked down one of the long pasture walkways lined by a hundred-year-old white spruce rail fence that Martha had imported, length by length, from Ontario, Canada. I knew this detail because it was explained in the tasteful two-color letterpress brochure and map of the farm that was handed out to each partygoer.

On one side of the path was a pasture with two miniature donkeys. They stood lazily about, wholly unimpressed by the high-powered guests in their summer finery trying to lure them over to be petted. The pasture on the other side of the path had several miniature cows of a rare heritage breed, according to the map.

Like the peony beds, every inch of the pathways, pastures, and patios were manicured to perfection. It was styled as if a photo shoot might take place at any second—right down to the galvanized tin bucket filled with carrots hanging from the antique fenceposts, waiting for guests to offer them to the donkeys. The carrots were perfectly straight and washed, of course.

As I reached the end of the path, I checked my map and realized that I was right next door to Martha's vegetable garden. I scanned around me, looking for a few tomato cages or cucumber trellises, but saw nothing but a cold frame greenhouse, another outbuilding, and a sturdily fenced-in area that I assumed must enclose electrical switchers or other industrial equipment.

"Hi, there!"

I turned around and saw a cheerful apple-cheeked woman whose sturdy size and composure instantly marked her as a midwesterner like myself. In the New York environs, any similar woman of her slightly overweight stature carries themselves quietly around, slouching a bit as if to avoid attention. But anywhere between New York and L.A. this woman would be considered an attractive, stylish MILF. And a happy one to boot, which made her stand out even more at this soiree. She was accompanied by a man in a touch-too-tight suit, who'd already loosened his tie and unbuttoned his top shirt button.

"I saw you earlier with Dr. Brent," the woman said excitedly.

"Yes, he's my partner," I answered.

"*You must be Josh!*" she practically squealed. "Dr. Brent is so adorable. I have every episode he's on saved on my TiVo."

"She does," confirmed her husband. "There's hardly any room for my shows."

"And I've tried your soap!" she added. "And I love your Web site! The farm is just so perfect! I tried your spring pea risotto recipe—I even used the pods, like you said." She lightly punched her husband in his bicep. "Jim ate it too, but he's kinda picky."

"I'm more of a hamburger kind of guy."

"I like a good hamburger too, Jim," I said. He looked a little uncomfortable in his summer soiree outfit. I had a feeling Jim didn't know a soiree from a sauvignon.

"You guys are so lucky," the woman said. "Oh, I'm Kerri, and this is my husband, Jim."

"Nice to meet you guys."

Lucky. I wasn't sure what to think about that. Fortunate, yes. Hardworking, sure. Lucky? Okay, maybe a little.

Kerri breathlessly launched into an explanation of how she found herself at Martha's party. She'd been selected as a sweepstakes winner through Martha's Web site, the prize being a trip and invitation to Martha's summer party. Jim, while obviously out of his comfort zone, seemed thrilled simply because his wife was thrilled. They were an endearing couple, and I envied them their easy excitement. In a way, they represented the midwestern part of me that I was pretty sure had been crushed under twelve years of day-to-day New York City living. I was happy to have stumbled upon them after playing the role of dutifully cynical work spouse.

"Are you guys having a good time?" I asked.

"Fantastic!" Kerri said. Her eyes sparkled in the setting sun.

"Have you had a chance to speak with Martha yet?"

"No, not yet," Kerri said. "We've mostly just been wandering around."

Knowing how cliquish the party was, I realized that they probably hadn't been included in many conversations. I think back to how badly I'd wanted to be invited to the birthday parties of my rich classmates who were lucky enough to live on the lake in Oconomowoc, Wisconsin. Would I have entered a raffle to do so? Probably. Would I have had a good time while I was there? Probably not. It was yet another reason to admire Kerri and Jim. To them a party was a party, and beautiful things were beautiful things. And they were thrilled to be a part of it all regardless of how well they did, or didn't, belong. As much as I didn't belong here either, I thought that perhaps if I stuck with them their enthusiasm would rub off on me.

"Have you seen the vegetable garden?" I asked Kerri, looking down at my map.

"I think this is it," Kerri said, pointing up to the tall fenced-in area on a slight rise.

"Really?" I said. "Why the Fort Knox treatment?"

"Probably deer trouble," Jim answered. "I just string up some clumps of dog hair and Irish Spring soap to keep 'em away."

"Let's go look," I said. I half expected giant floodlights to flare on us as we approached the wire fence. It must've been twelve feet tall. It almost looked like . . . dare I say it . . .

"I wonder if Martha comes out here when she gets homesick for the hoosegow," Kerri whispered, giggling.

At that moment I decided that I loved Kerri. Jim and I circled the tennis court–size garden, looking for a gate. I found it first.

"Should we go in?" I asked, suddenly worried if it was alarmed as well as fenced.

"Why not?" Jim said. "It's a garden, and this is a garden party, right?"

Even Kerri seemed a little hesitant, but Jim opened the gate and ushered us in.

"Oh! Look at this!" Kerri said, waving me over. "Here are some little tiny cucumbers. *Already! In June!* Can you believe it?" She picked one off the vine and offered it to me. No alarms. Good. I couldn't believe I was paranoid about eating Martha's cucumber—exactly how I felt cutting the celery at her house three Fourth of Julys ago.

This was a vegetable garden. True, it was better protected than most methadone clinics, but still, it was a vegetable garden. Just like ours at the Beekman. And just like the one I spent hours toiling in during my youth in Wisconsin. And a garden is for sampling. Anyone should be able to walk into any vegetable garden in the world and take a bite of whatever's ripening on the vine. People who grow vegetables know this. It's part of an unwritten universal code.

I realized that my fear of disrupting Martha's world vision with a bite from a cucumber was what differentiated her and me. I didn't know if Martha would truly mind if we nibbled on the cucumber from her picture-perfect garden. But whether she did or not, it still *felt* like stealing.

I took a bite of the cucumber. It was good. Cucumber-y. Not great, but it wasn't fully ripe yet. The garden didn't wither before my eyes as a result either.

"Worthless without salt," Kerri remarked, taking a bite of her own tiny cuke.

"Don't go criticizing," I said, "or you'll sound like everybody else here."

Kerri laughed. The problem with perfection, I realized, is that it leaves others with nothing to do but search for flaws. In the Beekman garden, which had been sorely neglected lately, guests can wander and admire the plants and occasionally pull a weed or two. It made them feel useful, helpful, a part of a bigger picture. If the portrait was already completely painted, then there would be nothing left to do other than pick it apart. Just as most of the other guests at Martha's party were doing.

After a half hour or so of wandering around with Kerri and Jim, I realized that I should really return to Brent. But first, the basil-infused gin and tonics I'd been sipping—responsibly—had found their way to my bladder.

"Have you guys seen any signs for the bathroom?" I whispered to Kerri, checking my map for a restroom symbol.

"No! Isn't it funny?"

"Funny or eerie?" I answered. "Maybe superrich people have bladder removal surgery."

"I think it's the regularly scheduled high colonics," Kerri said, giggling.

The thought of peeing in Martha's woods was terrifying to me, but it seemed like my only option. I imagined that there must be security cameras everywhere. Or roving border guards. I might get hauled away, fly unzipped, in front of the richest people in America, shouting in my defense that "Gin goes right through me!" Brent would get fired. Page Six would have a field day. "Martha Peeved by Peony Party Pisser."

"I'll stand guard for you," Kerri said. "Now go on, pee."

I made my way behind the gated garden and a few feet into the brush. Although in the past I have found more than one drunken occasion to flash my genitals at large audiences, I'd never felt more naked than standing with my fly unzipped on the edge of Martha's woods.

It took a moment, but finally it came—a steady stream released into the underbrush. If I felt like eating a cucumber was defacing Martha's perfect Peony Party, then surely peeing in the woods was an act of nuclear annihilation. But if I killed a few weeds and scrub seedlings, then at least at some future party, someone would have a true imperfection to bitch about. Really, I was doing Martha a favor.

When I finished, Kerri was waiting for me with her back turned, keeping watch for approaching guests.

"I should head back to the party," I said.

"Who said you ever left?" Kerri said, smiling, toasting me with her now-watery basil-infused gin and tonic.

Chapter Twenty-Two

Brent and I began arguing about every little aspect of the farm, our jobs, and the new business. With everything we were trying to accomplish, we spent whatever little free time we had pointing out what the other one hadn't accomplished yet.

On the way home from the farm the previous Sunday, we'd gotten into an argument about painting the house. We were able to get two sides done last year, but this year, with real estate booming, we couldn't find anyone to finish the job. It was only half perfect, which isn't perfect at all.

It was quickly growing impossible to keep up with the ever-lengthening list of chores. Each day we had dozens and dozens of soap orders flooding into our e-mail in-box—far more than Deb and ninety-year-old Rose could keep up with. Consequently we'd begun fielding nearly as many complaints about late orders as actual new orders.

The first flush of excitement as our business took off had been replaced by a constant terror of keeping up—and keeping up appearances. The now thousands of daily visitors to our Web site didn't want to hear about our house painting arguments. They came to read our stories and picture essays about bucolic farm life. They came for the step-by-step recipes of every meal that we made at the farm. They came for the weekly harvest updates. They came for the pastoral videos of the Beekman flower garden.

In our quest to create the perfect country place, we'd succeeded—if only fictionally.

We'd mutually decided to spend that late June weekend steering clear of each other since we seemed incapable of interacting without devolving into a nagging match. I resigned myself to the stony silence, with Brent trying to salvage our mishandled mail orders and me desperately trying to maintain and harvest a 7,500-square-foot vegetable garden.

Even John was in a bad mood. While we were selling as much soap as we could make, it still didn't make use of all the milk he was producing. Each day he was throwing away gallon after gallon of perfectly good milk. Because our farm hadn't yet gone through the byzantine legal process of certification as a grade-A dairy, we couldn't use our milk for anything other than soap or animal food. And the soap wasn't enough. John wasn't making the income he needed in order to keep all of his goats fed. And the chronic arthritis in his hip had been getting worse. Like most self-employed Americans, he had no health insurance.

Which was why we weren't surprised when he knocked on the kitchen door on Sunday evening to inform us that he'd taken a job in Schenectady . . . a full hour's drive away.

"Really? Doing what?" I asked.

"Data entry at an insurance company."

The thought of it pained me. I couldn't help but think that Brent and I had let John down. When he put that letter in our mailbox a year ago, he'd had such grand dreams of starting his life over—finally hoping to fulfill his dream of tending to a growing herd of beloved goats full time. Beyond providing his house, utilities, and a small stipend, we still couldn't afford to offer him the money he needed to survive as a full-time farmer with health insurance. Whatever money the soap was bringing in was being reinvested into the next, bigger batch.

Now all three of us were forced to work two jobs for the same relentless and demanding boss—the Beekman.

The three of us sat in the kitchen for another hour trying to figure out how to divvy up the chores John would now have to forgo for his new job. Who will mow the massive lawn? Hay the fields? Weed and water the garden?

"Fuck!" I said, suddenly standing up from the table.

"What's wrong?" John asked.

I raced over to the oven. I'd spent hours that afternoon photo-documenting the process of making a perfect lattice crust sour cherry pie for a blog entry. And now I'd left it in the oven a full half hour longer than it should have been. I pulled out the darkened brown mess. The juices had boiled over and burned onto the side of the pan and on the bottom of the oven.

"It doesn't look that bad," John said. "It'll still taste fine."

"I know. But I need to get a good picture of it for the blog."

"When my mother burns something, she always just dusts the top of it with powdered sugar," John offered, which sounded like the perfect sort of Martha Stewart tip, if only Martha Stewart ever burned anything.

While John and Brent continued to discuss the new chore arrangements, I cut a slice of pie from the least-burned side and tried to artfully arrange it on a plate. I only needed one halfway decent photo for the Web site. And we needed to leave for the train back to the city in fifteen minutes.

"That doesn't look good," Brent said, looking over at what I was doing.

"I know. It's not perfect. It's not going to be perfect. I'm just trying to get this done so we don't miss the train."

"I'd thought I smelled something burning," Brent added.

I'd reached my breaking point. I'd spent all afternoon making this pie for the blog—a pie that we wouldn't even be able to eat since we were leaving for the city—and he didn't say anything when he smelled it burning?

"*Then why didn't you say something!?*"

"*Because we're not supposed to be talking to each other!*"

"*Then why don't you shut the fuck up!!!*"

John swallowed the last swig of his beer and excused himself into the warm summer night. He had to start his new job in the morning. Now he, like us, had yet another life to juggle. I wanted to warn him about what he was in for. But what were his options?

What were *our* options?

Chapter Twenty-Three

The following weekend:

Divide and plant five hundred iris bulbs.

Write blog about iris bulbs.

Sweep up flies.

Weed garden.

Write blog about different types of weeds.

Pick, shell, blanch, freeze twenty-four quarts of peas.

Write blog about "Why We Blanch."

Pull gloppy algae from pond.

Decide that photo-documenting algae would turn off readers.

Tie up half of the sour cherry tree, which had fallen over during a summer storm.

Write blog ode to cherry tree.

Trim mock orange hedgerow.

Stake tomatoes.

Repair stone wall outside crypt.

Fix garden sprinklers.

Mow lawn.

Argue with Brent.

Argue with Brent.

Argue with Brent.

Chapter Twenty-Four

———

"Hi!"

"Nice to meet you!"

"So glad you could come."

"We're thrilled to help out."

It was the 2008 annual Sharon Springs Historical Society Tour of Homes. Doug and Garth had tried to warn us against taking part, calling it the "Snoop and Poop Tour." The last time they opened their own home for the historical society, someone went through their nightstand while someone else clogged their toilet.

But we were excited to meet even more of our neighbors. Brent, of course, couldn't bear the thought of actually being inside with all those people who no doubt came by for the express purpose of scratching his floors. So we stood on the porch outside greeting everyone who entered.

"I have to go weed the strawberry beds," I said, already tired of smiling. "Do you want to help?"

"No, I want to keep an eye on things."

"For what? It's the Sharon Springs Historical Society. I highly doubt they have plans to trash the place."

"I'm staying here," he said, ending yet another discussion.

We still weren't really speaking with each other. Brent was

growing exceedingly anxious about a possible visit from Martha. She'd brought it up several more times lately. To me it seemed as if it was her personal method of torturing him. I was growing more frustrated by the lists of chores that seemed to neglect the things I truly cared about. I didn't care if the fenceposts were perfectly straight, but I did care that the tomatoes were solidly staked before they tipped over.

This weekend was going to be particularly difficult to get through. And in addition to putting on our usual happy faces for the Web site photos, we also had to do it in front of real people.

We'd agreed last year that we'd open the home for the historical society's annual fund-raiser. In the weeks leading up to it, the president of the society gleefully informed us that they'd had more interest than ever. The Beekman hadn't been open to the public since the Selzners had renovated it. It was the first chance for many people across the county to see the interior. Plus there was the added benefit of meeting TV's own "Dr. Brent."

Oh, and the other guy.

Naturally, rumors had also been flying that Martha would be here this weekend. Little did everyone know that this actually was one of the weekends that Martha had tentatively scheduled for her visit. Instead she'd taken a last-minute jaunt to Russia to watch her billionaire boyfriend launch himself into space on a Russian spacecraft. She'd actually packed him lunches for the trip. America's lifestyle maven was going universal.

Even though Brent would no doubt disagree, the Beekman was in tip-top shape for the historical society tour. The row of white hydrangeas was standing tall and proud along the back of the wraparound columned porch. Dozens of different lily varieties were blooming in the flower garden, as were the delphiniums, irises, and poppies. John had been working late into the night, after arriving home from his new job, sweeping and organizing the barn so that the visitors could admire his goats.

It was a perfectly sunny day, and—even though I was dead tired and frustrated—I couldn't help but feel a twinge of pride for all we'd accomplished as I watched small clusters of visitors exploring the grounds.

There was a momentary lull in new visitors, which meant that Brent and I could take a break from greeting people and stand in stony silence instead.

"It was so much nicer when the Selzners were here."

"Oh, I know. Pat invited me over once. It was beautiful."

"There's not a single picture on the walls."

The voices were coming through the open window behind me. I had no idea who was speaking, but I continued listening in, my heart dropping with each word. I knew Brent heard them as well.

"They don't have any furniture! It's like an echo chamber in here."

"The previous owners had so many beautiful antiques."

"I don't like modern things. It seems so cold."

"Yuck. Look at all these flies."

"The flies are everywhere! It's filthy."

"Where's Martha?"

"They said that Martha was going to be here."

"I can't believe we drove out here for this."

And then:

"Those two act like their shit doesn't stink."

I couldn't believe what I was hearing. These were the people who smiled and waved at us as we drove by. These were the people who always told us how happy they were that we'd come to their village, and were building a new business there.

I suddenly felt as if I were standing on the porch naked.

No, we didn't have money to buy priceless antiques. We didn't have a staff to decorate, and clean, and make flower arrangements, and garden. Didn't they realize that the picture-perfect Beekman they'd read about on the Web site was entirely a product of myself, Brent's, and Farmer John's labor? And on top of it all, we all had full-time jobs during the week?

I knew their criticisms probably stung Brent even harder.

"C'mon," I said to Brent. "Let's go to the garden."

He knew I was trying to save him, and for once, he let me. Neither one of us mentioned that we'd overheard the insults. I tried to make small talk to distract us both.

"So did Martha give you any new dates she might visit?" I asked, stooping over to pull weeds from a seventeenth-century variety of French melon.

"No."

"Think it'll be this month?"

"Dunno."

"Well, she'll have to come by the end of August or she'll miss the best produce of the garden."

"*Look.* I don't *know* when she's coming. I *said* that already," Brent hissed at me.

We continued weeding in the silence we'd lately grown accustomed to.

"Oh, your melons are so far along for this time of year!" a voice called out from behind me. I looked up to see an older woman wearing a loose, bright purple sweater over a long denim skirt. On her wide straw hat she'd pinned a massive pink peony blossom. Her long gray hair hung over her shoulders.

"Do you think so?" I asked. "I kinda thought they looked a little spindly."

"Oh no, it's very difficult to grow melons this far north. I think you just might get a decent crop."

She asked us if it was okay for her to tour the garden. As long as you don't insult us, I thought.

Brent and I walked the woman around the beds, telling her the histories of each seed variety. She seemed quite knowledgeable herself, and explained that she had a fairly large garden of her own in the next county over.

"Of course it's not quite as neat and formal as this one," she said, laughing. "It's a little more Wabi Sabi."

"A little more *what*?" I asked.

"Wabi Sabi," she repeated.

All I could think of was Martha's tuna burgers with wasabi mayonnaise. Did this woman own a horseradish farm?

The woman patiently leaned against our potting table and began to explain the Japanese aesthetic of Wabi Sabi.

"Overly simplified," she explained, "it defines beauty as imperfect, impermanent, and incomplete."

Great, I thought. After waiting all week to work in the garden, now I had to stand here and listen to some kook and her philosophy. But her manner was so kind and open that she quickly won us over. If we'd learned anything from Sharon Springs, it's that trying to stop the constant flow of eccentricity was like trying to plug up the town's once famous springs.

"Take this basket of strawberries," she said, picking up the small pint-full I'd picked earlier in the morning. "These strawberries are smaller, and more misshapen than the ones you'd get in the supermarket. And because they're picked at the peak of ripeness, you know that they're decaying as we speak. And unlike supermarket berries, which you eat and never think about again, these strawberry plants need to be nurtured, year in and year out. They'll never be finished. It's all Wabi Sabi, and why many people believe these ugly strawberries are more valuable and beautiful than the most perfectly shaped supermarket berries."

I understood what she was saying, but it seemed too simplistic and perhaps a bit fatalistic. I was still striving to produce the most beautiful, perfectly shaped berries that I possibly could that also tasted perfect. By her standards, why wouldn't I just let the berry rows fill in with weeds and go unwatered until the strawberries are shriveled and ugly? Wouldn't that be super-duper Wabi Sabi? When I questioned this, she clarified.

"It's fine that one strives for beauty, but if one only finds it in perfection, then it will remain forever hidden. The Greeks pursued the aesthetic of the perfection. And still their marble statues chipped over time. Wabi Sabi would say their statues are even more beautiful chipped."

Something began to intuitively make sense. I remembered Martha's farm, and how every inch was so perfectly manicured that the guests entertained themselves by seeking out imperfections.

"Or take the Beekman itself," our new friend continued. This ought to be good. We were still stinging from other people's insults, and she was about to list our every flaw. "I've driven by it for years," she continued. "For a long time, when it was abandoned, its only beauty was in its decay. Then when the Selzners purchased it, they tried to restore it to the majestic beauty it once was. But they rarely visited. Since it went practically unused, it was easy to keep it looking 'perfect.'"

She paused to eat one of our Wabi Sabi strawberries.

"I read your blogs all the time," she went on, "and I've loved watching and reading about the place come back to life. When you two bought the Beekman, you began using it. And with use, comes decay. And with decay comes work. And with work comes dedication. And with dedication comes creativity. And on and on. You two will never be finished with the Beekman, it will never be perfect, and it will always be falling to pieces around you."

"So what you're saying," I clarified, "is that Brent shouldn't yell at me for not getting the house painted. He should thank me."

She laughed.

Brent didn't.

"I think what I'm saying," she concluded, smiling, "is that the Beekman is now the most beautiful it's ever been."

Chapter Twenty-Five

"Okay, great," the director said. "Now do the same thing only with more . . ."

"I know, I know . . . sizzle," I answered. I wasn't exactly sure how I was going to make kneading bread "sizzle" on film.

The cameraman was standing outside on the porch filming my hands and forearms through the open kitchen window as they kneaded the dough. After fifteen years in advertising, I was used to the repetitive boredom of shoots. But I'd never been on the front side of the camera.

We were shooting what we'd learned was called a "sizzle tape." It's a roughly ten-minute video that production companies use when they pitch television show concepts to networks.

This all came about when a friend of ours was having dinner with a noted daytime talk-show Celebrity who is not Oprah or Martha and her executive producer, and somehow the story of our hapless Thanksgiving turkey murder made its way around the expensive New York City restaurant table. The Celebrity felt that perhaps our life at the Beekman might make for an interesting reality show television series, and invited us to her Soho loft to discuss the possibilities.

We arrived at her loft bearing gifts of freshly laid eggs, home-made pickles, handmade soaps, and firmly bitten tongues. Brent and I hadn't exchanged a nice word in months. We both knew a television show about the Beekman would be a huge coup. It would basically be a half-hour commercial for the business. All we had to do was act as if we liked each other, which, lately, would demand an Oscar-caliber performance.

The Celebrity owned a couple of country homes herself, so she wasn't entirely unfamiliar with the charms of rural living. We gave our spiel about how most Americans had forgotten many of the simpler pleasures of life and how to provide for themselves. We discussed how the art of gracious living had largely fallen by the wayside.

We spent the next two hours brainstorming possible show concepts together, finally settling on something similar to *Green Acres* crossed with *Project Runway* crossed with Martha Stewart crossed with Paris Hilton crossed with *The Beverly Hillbillies* crossed with *I Love Lucy*. Apparently reality on its own is not a winning concept for a reality show. I knew we were probably veering off course when I found myself referring to my vision for "the Josh character."

"Maybe we should just send a director and cameraman up there to film for a day and see what comes back," the executive producer suggested.

"What happens on a normal day at the farm?" the Celebrity asked.

"Well," Brent answered, "this weekend we have to clean out the chicken coop."

"Great! What else?" the Celebrity asked, no doubt envisioning the two of us in our city suits and ties covered with chicken shit and feathers.

"Umm. That's about it," I said. "It'll take all weekend. Chickens are incredibly industrious manure makers."

The Celebrity looked a little worried. I'd come to realize that while most Americans don't have any idea what actually happens on a farm, they all *think* they do. Having spent hours as children with their Fisher-Price farms and pull-string toys that make animal noises, people have created a tableau of farm life in their heads that couldn't be further from reality. They envision Brent and me spending our weekends driving a big red tractor aimlessly around the barnyard, taking breaks to milk things and perhaps tote a bale of hay somewhere. Fisher-Price seems to ensure that every little kid grows up with a false perception of the lives of firemen, policemen, and farmers. Maybe if they made more accounting office play sets and little middle management figures, they'd hit the mark better—or at least be more demographically accurate.

"Well, why don't you come up with a list of chores," the executive producer suggested. "We'll film a little bit of all of them."

Coming up with a list of chores was hardly a problem. Coming up with a list of chores that America would want to watch us doing would be more challenging.

But if we were going to create a successful television show, I guess that's the kind of reality we'd have to learn how to fake.

"Go ahead and talk to each other more," the director instructed. "Just pretend we're not here."

If you weren't here, I thought, we wouldn't be talking at all. Even if we weren't fighting, it's really unnatural to be continuously speaking with one's partner. As far as I'm concerned, the whole point of being with the same person for many years is not so that he or she can finish your sentences, but so that you rarely have to start one to begin with.

"So," I began awkwardly, trying to fake a real conversation with Brent, "this bread seems to be coming out very nicely."

"Yes," Brent replied, "it looks very good."

What the hell else is there to say?

"I'll be kneading this bread for about eight to ten minutes," I added.

"And then will you bake it?" Brent asked.

"Yes, then I will bake it at four hundred twenty-five degrees for about twenty minutes."

"Or until it sounds hollow when thumped," Brent added.

"Yes."

I was out of words, and we were only forty seconds into the take. This didn't bode well.

The next several staged chores and resulting dialogue seemed similarly stilted:

"Josh, did you know that this is a common thistle plant? It should always be pulled before going to seed . . ."

"Brent, one of the wondrous properties of goat manure is that it doesn't need to be composted."

"Say, Josh, many people don't realize that turkeys raised in factory farms are often sickened by rhinotracheitis and colisepticemia."

At some point during the morning, I realized that the most exciting moment of our potential reality show would be the copyright notice in the credits. To compensate, I came to the conclusion that if I ran everywhere—physically moved my body faster—the film might seem more engaging. I galloped out to the end of the drive to get the mail. I trotted to the garage to grab a trowel. After we hooked up the tractor to spread some manure, I ran alongside Brent as he drove it across the field.

For even more "sizzle," instead of simply leading the goats out to graze as we usually did, I raced out in front of them, hollering

an improvisational goat call that made me sound like a yodeling
hillbilly. I turned back toward the barn and saw that the goats
had stayed back, huddled together in fear in the barn doorway.
They obviously preferred to skip dinner rather than get too close
to the retarded scarecrow suffering a grand mal seizure.

But there still wasn't enough sizzle for the director. Maybe,
I suggested, we should try some other reality show tactics. Perhaps I should admit to an affair while canning green beans. Or
threaten to vote Brent off the farm by forming a secret alliance
with the goats. Or maybe we needed some sort of catchphrase,
like "Now that's good livin'!" or, "Manure, schmanure!"

The director finally decided that interaction with the animals
"read well" on camera, so Brent and I took turns cuddling every creature we could lay our hands on—even the turkeys, who
flailed and flapped their wings in objection as if we were colisepticemia carriers.

I was exhausted by noon. Doing five-minute snippets of a lot
of chores was harder work than actually finishing one of them.

"Well, Brent," I emoted, trying not to run into the cameraman walking backward in front of us. "Shall we rustle up some
lunch?"

"Sure, Josh. Let's see if that bread's ready yet!"

I broke into my trademark gallop back toward the house.

By late afternoon, I was so bored with my own reality, I wished I
could aim a remote and shut myself off. When I was growing up
in Wisconsin, I would daydream about becoming a television celebrity while spending hour after boring hour weeding the family garden. Now that we had a shot at being on a television series,
all I wanted was to be left alone so I could go weed my garden.

As both Brent and I grew tired and bored, it became harder

to hide the tension between us. My cheerful extemporaneous dialogue was growing more transparent.

"Hey, Brent," I'd say. "Did you notice that you left the barn door open *again* even though I've told you a thousand times not to?"

When the director and cameraman took a break to change the camera batteries, Brent pulled me off to the side of the porch.

"What are you doing?" Brent hissed through clenched teeth, covering the tiny microphone clipped to his collar. "You're going to ruin it."

"Look, I'm getting tired," I said, sighing. "If they don't have enough sizzle after six hours of shooting, they never will. Maybe we're just not all that sizzly."

"Just stop being such a dick," Brent said. "That's not our brand."

"Our 'brand'?" I echoed, laughing. "You just called us a *brand*?"

"You know what I mean."

"Yes, I know exactly what you mean," I said. "You mean that not only have we turned our weekend getaway into a second job, and not only have we been arguing about absolutely everything for the past two months, but you've now reduced our relationship to a marketing term."

"Look," Brent said, "it was your idea to—"

"If you say that one more time, I'm leaving you."

I'd crossed the line. The line I promised myself I'd never cross. Brent's father had died when he was only eleven years old, and I knew within moments of meeting Brent that he had a fear of abandonment, even if he didn't know it. I also instinctively knew that I should never ever exploit it. But I just did.

At that moment all I wanted to do was escape everything. I was sick and tired of the Beekman. It had completely taken over our lives. The Brent and Josh that so giddily crossed over the threshold just over a year ago were as dead as Mary Beekman and the rest of the ghosts. They'd been replaced by a brand. Two smiling gentlemen farmers sharing picture-perfect snapshots of their picture-perfect lives with the rest of the world.

As Brent kept repeatedly pointing out, it *was* my idea to find a way to leave advertising behind me to live full time on the farm. But what he didn't realize was that his chronic Martha Stewart–like quest for perfection had done nothing more than turn the Beekman into another job.

Now I wanted to quit two jobs.

"Okay. We're ready," the director said. "We were thinking that maybe we'd shoot you two separately for a while. Josh, you first."

I realized that the director had heard every word of our argument through his headphones. They'd probably use it in the sizzle tape backed by ominous music and B-roll footage of storm clouds. I could honestly have cared less.

Brent asked the soundman to take off his microphone. As soon as he was free, he disappeared inside without even looking at me.

"Okay," the director started with his interview. "Why don't you start by telling us how you and Brent came to buy the Beekman."

"Because we thought we were something we weren't," I answered.

"I'm sorry," the director said. "Because my question won't be in the edit, I'll need you to say that again as a full sentence."

"Brent and I came to buy the Beekman because we thought we were something we weren't."

"Can you elaborate on that a little?" the director probed.

"Brent and I came to buy the Beekman because we thought we were something we weren't. We thought we were the perfect couple with perfect taste who were perfectly suited to a life of happily ever after."

"Would you say that your relationship is in jeopardy?" The director asked.

"Maybe," I answered.

"Again, I'll need you to repeat that as a full phrase," the director said.

"Maybe our relationship is in jeopardy because we keep putting ourselves in situations where people expect us to be perfect . . . Say, for instance, on a reality show where the director would like our relationship in jeopardy because it would help him create the perfect sizzle tape to sell to a network, which would then put even more stress on us to be the perfect couple."

"You can't refer to the show in your answers."

"I think I want to end this now." I unbuttoned my shirt to take off the microphone.

I wasn't just referring to the interview. I wanted everything to just be done. Over. Somewhere along the way my reality had become a nightmare of a fantasy, and I wanted someone to yell "cut."

Chapter Twenty-Six

_____

"Ha . . . ee . . . urth . . . ay." The voice was crackly and broken on the other end of the phone.

I stepped outside on the porch to see if I could get a better signal. Not much, but a little better.

"Happ . . . birth . . . ay," Brent repeated.

"Thanks," I answered. I didn't know what else to say. He was clearly calling me on my birthday as a formality. As long as we still shared a mortgage—two, actually—it probably seemed like a good idea to celebrate the fact that the person who shared half your debt was still alive.

Then, either because he was calling from Martha's jet or because the Beekman never had a strong cell signal, the call dropped. Either way, it was a relief to both of us. We'd fulfilled our respective obligations. His: to go through the formalities of our relationship. And mine: to turn thirty-nine with a respectable amount of dignity and forced good cheer.

Since my birthday fell on Labor Day weekend, I came upstate alone to celebrate on the farm. While I wasn't thrilled about being alone to celebrate the first moments of my thirty-ninth year on the planet, I was happy to have the farm all to myself. Even though Brent was scheduled to return to the city on Friday night, he'd decided that he'd be too tired to make the trip up—even for my birthday. For a change, we didn't argue about it.

As always, there would be weekend chores for me to accomplish from sunup to sundown. But at least no one would be waiting for me at the end of the long day to tell me what I did incorrectly, or finished too slowly, or had forgotten about completely.

Brent's call came just before dinnertime. Most likely he and Martha would soon land in whatever city they were heading to and be whisked away to the fanciest restaurant in the area, where they'd meet up with other interesting and famous people. They'd pass the evening with special dishes being sent to their table by the chef, and bottle after bottle of the cellar's best wine. It would be, of course, picture perfect.

My birthday evening would be somewhat different, although I considered Bubby the Barn Cat and the goats as pedigreed of guests as any. I was going to enjoy my thirty-ninth birthday feast in the garden—just Bubby and myself—at the potting table, with a couple of candles and a few late-season fireflies for ambiance.

While Martha and Brent were riding in their limo to wherever, I gathered the ingredients I'd prepared for my self-celebratory dinner, including a few items I'd already cooked earlier in the afternoon. I loaded up a tray with the ingredients, food, wine, and utensils I'd need, and headed outdoors.

As I crossed the yard with my loaded tray, a surprisingly cool breeze came across the pasture, cutting through the humid late-summer air like a piece of ice being dropped in warm tea. It was the first gentle reminder that summer was nearly over. Looking back, I couldn't believe how much of summer I *didn't* have. Between the soap, Web site, magazines, television show, and my day job, it didn't feel like I'd sat down once, let alone enjoyed an entire lazy summer afternoon. I didn't allow myself to dwell on this. If I started listing regrets, my thirty-ninth birthday would certainly deteriorate quickly.

This will be the last year in which I could deny, with any sort of credibility, the fact that I am middle-aged. Thirty-nine has the thinnest remaining veneer of the potency and possibilities of youth. It's when the best I could hope for in the future was looking good *for my age*.

The clouds had been gathering throughout the afternoon—not threatening rain—merely dulling the day and erasing the shadows. Farmer John finished his afternoon chores early to attend a picnic in the next town over. I was officially by myself. I set the tray down on the potting table and spread out my dinner ingredients.

I was going to make myself a completely improvised salad. I'd baked a crusty baguette earlier in the afternoon, which I now ripped into small cubes and threw into a large bowl. Next I took the thick steak that I'd briefly seared on the kitchen fireplace grill and sliced it on the diagonal, paper thin.

It would be my first taste of "Cow." We'd eventually gotten around to butchering him after John got his new desk job. With John's limited time, Cow was simply too much to take care of, though we'd put off his butcher date repeatedly because we thought it looked good to have a cow on the farm. "Cow" was "on brand." At least his brand appeal kept him alive a good seven months longer.

I wasn't the least bit emotional about eating Cow. Being overly sentimental about his life would be an insult to both him and ourselves. We did our jobs as responsible and humane farmers, and he did his job as a responsible and healthy farm animal. Even though we have a close relationship with our animals, at the end of the season it's still primarily a professional one.

I added the slivered steak to the bowl of crusty bread. Then I circled the garden, snipping off whatever I fancied directly into the bowl: A little parsley. A couple of thinly slivered celery leaves. Some purple basil. Chives. The endive heads, though small, were crisp and a beautiful pale white-green that almost glowed. I took a satisfyingly bitter bite of one before adding the rest of its leaves to the quickly filling bowl. I picked and tossed in some early blossoms from our fall pea planting and some peppery bright orange nasturtium flowers. The lemon squash blossoms tore like wet tissue paper as I plucked them, along with some of their tiniest fruits. The purple scallions filled the air with a biting pungency the moment I pulled their reluctant roots from the earth. I sliced them so thin they were translucent.

The bowl was brimming with every color imaginable, and when I added a drizzle of olive oil, the colors seemed to magnify even more. The salad was so bright and cheerful that it actually made me smile for the first time in weeks.

It was my birthday party in a bowl. I tossed the colorful streamers and tiny balloons with a little of our own homemade apple cider vinegar.

I saved the main ingredient for last. The true guest of honor: the summer's first Cherokee Purple heirloom tomato.

The Cherokee Purple had become almost mythological for Brent and me. Dark burgundy with green shoulders, it was the centerpiece for the very first meal he and I had prepared together as a couple. Nearly ten years ago, we were walking through the Union Square Greenmarket on one of our first dates, when we spotted a wooden crate with the largest, most luscious tomatoes we'd ever seen. The sign read CHEROKEE PURPLE. The farmer at the stand explained that they were rediscovered in the early 1990s when a gardener received a mysterious envelope in the mail containing seeds. An accompanying note claimed that the seeds had been passed down for generations, and were originally grown by Cherokee Indians.

Thinking back, our Cherokee Purple tomato story was probably why I was so insistent about putting in such a large heirloom vegetable garden.

Brent and I bought half a dozen that day, and took them home to my small apartment on Twenty-third Street. We brought the tomatoes and a saltshaker out onto my rickety fire escape, six stories above the sidewalk, and ate all of the tomatoes, one after another, like apples. The juice and seeds dripped from our chins down to the street below. It's probably one of my most vivid memories of summer in New York City, and one of my favorite memories with Brent.

Naturally, Cherokee Purple was one of the first plants to go into the Beekman garden. Because of an early frost our first year, we hadn't had any ripen. But last weekend, after I'd sent the television pilot crew packing, I spotted the first Cherokee Purple tomato nearing perfect ripeness tucked away in a leafy giant bush. It had barely the first blush of burgundy red on its cheeks. I knew that it would reach perfection just in time for my birthday.

The tomatoes had been planted in the back row of the garden beds so that the towering plants didn't shade the rest of the crops. I wound my way through the paths to the bush that held the hidden treasure. I walked past the black cherry tomatoes that were Brent's favorite, and the pure white globe tomatoes that always fascinated our dinner guests. I shunned the Pink Brandywines, long considered to be the best-tasting tomato, as well as the heart-shaped German Red Strawberry variety. The Wapsipinicon Peach tomatoes, with their fuzzy yellow skins, were as sweet as apricots, but they were not my target tonight. The Green Giant tomatoes with their lime green skins hung heavily from spindly vines, as if all of the plant's vitality had been expended on producing the huge two-pound fruits. I walked straight past the over two dozen varieties of tomatoes we'd planted, each with their own charms and temptations. I would not be distracted.

There, in the farthest corner of the garden, stood my target. An immense, verdant bush that stood over six feet tall and wider than I could wrap my arms around—which I would, if possible. I'd waited a full year for this moment. The Purple Cherokee tomato is beyond mere tomato-dom. It's as if the taste of six tomatoes were squished together into one. The fruits are larger and more perfectly round than any other heirloom variety. There are frequently small scars or cracks around the stem, and the skin in that area has a deep green tinge, almost black. The flesh inside is mottled with deep purple and burgundy streaks, not unlike Cow's. Even more so than other heirlooms, it's a finicky plant, with little pest and disease resistance bred into its genes. Many gardeners avoid the Cherokee, since it isn't a very prolific plant. We'd be lucky to get a good half dozen in our short growing season. And of the ones that do ripen, they need to be picked at exactly the correct moment. In the course of one hot afternoon they could go from underripe to rotting on the vine.

Hopefully, I'd timed my treasure just right.

I stooped over to search through the leaves in the general proximity of where I remembered spotting the jewel last weekend. I caught a whiff of the peppery smell of the tomato leaves, something I love nearly as much as the tomatoes themselves.

It was there, huge and impressively round. I hefted it in my hand before picking it. It was heavy, full of water from the week's rain. I carefully twisted it clockwise to loosen the stem, which separated easily, as if I'd picked it mere seconds before it would have dropped to the earth on its own accord.

Holding it in my hand I marveled at how many things had to go right for such a perfect present on my thirty-ninth birthday. The serendipity went beyond an adequate seasonal rainfall, correct temperature range, or the nitrogen in the goat manure used to fertilize the beds last spring. It extended all the way back to the chance envelope that arrived in a gardener's mailbox all those years ago.

While the line connecting my rural Wisconsin youth to my drunken drag queen nights to my fledgling goat soap empire might not seem obvious, at that moment I was convinced that it led directly to the simple, decadent fruit I now held in my hands.

Like the slowly ripening tomato, I seemed to embody far more excitement and possibility during the years leading up to this quiet evening. Also like it, perhaps the kindest label for me in the coming years will be "overripe." I don't subscribe to the "fabulous at fifty," or "sexy at seventy" philosophy espoused by our daytime talk-show hosts and aging celebrities. I don't buy it, well, because I sell it. After this many years in advertising, I know the art of deceiving marketing speech even better than a sixty-year-old underemployed actress touting that she's sexier than ever. It's just not true. I see it in my face. I see it in my hands. I see it in my thoughts, desires, and goals. And I see it in this perfectly ripe Cherokee Purple tomato. It will only have one perfect moment on its vine, and then it will be plucked and savored, and ultimately it will be gone.

I might have just slipped past that moment in my own life, I thought. But that's fine. That's how things are. Flowers don't blossom then disappear into thin air. They fade. Then the plant drops its leaves. Then the stem browns. And then the whole thing topples over. I figured I was lucky to have been as colorful a bloom as I had been, and, if all goes well, I'm still several decades from toppling over. My own personal Peony Party might be wrapping up, but there's still a little summer left before the fall.

I sliced up my prize and added it to the bowl before tossing all of the ingredients together. I forewent the plate I brought out and decided to eat my dinner directly from the large bowl.

The first Cherokee Purple bite was everything I expected and remembered it to be.

Last year at this time Brent and I were at our happiest in the chaos of building our new farm. It was pure Wabi Sabi. But then—seemingly so naturally—the chaos turned orderly . . . and demanding . . . and destructive. We didn't even notice how it happened. But somehow the Beekman had brought out the worst traits in both of us, which were also the very same traits we once respected and admired each other for. His drive and perfectionism. My love of a good time and true experiences.

In short, he was Martha.

And I was Oprah.

It was the growing realization of the half of my life that was gone that was making me so determined to enjoy the half that was left of it. What wasn't obvious was whether I had the patience to include Brent in it. He had his own Martha goals to achieve. My years with Brent represented the happiest, healthiest, sanest years of my life. And I think he felt the same. Before Beekman, when we had our separate lives and jobs, the two were complementary. Now that we were trying to merge our lives into one life at the farm, the differences in our approaches toward living were becoming insurmountable.

He was *Martha Stewart Living*.

I was Living My Best Life.

It wasn't Wabi Sabi anymore. Sometimes yin and yang is really just black and white. Or oil and water.

I finished my birthday meal and stood in the darkening garden, watching almost four decades disappear behind me and nothing but fog ahead. When first cultivated in America, tomatoes were originally called "love apples" and were considered to be mildly poisonous.

Like love.

Book 3

Chapter Twenty-Seven

Rather than return to the city on Labor Day evening, I decide to take a 7 A.M. train on Tuesday and head straight into the office. Part of my reasoning is that I wanted to avoid the post-holiday Monday-night rush. But the bigger part is I couldn't face getting into yet another argument with Brent. I'd had a fairly relaxing birthday weekend while he stayed in the city, and I just couldn't face returning home to his to-do lists and exasperated sighs at my lack of productivity.

"Call me."

Brent's text message comes through at 9:32, just as my train is pulling into Penn Station. I don't want to call. I'm already late for yet another agency meeting about how to save our giant airline client. The price of fuel has more than doubled in the last few months, and the already strapped airline is being forced to cut corners. One of those corners is rumored to be advertising—which means our agency. As someone who flies fairly frequently, I suppose I agree that if an airline has to cut corners, I'd prefer it to be from the marketing budget rather than, say, rivet allocation.

But the text's brevity conveys its importance. Since we're barely communicating at all, two words speak volumes.

I climb the stairs out of Penn Station and stand in a sliver of warm September sun.

"Hey," I say after Brent answers on the second ring. "What's up?"

"I got a pink slip."

"What? Really?" I'm actually more surprised that he used the phrase "pink slip." Who uses that anymore? Where does it come from? Did Martha really walk around the office with a little pad of pink paper, pausing at everyone's door to neatly inscribe "you're fired" on individual slips?

"It's a bloodbath," Brent says. "Rumor has it that there's another dozen or so going down today, and more during the week."

"Wow. That's terrible. Are you okay?"

"Yeah, I'm fine," Brent says in his normal, cool MBA/MD tone. "It's not like I didn't see it coming."

It's true. Even though we really hadn't talked about it, we'd both seen it coming. The constricting economy had been especially rough on media companies like Martha's. Ad sales had been plummeting, her television show was losing ratings, and stores that carried her merchandise were reporting steep losses. There'd been several layoffs already. And since "Dr. Brent" wasn't directly tied to any one revenue stream, it was only a matter of time before the company began questioning its commitment to Brent's initiatives. In the face of declining profits, Martha Stewart is not the kind of woman to utter, "At least I have my health."

Brent explains how the news was broken to him by the publisher of one of Martha's magazines. They gave him the option of continuing to write his articles and appearing on Martha's television and radio shows as "Dr. Brent." The company still wants to have the veneer of health. Which, I suppose, doesn't surprise me. As long as everything looks well in Martha Land, everyone else will think that it is.

"What did Martha say?" I ask.

"She's not here."

"You mean you just spent two days with her, flying on the jet and eating meals together, and she never mentioned that you were going to be let go the minute you got back to New York?"

"Martha doesn't really handle layoffs."

I find myself growing enraged. While we may have been drifting apart, I still can't help but want to defend him against others.

"That's not right. I'll be interested to see what she has to say to you."

"I suppose she'll come by later in the week," Brent answers. "I've got a lot of projects under way that I'll have to figure out how to have someone else handle."

"Is there anything I can do for you?" I ask.

"Nah. It's for the best, really. The stock is plummeting. I'll never get anything done here in the long run."

"Okay."

"See you tonight."

"Brent, wait . . . You there?"

"Yeah."

"I'm sorry about this. I really am."

"Yeah. Me too."

"Love you."

"You too."

When I hang up the phone I start to do the calculations in my head. We've been good savers. We have our emergency fund. We've always been very careful to budget so that we could get by on only one of our incomes. It would be tight, but we'd survive. Financially, at least.

But I also feel more trapped now, as I suspect Brent does too. I'm certainly not going to part ways with someone who's just lost his job. We've been together for almost ten years. We can survive a little longer together. At least until he gets back on his feet. He's an MD with an MBA from some of the most prestigious schools in the country. He'll probably wind up making even more money. At which point he'll dump me for his twenty-year-old executive assistant.

We were going to have an even harder time faking perfection now than ever before. But at least now we didn't have to worry about Martha coming to visit to rub it in.

Chapter Twenty-Eight

September 18: The Dow loses one-third of its value.

September 23: It loses even more.

October 5: The stock that Brent had received for the past two years' bonuses has lost 87 percent of its value.

"Wow, these apples are pretty deformed," Brent says, holding one up to the sun.

"Well, it's their second year being organic," I answer. "The bugs have really had time to entrench. It doesn't matter anyway. We're pressing most of 'em."

With Brent having wrapped up most of his work at Martha, he'd been spending more and more time at the farm. I'm both jealous and a little angry. He's living *my* fantasy. As he was always so fond of pointing out, it was *my* dream to move to the country full time. While I know this is not what he wants either, I can't help but feel resentful. While I've been in the city trying to hold the advertising agency together in the face of a global economic meltdown, he's been up at the farm canning five times as many tomatoes as last year, along with pickles, pumpkin butter, pear sauce, pickled green beans, and mashed pumpkin for

Thanksgiving pies. To me, these chores would seem like a vaca-tion. But to Brent, they're boring. Plus they don't involve social interaction. To Brent, a day without a business meeting is like a day *with* a business meeting is for me.

If there is an upside to the situation, it's that Brent is using his time to grow the Beekman business. Now that he can work on it full time, he has less to nag me about. I have no idea whether we're going to even keep the Beekman, but for now at least it keeps him busy. In his first few short weeks of unemployment, he already has a new business plan involving cheese, confections, home decor, and garden supplies. He's using all of his media con-tacts to get us even more PR than ever.

Except there are fewer and fewer orders.

If we superimposed a chart of our revenues over a chart of the Dow, I suspect they would match up perfectly.

"Well," Brent says, "we'll have to find a few perfect apples for blog pictures."

Even though our sales have fallen, traffic to the Web site has exploded. A lot of out-of-work people are sitting at home with nothing to do, I suppose. Not that this helps us in any way. We don't make a cent unless people buy something.

"What constitutes 'perfect' in your mind?" I ask.

"You know what I mean."

"Yes, I know . . . like a Martha photo."

"People like to see perfect things," he says. "It's aspirational."

"I think right now this country could use a little less aspi-ration and a little more perspiration," I say. "Aspiration is what got this country into credit card debt and underwater subprime mortgages."

"You're one to talk."

Here we go again.

"What do you mean?"

"You've spent thousands of dollars putting in your heirloom

vegetable garden, and your French canning jars, and native pe-
rennial flowers for the garden," Brent says.

"But those are *valuable* things. It's better than spending money
on gas-guzzling cars and McMansions."

"No, instead we bought a *real* mansion."

It was true. Were we as guilty as the rest of America for getting the country into this financial mess? We weren't like the
suburban house flippers I see on HGTV who took out some
crazy Rube Goldberg mortgage. We got the standard thirty-
year fixed delayed gratification of the American dream that
our ancestors bought into. We also paid cash for a four-year-
old used Ford pickup, not a Hummer. Instead of eating out every night, we lugged fifty pounds of our own vegetables back
into the city each week. Plus we still wound up putting the appropriate percentage into our savings account each month. At
least we did until Brent lost his job. We're not supposed to be
in financial jeopardy according to the news. We did everything
the right way.

It seems no one is immune to the downturn—even Martha.
With over 90 percent of her wealth reportedly tied up in her own
stock, she's lost nearly 84 percent of her net worth. Not only that,
but according to her blog, both her houses in the Hamptons and
in Bedford were struck by lightning the week after Brent and
many of his colleagues had been laid off. To add to her string of
bad luck, a Web site reported that Martha learned that the man
she'd called her boyfriend for a decade had become engaged to a
Swedish model in her twenties. And that Martha first found out
about it from a gossip site.

Brent, the consummate businessman, harbors no ill will about
his termination. Had he been in the CEO's place, he'd have made
the same decision. MSLO, like all media companies, is hemor-
rhaging money.

But I can't help but wallow just a little in schadenfreude for

Martha's recent misfortunes. She never once e-mailed or called Brent after his layoff. In all my years as an employee, and later as a manager and partner, I have never let a terminated colleague disappear without privately acknowledging her or his contributions, and offering to help in any way that I could. For a woman who has publicly lamented her lack of friends, it's hard to believe that her sixty-nine years of human interaction haven't illuminated the cause.

But it's hard to dwell too long on unpleasantness on a bright fall day at the Beekman. Even our relationship troubles seem to have melted away a little.

"This one looks pretty decent," I say, holding up one of the apples off of our Golden Delicious trees for inspection. "If we shoot it from this side." I hold up the unblemished side for his inspection.

"It has that little warty, crackly thing there," Brent says, pointing.

"That's hail damage." After noticing the strange defects on many of the apples a few weeks earlier, I'd researched their origin online. "It doesn't affect the taste. It's going to be on most of them."

"Maybe we'll just retouch it out," Brent says.

"I'd rather spend the afternoon making the tarte tatin than retouching photos of apples." We've planned for our weekly "How-To" blog entry to be a step-by-step photo slide show of the method for making the classic French dessert. And, since it's a beautifully warm Indian summer day, we've invited some of our friends to come by and share dessert and coffee on the porch. It will probably be the last outdoor entertaining we do for the year. Of course it will all have to be perfectly documented for the Web site, just like all of Martha's parties. Well, maybe not exactly like her parties. Hopefully our guests won't skulk around, bitching about us behind our backs.

About a dozen people show up for our "impromptu" dessert party on the back porch. We haven't seen many of them for several months, having sacrificed our social life all summer as we chased the chaos of building the Beekman brand.

Everyone has gathered on the porch, and I shuttle between the groups of friends and neighbors taking "candid" pictures for the blog. Our friends know the drill and do their best to look natural. They've grown used to posing for the Web site. In the last six months we've enlisted nearly everyone in the town for some sort of project for Beekman 1802. If not to work making and wrapping the soap directly, they've been asked to open up their homes for blog entries, or to be interviewed by journalists to whom we've successfully pitched Sharon Springs/Beekman stories.

Doug and Garth are dressed in neatly pressed autumn flannels, and Michelle is wearing a chic peasant top. Heidi, the manager of the American Hotel, crosses the porch toward me. Spending most of her days surrounded by the whirlwind of Doug and Garth has made her equally quick and acerbic.

"Where have you been?" Heidi asks, pausing to hold her plate up to the camera for me to take a better shot.

"You're a local. You should know," I answer, angling in with the camera for a luscious close-up of the tarte on her fork. "We've spent the last three weeks trying to preserve every last tomato before the frost hits."

"If you were really like the locals," Heidi says, "you would've been down at the bar having a drink with a trunk full of Del Monte and a garden full of tomatoes rotting on the vine." She adjusts her plate. "Did you get a good shot of that apple sliver on the edge there?"

I zoom in on the close-up.

"Can I get a shot of you leaning on the porch railing with the plate? The sun is perfect."

She maneuvers herself between two other guests, leans against the porch pillar, and stares just over the camera lens.

"How's this?" she asks.

"Great. Perfect. Hold it."

I snap away. I hear Brent behind me, talking with some neighbors about . . . yep, Martha. She's become as ubiquitous a topic as the weather around here.

"Are you and Brent doing okay?" Heidi asks.

"Sure, why?" I answer, trying to cover my surprise.

"I dunno. No one saw you both all summer. And now Brent's spending all his time up here alone."

"No, everything's fine. I've just been really busy at work."

"Okay, my thigh is numb," Heidi says. "And I'm out of pie."

"It's tarte tatin."

"You say 'tomato,' we say 'tomater,' " Heidi quips. "Did you make it yourself?"

"Yep."

"It's good stuff."

"Really?"

"You didn't taste your own pie?"

I realize that I hadn't. The tarte had taken the entire afternoon to make. I probably could've made it in an hour and a half or so, except for all the photos. Wash, *snap*. Peel, *snap*. Slice, *snap*. Caramelize, *snap* . . .

I head back into the kitchen to grab a piece for myself. The kitchen is still filled with the scent of baking; my mouth salivates. I also hadn't eaten lunch or dinner, I realize. Nor a single bite of any of the apples we'd picked all morning. We were so consumed with inspecting them, trying to discover the "perfectest" one. Except for the small number we needed for the tarte, we'd sent the other bushels of apples with a neighbor to be pressed at Sharon Orchards.

On the kitchen table, the platter that held the tarte is empty, save for a few picturesque crumbs.

Brent's and my annual apple-picking weekend has passed by and I haven't had a single bite of an apple.

Brent insists on cleaning up after every party before we go to bed. In his mind, I'm sure he's worried that someone might drop by for breakfast and see the mess. But as we walk our guests to their cars, Brent seems kind of distracted. When the final tail-lights vanish out the driveway, I turn back toward the house. Brent doesn't follow.

"Whacha doin'?" I ask.

"I think I'm gonna go for a little walk."

Brent's not the type of person who goes for little walks. No more than I can picture Martha simply taking a stroll to nowhere.

"Okay," I say warily. "Don't let the coyotes get you."

It takes me nearly an hour and a half to clean the kitchen. I start worrying about Brent after about a half hour, and by the hour mark I was planning on calling all of the local hospitals like I'd seen done in Lifetime movies. Except that there's only one hospital in a fifty-mile radius. If Brent had somehow been hit by a passing car, he wouldn't have even made it to the hospital yet.

I hear footsteps on the porch. Brent passes by the kitchen window in front of me, throwing a shadow against the counter. I hear him take his shoes off, one by one, by the door. *Clunk. Clunk.* He enters.

"Where were you?" I ask. He looks strangely blank.

"I was just weeding some. In the garden."

"At ten o'clock at night?"

"It's a full moon. Or nearly."

He crosses to the refrigerator and takes out a small bottle of Diet Coke. Diet Coke is his secret shame. It goes against everything he preaches, but he can't break the habit.

"You know, the weirdest thing just happened," he says. He's holding the refrigerator door open so I can see his face.

"What?" I ask, leaning against the sink. Weird things don't happen to Brent. He doesn't allow them to.

"I was kneeling in the garden, weeding," he says, "and then I just broke down crying."

This *is* weird. Weird enough to actually frighten me a little. In the almost decade we've been together, I've never seen Brent cry. I'm the dramatic one. He's the autistic robot MBA MD.

"What were you crying about?" I ask tentatively.

"I dunno," he says, taking another swig of Diet Coke. I believe that he actually doesn't know. He's mentioned to me in the past that the only time he'd shed a tear in his life was when his father passed away.

"Is it your job?" I ask.

"No. I don't think so," he says, screwing the top back on the bottle and replacing it. Bathed only in the light from the refrigerator he looks sickly, and small, and so alone that he seems half made up of shadows.

"It's just weird," he says again. "It just seems as if everything's ending and we weren't ready for it."

He closes the refrigerator door and heads upstairs to bed.

The following Tuesday, during the agency's weekly partner meeting, it becomes apparent that our shrinking revenues will not support most of the company's salaries for much longer.

Including mine.

By the end of the year it looked like we would both be jobless.

Chapter Twenty-Nine

The day before Thanksgiving is the first time Brent and I have seen each other in over a month. I've been working nonstop, including weekends, to try to lure new clients to the agency. But it's in vain. Wall Street has collapsed, and with it, businesses all across America. Every business is slashing its marketing budgets. Every ad agency is laying off swaths of personnel.

Brent, likewise, was working overtime at the farm. As the country's fortunes and mood slipped further and further into a depression, and our soap sales continued to plummet, he valiantly fought back the only way he knew how: with Martha-like perfectionism.

The Beekman blog entries became brighter and more aspirational than ever. The photos were crisper and more colorful. The newsletters more frequent and inspiring.

I found myself checking the Beekman Web site each morning to read about the beautiful and wondrous life I was apparently living.

Unlike last year, I was dreading the holiday season. With bleaker news coming every day, it was hard to find much to be thankful for. I felt as if I were simply stumbling forward, trying to find solid footing each day, but slipping farther behind. We'd paid for holiday soap inventory in advance, but with the recession hitting so quickly, a good deal of our savings sat unpurchased on the shelves in Deb's shop, smelling faintly of lavender and regret.

We'd also just learned that the three networks that had looked at the pitch video for our proposed reality show had passed. Our sizzle never sparked, apparently, which, looking back, doesn't surprise me. The show was supposed to be about Brent and me "having it all," which, given the new economic climate, now seems simply vulgar and untrue. Nevertheless, we'd been holding out hope that the show and resulting publicity might be our best, last chance to salvage our soap business.

I arrived at the Beekman just an hour or so before the rest of my family. I invited them to spend Thanksgiving with us last year, so they'd booked their trip earlier in the summer. I haven't told them that Brent had lost his job and that I'm about to lose mine. There's nothing to gain by it. It will accomplish nothing but cast a cloud over the entire visit. I'm hoping that maybe their presence will alleviate some of my anxiety over money, my relationship, and the mortgages. Brent's been doing a good job pasting a happy Beekman face on the Web site, but to do it in person will be a much larger challenge.

Having not seen each other for so long, Brent quickly tries to catch me up on everything I've missed. As I rush around trying to determine what groceries are in the pantry and which will need to be bought for tomorrow's feast, and which beds Brent has made and which need their sheets changed, it feels like opening night for a show we hadn't rehearsed for.

Brent has purchased the turkey already. Given the presence of three nieces and nephews, we decided to pardon our turkeys this year, opting instead to purchase a fully dressed one from our neighbors. It's a giant twenty-two-pound monster, grass fed and hormone free. But the rest of the feast comes entirely from the farm again, just as last year. We plan on having roasted beets with goat cheese, Brussels sprouts with cream, stuffing made from homemade bread with onions and celery from the garden, garlic mashed potatoes, apple cider–glazed parsnips and celeriac, baked Green Hubbard winter squash, and three different homemade pies for dessert with homemade ice cream and slow-cooked goat milk caramel sauce.

I'm determined to throw my family an iconic Thanksgiving—just like the one Brent and I celebrated last year. My family loved Brent from the very first time they met him. And over the years, their closeness has only grown. Brent probably e-mails my mother more than I do, and my mother scolds me if she feels I've slighted him in any way. She once told me that she spoke about her three "sons" so often that many people at her church think Brent is her biological offspring.

I don't want them to realize that there is a distance that has grown between Brent and me. I'm having a hard enough time myself dealing with it. In fact, I'm not dealing with it at all. Neither is Brent, I don't think. It was as if we believed that if we simply stayed busy in our own respective worlds maybe nothing would change. But it has, and it's palpable to me.

Naturally, I overcompensate when my family arrives. Brent and I join them outdoors for an impromptu football game. We run with the goats in the field. Before everyone heads to bed, we huddle with my nieces and nephew in the attic telling ghost stories about Mary. It's the most time Brent and I have spent together since late spring.

On Thanksgiving morning, we rise to put the giant turkey in the oven at sunrise. The morning ticks away as Brent and I are consumed with baking, glazing, deglazing, peeling, pitting, chopping, measuring, stirring, basting, mashing, mixing, boiling, burning, and sweating.

My nieces and nephew spend hours in the hayloft, stacking and excavating hay bales to create the world's largest and most intricate life-size maze. I know this because every time one of them comes inside to use the bathroom or get a glass of cider, they try to cajole the two of us into joining them. We promise that we will after dinner. When they grow tired of the maze, Farmer John revs up the tractor for rides through the fields. It's shaping up to be exactly the sort of holiday that I'd hoped for them.

My mother joins us the kitchen, but curiously keeps out of our way, sitting on a bench, knitting and chatting as Brent and I flit back and forth. We're cooking several things on the open hearth, as the Pilgrims must have, which requires an enormous amount of attention and patience.

By early afternoon, the windows in the kitchen have steamed over completely. I can barely make out the blurry bloblike out-lines of the kids running along with the goats in the field. Brent is frustrated that the centerpiece he'd planned using wild grape vines and fallen birds' nests wasn't holding together the way he'd hoped. He asks me to help, but after fifteen minutes of holding two vines together waiting for the glue to dry I snap at him.

"I have to get back to the kitchen."

"Just hold it a couple more minutes," Brent says. "It's almost dry."

"Believe it or not," I snarl, "we can have Thanksgiving din-ner without the perfect Martha centerpiece. But we can't have Thanksgiving dinner without dinner."

"Shhhh . . . Your mom can hear us," Brent hisses.

"So?"

"Just go back to what you were doing," Brent says. "I can do it myself."

Back in the kitchen my mother looks up from her knitting. She's heard our little argument but has chosen to ignore it. It's strange to see her so . . . not busy. My memories of family Thanksgiving feature her running around the kitchen all by herself. With a husband, two sons, and no daughters, she had almost no help in matters of cuisine. I thought for sure she'd be shadowing me all day, helping me to make some of the same dishes that she'd made for years.

"Oh shit," I say, suddenly remembering.

"What, honey?"

"I forgot the fucking Waldorf salad."

"Well, that's not a big deal," she says. "We have plenty of food. More than plenty."

"No, there's still time," I say, looking at the clock. "The turkey won't come out for another hour."

Mom turns back to her knitting. Why isn't she offering to help? My mother offers to help strangers put grocery bags in their trunks. She accepts every post on every church committee that no one else will take. When my father gave her the services of a cleaning woman one year, she not only insisted on cleaning right alongside the woman, but also wound up cleaning the cleaning woman's house several times when the woman fell ill.

But today, the most familial culinary day on the calendar, she's just sitting there.

"Do you think you could help me make the salad?" I finally ask. She looks a little startled.

"I guess," she says. "What can I do, honey?"

"Can you chop this up while I go out to the chicken coop to get some eggs to make the mayonnaise?"

"Okay. Sure," she says.

When I return from the coop, she's back in her seat, knitting. The celery is untouched on the counter.

"The knives are in the holder over there," I say, confused.

"I know," she says. "I just wasn't sure how you wanted it cut."

My mother has made Waldorf salad probably more than a hundred times in her life. Its appearance on our dinner table signaled a "fancy dinner," as we called them. She could make a Waldorf salad easier than the sous-chef at the Waldorf itself. It was a holiday staple at our house, which is mostly the reason I'd decided to make it today.

My mother gets up and walks over to the knife holder.

"Which one should I use?" she asks, fingering the handles.

She can't just pick a knife?

"Just grab any one," I say. She pulls one out. "No, not that one. Take the chef's knife, there, on the right."

She slides it out and places it on the cutting board while she rinses off the celery in the sink.

"Make sure the water's cold," I say.

When she's finished she returns to the cutting board and holds up the knife. Right before chopping she stops.

"What's the matter?" I ask.

"Well," she says, contemplating. "Do you want me to cut it straight across, or on an angle?"

For a moment I'm annoyed with her constant questioning. How hard can this be? It's celery, for God's sake. I was the one who had to grow the damn thing from seed, starting each bunch in tiny little peat pots in the middle of March. I was the one who spent hours one afternoon tying each bunch up with string so that they'd grow tall and straight. I grew the most perfect bunches of celery on the eastern seaboard all by myself, and now I can't even get a hand chopping it up?

I nearly snap at my mother as I had with Brent a few minutes ago. But then I remember Martha—Martha's kitchen, to be exact. I think back to the Hamptons on the Fourth of July three years ago, when I was petrified about chopping the celery for the tuna wasabi burgers.

In the face of uncertainty, I'd tried to paint an iconic picture of the perfect family Thanksgiving. I'd become as exacting as Brent. And Martha.

My own mother is scared of me.

My family returns to Wisconsin Saturday evening. After they leave, Brent's and my facade of togetherness fades away like the green of the Beekman fields before winter. We turn the heat down to forty-eight to save money as we clean up after my family in silence. By the time Brent and I are finishing folding four guest rooms' worth of sheets, towels, and washcloths, it's almost midnight.

"You know," Brent says. Neither of us had spoken in so many hours that his voice nearly startles me. "I was thinking that maybe, given our money situation and all, maybe we should close up the Beekman after the holidays to save on heat."

Over the last few weeks, as it became obvious that neither of us was going to replace our income anytime soon, I'd begun thinking the same thing. We'd save probably a thousand or so dollars a month on heat, train tickets, and gas for the truck. It would be hard to argue against that plan. I just hadn't wanted to be the one to suggest it.

"Why wait till after the holidays?" I ask, resigned.

Brent reminds me that one of our neighbors had asked if we'd host a New Year's Eve party and concert at the Beekman, to help one of her musician friends satisfy a grant requirement. She'd asked months ago, before Brent had lost his job and I lost mine, and then all of Wall Street lost theirs. Throwing parties seemed like a fun idea back then, so we agreed.

So we'd close down the Beekman on New Year's Day. That meant that we would have to be together in our cramped eight-hundred-square-foot apartment in the city all winter . . .

unemployed . . . together 24/7. I was fairly certain that would mean the end of Brent and me. Over the past year, his essential Martha-ness and my inner Oprah festered to the surface and erupted. There was no hiding our differences any longer. If it had grown impossible to stay together this past year when we were apart so much of the time, how could we possibly survive being trapped together in our tiny apartment?

I'm overwhelmed with grief. As crazy as my life may have seemed to people from the outside—the nightclub days, the drinking, buying a farm on a whim—I'd always known exactly what I was doing and where I was going. There wasn't a single morning of my life, including the ones where I'd woken up in strangers' apartments, that I didn't feel completely in control of my fate. But now for the first time I don't have a clue how I came to be wrestling with a fitted sheet in a 206-year-old farmhouse that we were probably going to have to sell off as my relationship fell to pieces smaller than the bone fragments in the crypt.

"Goddammit," I say.

"What?" Brent says, still thinking I was referring to something as trivial as closing down the Beekman. "You want to waste all that money heating it during the week when we're not around?"

"It's not that."

"What is it then?" Brent asks. He sounds sincerely interested.

"I dunno. Everything." I sigh. "It seemed the only thing I had left to look forward to was Christmas."

"We still have Christmas. We're here through New Year's."

"That really makes for a wonderful holiday," I said, sighing again. "Sitting around in the cold with no money to give each other presents and draining the pipes to close down the house."

"Well, there certainly wasn't anything that great about last Christmas," Brent says, smoothing a still warm pillowcase against his chest. "We froze our asses off getting a Charlie Brown tree in the wilderness that we didn't even use, we never finished getting all the garlands strung and hung, and we spent the entire vacation making batch after batch of soap for our friends."

"That's my point," I say, ironing out a stubborn puckered wrinkle on a sheet.

"What's your point?" Brent says.

"It wasn't perfect."

"Far from it."

"And we weren't even smart enough to enjoy it."

Chapter Thirty

Brent and I are lying in bed watching the annual airing of *Rudolf, the Red-Nosed Reindeer* using the rabbit ear antenna on the TV. Neither one of us has said one word about Christmas plans.

"At least you don't have to come up with a present for Martha this year," I say during a commercial break.

"What you mean to say is at least *you* don't have to help me make one," Brent replies.

"True."

"Why don't we just ignore Christmas this year," Brent says, flipping the channel to a rerun of some horrible reality program. It's actually not a bad idea, I think. Every mention of Christmas in the newspapers and on television this year is attached to plummeting retail sales and stories of families forced to spend Christmas Eve in their cars. Several people have already died at large retail chains as people stampede to take advantage of clearance sales. As a country it seems we're not ready to give up the ghost of Christmas past. People collecting unemployment are still concerned about having the same number of presents under the tree for their children as they had last year. It doesn't seem to even matter what the presents are—just that there are a lot.

This, I think, is what worries me most about the future—about Brent's and my future. America has always been able to sentimentalize the holidays. Through every trial and tribulation of this country, we've been able to take a few weeks vacation from our stresses to create a homespun holiday memory. In 1897, America was still struggling to recover from our devastating civil war in the midst of the longest global depression in history. Then our hopes were buoyed by a *New York Sun* editorial assuring us that despite a worldwide outbreak of cynicism: "Yes, Virginia, there is a Santa Claus." World War I, the "War to End All Wars," was marked by spontaneous Christmas truces on front lines around the world. Even the modern version of our jolly, fat, apple-cheeked Santa Claus was hatched in the middle of the Great Depression as a series of illustrations in Coca Cola advertisements.

But this year's Christmas season seems to have no redeeming or restorative qualities. The stories aren't about homemade presents and the joy of family. They're about humans being literally squished to death by other humans at clearance sales, and about struggling to fill the space under the $450 artificial tree purchased during better times.

Maybe this downturn of Christmas spirit is what happens when half of the country's advertising and media executives are laid off. When *Martha Stewart Living*'s December issue is slimmer than ever, how are people supposed to know how to celebrate? People may gripe about the commercialization of Christmas, but all evidence points to the fact that Christmas is quite possibly the most powerful brand in America and has been for a long time.

If Christmas itself isn't selling, then perhaps we really are doomed.

"Yes," I agree, as the credits roll on *Rudolf.* "Let's ignore Christmas."

I'm surprised at how easily I agree to this. Brent and I love Christmas. Even when things don't go exactly as we planned— like last year's cut-your-own-tree debacle—we still love everything about Christmas, and Christmas Eve, and the weeks leading up to it all. The first year we were together, Brent surprised me on my birthday (in August) with a shopping bag full of Christmas ornaments. He was a medical resident at the time with barely enough money to eat, and he'd gone to every expensive New York City department store on December 26 to buy their clearance ornaments. He'd done the same thing every year since. We had a huge collection—hundreds—each one with its own story.

This year they wouldn't even make it out of the attic. I wondered if they ever would again.

Chapter Thirty-One

Heading into the office every day leading up to Christmas is like opening advent calendar doors in which each day isn't a kind biblical verse but an ancient Gypsy curse.

We seem to be losing clients and revenue daily. We're not alone. The economic meltdown is bringing the entire advertising industry to its knees. Of course the advertising industry is accustomed to spending a lot of time on its knees, but this is something quite different. Even the old-timers have never seen it so bad. I've had to let go several more employees, bringing the grand total of lives I've had to personally ruin this holiday season to eight. The agency has lost a total of twenty-eight employees. The odds of any of these people finding new places of employment right now are nonexistent—or, in other words, roughly equal to mine and Brent's.

Any fleeting hopes of somehow turning the agency around by the end of the year has vanished.

Tonight is the agency holiday party, which we'll be hosting in our own office this year rather than at a fancy venue. The decorations are handmade, the booze cheap, and the food scarce.

For the sake of the company party, I've forced myself to dress festively this morning, which I'm regretting now as I trudge through the gray sludgy mess on the sidewalks of Wall Street.

The street is practically deserted. In the last few years, Wall Street at Christmastime literally felt like a candy store full of children. High-end retailers like Tiffany and Thomas Pink built some of the first retail shops on Wall Street simply to take advantage of the two or three days each year when bankers and brokers received their multimillion-dollar yearly bonuses. Their rationale, quite simply, was to put diamonds and luxury goods right outside the revolving doors of the banking and brokerage institutions in hopes of intercepting even a small fraction of employees walking out with pockets stuffed with bonuses far greater than the lifetime earnings of 99 percent of Americans.

I smile remembering a marketing promotion Porsche tried last year. Eight new shiny red Porsche 911s drove up and down Wall Street all day in reindeer formation. Directly behind them followed a black Porsche SUV with Santa Claus sticking up through its moon roof, loudly ho-ho-ho-ing and encouraging the newly flush pedestrians to visit their local tristate Porsche dealership.

What seemed ingenious then seems morally bankrupt now. Not that I had any right to be judgmental. After all, I'd made a career out of making people want.

This year, the three-story-tall Christmas tree standing outside of the New York Stock Exchange seems brave but battered. The retail stores in the neighborhood all have CLEARANCE SALE signs posted in their windows going unread by the nonexistent crowds of unemployed Wall Streeters. Every day there seems to be more and more television satellite trucks lining the side streets waiting for another global capitalist behemoth to go belly-up.

As I step off the sidewalk to cross the street in front of our office tower, I misjudge the location of the edge of the curb, hidden beneath the sooty slush. I land, ass first, in a puddle caused by a backed-up sewer drain. The man right behind me reaches out his hand to help me up, but in my embarrassment, I'm already halfway back on my feet again.

"Thanks," I say to him, "but I'm fine."

As the cold of my wet jacket and pants seeps through to my skin, I realize just how not fine I am.

I have two mortgages, a job that is about to end, and a jobless spouse. I have an unsellable mansion in the middle of nowhere, a co-farmer who relies on us for a stipend, eighty-five goats who rely on the stipend for grain, five barn cats who rely on the grain for mice, and sixty-five million cluster flies who rely on the goats to supply the manure for them to lay eggs on and hatch from to then die inside of our unsellable mansion.

If I counted my blessings, they'd come up in negative territory—just like the Dow.

My BlackBerry buzzes. It's a text from Brent.

"U 4got to say I love you b4 u left."

As awful as we'd been to each other the last seven months, we never forgot to say that we loved the other whenever we hung up the phone or walked out the door. It may have just been force of habit or avoiding our problems, but we still did it—until this morning.

I turn away from my office's front door. I'm not going in ever again. I quit. I'll phone my partners and colleagues later and finish up whatever paperwork I need to finalize a clean break. This endless dribbling away of everything in my life has to stop. Even if that means that I have to swing the hatchet on my own neck before someone else does.

I quit.

I have to go back home to tell Brent that I love him. It might just be a pointless, questionably sincere habit. But then again, it's not like I have much else left.

Chapter Thirty-Two

Sometimes we wonder whether Bubby sits on the porch steps of the Beekman 24/7 from the moment we leave on Sunday until the moment we return on Friday. No matter what time, day or night, we pull into the Beekman driveway, his goldenrod-yellow eyes greet us and gleam with the reflection of our truck headlights as they sweep across the darkened porch.

The ground is completely frozen. I can tell just from the feel of the gravel under the tires. The thermometer on the dash of the truck reads 4 degrees. I almost already regret leaving the city early to come up here. What made me think that Christmas at the Beekman was going to be any more palatable than in the city? We should have just come up New Year's Day to shut the house down. Hell, we should have shut it down after Thanksgiving.

"The light's burned out again," I say, noticing that one of the lamps mounted on the twin stone pillars at the end of the drive is dark.

"Well, that'll save us a quarter a month," Brent says jokingly. It's precisely the sort of repair that would have thrown him into fits of distraction just a few months ago. But now, with neither of us bringing in a single penny of income, the price of fixing even the slightest imperfection is too high.

Neither of us commented on the different Christmas light displays decorating many of the houses on the drive over. It's so unlike us, especially Brent. Last year, he sang along with the radio's Christmas carols the entire forty-five miles back and forth from the train station during the month of December. I like it when he lets his guard down. When I watch him sing along to silly commercial holiday songs about Grandma getting run over by reindeer, it's as if I get to see what he must have been like as a ten-year-old boy. Before he met Martha. Before he got his MBA. Before he was a doctor. Before the global economy began collapsing. Before his father died.

The Beekman is pitch black.

Last year so many townspeople commented on how nice it was to finally see a Christmas tree lit up in the large Palladian window. Before us it had been decades since anyone spent Christmas at the Beekman.

John's little house is dark too. He's probably at a holiday party with either his family or his new boyfriend. Since we hadn't planned on being here, I hadn't bothered asking him what his holiday plans were. I hadn't bothered asking anyone what their holiday plans were. I was afraid that someone might want to include us.

As Brent pulls open the screen door, a clutch of Christmas cards falls to the porch floor. I'd forgotten how many we'd received from our neighbors last year. And how we'd gleefully spent the week before Christmas driving around, putting Beekman Christmas cards in every mailbox within a ten-mile radius. In addition to the cards, we find two tins of homemade cookies and an assorted basket of very cold homemade preserves stacked near the door. I pile them up in my arms without even bothering to check who they're from.

The inside of the mansion is freezing. I go to turn the heat up . . . slightly.

"Keep it at fifty," Brent warns. "Or lower."

The mansion barely feels warmer than outside. It also feels much emptier, lonelier. I realize how intricately woven together cold and loneliness really are. The loneliness is as visceral as the temperature. I think even Mary, our little friendly ghost, has gone.

I know there must be some sort of physical explanation for the change in sounds inside the house. Brent's footfalls echo through the upstairs hallway as he checks that none of the bathroom pipes has frozen. The cold must magnify the sound waves. Perhaps the wood floors contract and harden into a louder percussive instrument. But in addition to the booming loneliness, something else feels different. Something more tactile is missing. Something . . .

"Josh?" Brent calls from upstairs.

"Yeah?" I shout back.

"Did you have a cleaning lady or something come in here?"

What is he talking about? Why, with both of us out of work, would I have hired a cleaning woman?

"No, why?"

"It's just," Brent's footsteps cross the wide upstairs hall above me and enter the guest bedroom across from ours. "It's just that . . . There are . . . There are no *flies*."

I look down at the kitchen counter where I've just set down the holiday gifts from our neighbors. He's right. They're gleaming white. Not a single zombie fly corpse.

For us, the lack of flies is far spookier than the presence of ghosts.

I hear Brent cross into the other guest room. *"None in here either!"*

I run up the stairs and find him standing at the top waiting for me.

"Did you check the attic?"

We head to the attic stairs together. I reach the door first, and to be honest, I'm a little afraid to open it. I've seen this horror movie before. There are probably a million flies piled up on the other side, waiting to spill out on top of us or, even worse, one giant queen fly ready to burst with trillions of replacement zombies. I open the door slowly.

Nothing.

Brent heads up the stairs just far enough to survey the attic floor.

"Nothing," he says incredulously. "Absolutely nothing."

"Maybe John swept them up."

"Why?" I ask. "He doesn't even come in the house when we're not here."

"It's spooky."

"I know."

"It's a Christmas miracle." A smile crosses his face.

"Praise baby Jesus," I say. "Or is there a patron saint of flies?"

We putter around the empty house for the days leading up to Christmas, doing nothing much other than reading tabloid magazines and surfing gossip sites. The constant wind drifts the snow across the driveway, making it completely impassible, but we barely even notice. There's just enough left in the pantry, root cellar, and freezer to last us till New Year's.

We keep the thermostat hovering around forty to save money and traipse around the house wrapped in quilts and blankets that trail behind us like wedding dress trains. We look like ghosts in our own house, trudging from our bed to the kitchen and back to bed. Occasionally we shower, but with the house so frigid, we even try to avoid that for as long as possible. We seem caught in an endless loop of nothingness between our past lives of constant activity and our future lives of . . . *what?*

We've never been this un-busy.

I suppose we could find some chores to do—maybe something in the barn? It's too cold, really. Normally this time of year would find us in a shopping, decorating, or baking frenzy. But I'm realizing that if you decide to ignore Christmas, the entire second half of December is sort of dead air. It's like being caught in between stations on a radio. The thought crosses my mind that with our sloth combined with the frigid temperature of the house, we might just fall asleep and never wake up.

We continue this lazy rinse and repeat pattern until the morning of Christmas Eve, when my cell phone rings.

"Is the lady of the house home?" comes the chipper voice from the other end of the line. It's Doug. I smile for the first time in days.

"Speaking," I chirp, eager for battle.

"Oh, I'm sorry," Doug replies. "The voice was so masculine, I thought I had the wrong number for you."

"No, you just have a number of things wrong *with* you."

"Yes, according to my friends I'm a horrible judge of character."

"You're so funny," I say. "I guess it's true that people develop good personalities to compensate."

"How flattering. I'm being lectured on compensation by a whore."

"Consider it my Christmas gift."

"Speaking of," Doug says, finally turning somewhat serious. "Rumor has it that there are lights on at the Beekman but nobody's home."

"Yes, we decided to come up for the holidays after all. But we're not really celebrating."

"At your age it's birthdays you don't celebrate. Not Christmas."

"It's just been such a bad year," I explain. "You have no idea how terrible things are down in the city."

"It's been bad up here for the last hundred years, city slicker," Doug says, putting on his pretend hick voice. "Why we locals have been known to celebrate Christmas with nothing more than a baby Jesus made outta corn husks and goat poo."

"Enchanting."

"C'mon, everyone knows you're in town. You'll have to come by for our party tonight. Doug's mom is making her Christmas Eve margaritas. And I have a brand new pair of footie pajamas."

"I don't know. We're kind of just lying low."

"If you don't, I'll tell everyone that you're not coming because Martha's at your house for Christmas. The road in front of your house will be like the parking lot at Walmart on food stamp day."

"I'll check with Brent."

"Okay, we'll see you around seven-ish."

"Maybe."

"And hey . . . Merry Christmas."

In the end, we don't go to Doug and Garth's Christmas party because we wanted to. We went because we were afraid that if we spent one more minute in bed we'd wind up with deep vein thrombosis.

We pull up in front of their rambling 1874 village house, which, with the windows glowing and silhouetted partygoers visible from the street, looks exactly like the sort of holiday scene we've been trying to avoid.

"Ready, Grinch?" I say.

"Let's get this over with."

It's even worse than we feared inside. The holiday cheer

nearly knocks us over when Doug greets us at the door in his best holiday kilt.

"You made it!" he says. "I was getting worried. I was just about to send Michelle to the bottom of the hill to watch for you. Okay, to be fair, I was actually going to send her out because she's drunk as an Irishman and I thought it would be fun to watch her try to stumble down the hill on the ice. But still, it's nice you came."

I give Doug a quick kiss on the cheek. It is nice to actually converse with someone after several days of muttering only to Bubby, Brent, and the television. Garth comes around the corner with his arm around his mom, who's holding her holiday pitcher.

"Hi, boys," the woman says. "Salt or no salt?"

"Slow down, Mom," Garth says. "Let them get their coats off."

"Hey!"

"Merry Christmas!"

"So good to see you!"

Everyone is full of proverbial good cheer and Mama Garth's margaritas. The house is so warm compared to the Beekman. The air is filled with the scent of woodsmoke from the fireplace. It seems like there are even more villagers here than last year.

George the mortician/bartender and his new bride are talking about their record garlic harvest in one corner. In another Heidi and Michelle (who is nowhere near as tipsy as Doug mentioned) are complaining about the lack of good-looking straight men in the county. Our neighbor Peter, from D. Landreth Seeds, is comparing notes on one of his favorite new wine discoveries with another wine buff from down the road.

It's so *festive.*

What's wrong with these people? Don't they know that the world as we know it has ended? That one-hundred-year-old department stores are getting ready to shutter their doors right after the holidays? That a deserted Wall Street now attracts more somber and reverent tourists than Ground Zero? Where do they think the state is going to get its tax revenue this year? Why are they so damn oblivious?

"Hey. Happy holidays." It's Farmer John. He's here with his boyfriend, Jason. The two are wearing colorful, almost matching sweaters and neatly pressed jeans. I hardly ever get to see John in anything other than his barn clothes and muck boots. "I've seen the lights on in the mansion," John says. "I didn't think you were coming up till New Year's."

"We just wanted to leave the city," I say. "It's so horrible there right now."

"Oh, I know," John says. "Somebody was talking about it all at the Agway." If they're talking about Wall Street in the Cobleskill Agway, things must be really bad.

"So are people worried?" I ask.

"About what?" John says.

"You know . . . jobs, the market . . ." I nearly say "trade deficit" but even I realize how ludicrous the words sound in Sharon Springs. The closest thing to a trade deficit Sharon Springs has ever seen is when someone opened a rival roadside ice cream in nearby Cherry Valley two summers ago.

Of course these people are celebrating Christmas like they always do. There's really no measurable difference between this Christmas in Sharon Springs and any other. There's really no measurable difference between any two given days in Sharon Springs.

But Sharon Springs' nonchalance stems from more than just being far removed from the epicenter of the financial maelstrom. Ever since Mayberry, we like to think of small towns as separatist utopias. But our small towns are not blissfully ignorant; they're weary and pragmatic. Sharon Springs, once one of the leading spa destinations in the world, is, frankly, *over it*. It's been collapsing—quite literally—for years, with nary a rebound. The town that once hosted the Rockefellers and Oscar Wilde was dealt its fatal blow decades ago when the train stopped coming to town and the thruway bypassed it. It had to deal with social, financial, and cultural ruin way back then, without any billion-dollar bailout packages. And after you've been essentially dead for fifty years, it takes a lot more than global market collapse to get under your skin. If or when this whole mess is over, life ain't gonna be much measurably different here in Sharon Springs.

Garth's mom swings by with a fresh pitcher. She makes them stronger as the night goes on. Everybody knows this. They've been coming to this party for years. This village of misfit toys will get drunker and drunker and drunker, until Doug, seated in his fuzzy pajamas, begins the annual reading of " 'Twas the night before Christmas."

And afterward, as they do every year, these two gay innkeepers will kick everyone out into the frigid wind of Christmas Eve, waving as everyone stumbles through the village streets, weaving in sync. God help any pregnant virgins wandering around.

Michelle's lucky. She only has to walk a few hundred yards to get to her mansion on the hill—where only a few hours from now, she'll wake with a hangover to host the same exact group of people at her annual Christmas Day brunch, which I'm sort of strangely looking forward to, I realize. Even in my dark, Grinch-like mood, my heart seems to be growing at least a couple of sizes bigger.

Maybe it's the ritual of it all. Not knowing what will come of my life in the new year, any certitudes—no matter how fleeting or minor—are welcome.

Or maybe it's just the margaritas.

"Hey, everybody!" Michelle shouts into the night air as everyone stumbles out of Doug and Garth's house. We can barely see

her slight frame in the distance on the darkened tree-lined side-walk. *"Don't forget tomorrow! I'm making PINK STUFF!"*

According to the thermometer in the truck, the temperature has dropped even further. Back in the Beekman, while I'm brushing my teeth, I notice that frost completely covers the *inside* of the window panes. After I've washed up and decided what would be my warmest sleepwear, I climb into bed where Brent is already lying half asleep. He rolls over, opens his eyes, and laughs. A puff of steam comes out of his mouth.

"You're not really going to wear that to sleep in," he says.

"Why not? It'll keep my nose and ears warm."

Brent gently traces the eyeholes on my ski mask, and picks his head up to give me a kiss on my barely exposed lips.

"Merry Christmas," he says to me for the first time this season before closing his eyes.

Chapter Thirty-Three

"Check out this e-mail," Brent says to me the morning after Christmas. I'm still a little hungover from Doug and Garth's party two days ago, and Michelle's follow-up brunch. It seems like the local strategy for dealing with the long, hard winters is to be blacked out for most of it.

I shuffle over to his beanbag, wrapped in the comforter from our bed.

"She's from the *Times*?" I ask.

"That's what it says."

"And she wants to come up here?"

"December thirtieth."

"That's the day before the damn party."

The idea of hosting any guest, let alone a reporter, seems completely unfeasible. We were barely surviving ourselves. All we want to do is open up the Beekman for visitors one last night for the promised New Year's Eve party, and then pack up to head home. We needed to sit down first thing in the New Year and face the fact that we were income-less. We had some tough decisions to make—not just about the Beekman and our finances, but about ourselves. Us.

"Should we do it?" Brent asks.

"Brent, I can't," I say. "We brought ourselves to the brink of insanity this year trying to create bright shiny Beekman World. We lost. I don't want to do it one last time for old times' sake."

"Well, we obviously did a good job if the *New York Times* noticed us," Brent says.

"*You* did a good job," I say. "I just complained a lot."

"And you were very good at that," Brent confirms. "But this could be a really big opportunity. Our biggest since the *Martha* show."

"I don't know, Brent."

"Look, it was your idea—"

I immediately cut him off. I can't do this again.

"So help me God, Brent—"

"*No, no,* wait a second," Brent continues. "It was your idea to find a way to live up here full time. And I tried—*we* tried. We really did. Walking back into this empty house last week felt like the biggest failure of my life. But it wasn't. My biggest failure was not making you happy."

"Come on, Brent. Don't make it such a big deal."

"No, it is," he went on. "That night when I broke down in the garden? Do you know why? It was because I wanted to make your New Year's resolution happen for you. I thought I could do it, and I couldn't. I never fail. You know that."

It's true. Through high school, med school, and business school, Brent has never received a grade lower than 4.0. And he had perfect attendance to boot. "Perfect." There was that word again.

"It was my fault too," I say to Brent. "Mostly my fault. I told you what I wanted, you kept trying, but I couldn't keep up with you. No one can keep up with you. Then somebody went and broke the whole world and there was nothing either of us could do about that."

"This *Times* piece could be our last chance."

"I dunno."

"It's still your resolution. And it's still the same year."

"It's just that when I said I wanted to live here full time, it was because I wanted to do something *real*. You know?"

"I don't know what you were doing, but I was doing real work."

"No, we were creating images—images of the perfect farm, the perfect life, the perfect couple. It wasn't anything different than I do in advertising . . . just more of it—and with the added punishment of torn ligaments and sunburn."

"That's just how the world works," Brent says. He's genuinely confused about what I'm saying.

"No, that's how Martha World works. I wanted to live in Oprah World. The world where you chase your dreams, strip away all the bad energy, get in touch with your real self, and Live Your Best Life."

"What if the 'best you' is putting a shiny, happy spin on the world."

"No, that's the advertising me."

"*And* when you were doing drag," he adds. "Back then you pasted sequins on reality so that everyone would want to party with you, to have what you had, to be sparkly." He paused. "Face it. Making things sparkly and seductive is what you're good at."

"But I'm tired of that. That's work. I just want to dig in the dirt."

"Look. When William Beekman got tired of being a farmer, do you think that there was some ye olde Oprah telling him to chase his dreams? To 'be the best Beekman'? No. He was a farmer with eight kids. You can't feed eight kids on self-help maxims and dreams. Oprah World is just as false and shiny as Martha World."

He had a point. I could dig in the dirt all the way to China and I still couldn't save the farm. We have neighbors on both sides of us digging in the dirt eighteen hours a day trying to make a profitable living from their farms. And they aren't. We were making more money off of our dwindling soap sales than they were off of their hundreds of acres of land. There's an old local joke around here: What's the best way to make a million dollars? Invest three million in a farm.

Sadly, I've learned that farming is probably the least viable way to save a farm. *Farming!*™, however, just might be our best, last chance. Could I really get it up one more time? Create the sparkliest version of Beekman for our visiting reporter? Could *we*, Brent and I, present the press-worthy version of ourselves as an endearing couple? Having grown apart for the better part of a year now, could we really be able to fake it well enough?

I'm entirely conflicted. And a little dizzy. These three weeks of almost near inactivity have lulled my brain into a slushier mess than goat pee in the snow. Since I walked away from my job I hadn't had a single marketing twitch, not a single spark of sparkle.

Maybe Brent's right. If we're going to save the Beekman, we're going to have to sell harder and smarter than ever before. It's obvious that the last thing this 206-year-old farm needed to survive was another farmer—and especially not two gay New York City ones. Maybe what it *did* need was a good PR agent, a decent ad campaign, and more blinding sparkle than a drag queen under a disco ball.

I thought I wanted to leave advertising for life at the Beekman. I didn't realize advertising was how I could save it and, in turn, possibly save myself.

"Okay," I tell Brent. "We can invite the reporter."

"Really?"

I take a deep breath and put on my invisible wig and high heels.

"And let's not leave a single sequin unpolished."

Chapter Thirty-Four

"Josh?"

I hadn't seen the reporter approach. The Albany train station lobby was crowded with people traveling to New York City for New Year's. The few arrivals from the other direction were easily lost in the crush.

"Hi!" I say beaming. "Welcome!" To help her find me, and to create just the right impression, I'm wearing my best gentleman farmer costume—neatly pressed jeans, stylishly plaid flannel shirt, and shiny Agway barn-mucking boots. It's my farm drag.

I'd agreed to pick the reporter up at the train station by myself. Brent needed to stay behind to let the musicians set up in the wide center hallway and rehearse for tomorrow's New Year's Eve concert. The caterers would also be dropping off their tables, along with other people who would be traipsing in and out of the house to set up folding chairs and decorations.

Having strangers invade the house while entertaining a reporter from the *New York Times* is neither Brent's nor my ideal scenario, but since it's unavoidable we decide to play off the chaos with a certain manufactured insouciance, as if hosting formal holiday concerts for seventy-five people was just another simple fact of country living.

On the ride back to the Beekman I regale the reporter with

stories of how Brent and I stumbled on the Beekman and how we fell under its spell from the first moment we saw it. I tell stories about its long impressive history—the visits from a young James Fennimore Cooper, the savage Indian attacks, and its years as a safe haven for runaway slaves. By the time we reach the Beekman, I'm worried that perhaps I may have colored the picture too brightly, or as we say in advertising, I'd "failed to manage expectations."

But as we drive over the hill and the Beekman comes into view, I couldn't have manufactured a more perfect beauty shot. The gray snow-laden clouds had parted just enough to bathe the mansion in bright late-afternoon winter sunlight. The white clapboards shone even brighter than the snow drifts surrounding the house.

"Wow, this place really is stunning," the reporter remarks as we pull into the driveway—freshly plowed by Farmer John. We pull up behind the caterer's van, which is behind a station wagon, which is behind a pickup truck full of folding chairs.

"Who are all these people?" the reporter asks.

"Oh, we're just having a small get together," I explain, with just the right soupçon of insouciance. As if cued by a television commercial director, Brent appears on the side porch, also dressed in his best gentleman farmer drag.

"Hi!" he hollers with his broad TV-appearance grin. "Welcome to the Beekman! Sorry about all the ruckus," he says, gesturing toward the men carrying folding tables and chairs in through the porch's side door. I can't believe he just used the word "ruckus." If he "reckons" something next, I'm going to have to get him to tone it down a little. "We're having a little New Year's Eve concert tomorrow. We'd love it if you could stay."

"I'd love to," the reporter answers as she pulls her overnight bag from the backseat. "But I have to get back into town to finish another story."

"That's a shame," Brent says. "We were going to open the first bottle of Beekman hard cider at the stroke of midnight."

Brent's so *on* that he's not even shivering while standing in the 5-degree weather wearing just his flannel shirt.

I carry the reporter's bags up to her room, where Brent has built a roaring fire. Brent's turned the heat back on for our guest, so the whole house is toasty warm. It's a welcome relief. I was tired of coming in the house and putting *on* more layers.

Everything in the guest room is as spotlessly clean as when I left for the train station, but something seems different. I look around the room as she unzips her bag on the bed. What is it?

I realize it's not some *thing* out of place. It's a sound. A buzzing.

The zombie flies.

They're back.

I can see them crawling in the corners of the windows. Where do they come from? They seem to be hatching before my eyes. I look out into the hallway. They're there too, buzzing around in haphazard circles in every single pane of the huge Palladian window.

"Why don't you relax a bit," I say, with a trifle less insouciance, "and come down and join us for a snack when you're ready."

I race down the stairs. Brent's already thwacking away with the flyswatter in the kitchen.

"Where are they all coming from? And why now? This place is fucking haunted," I say.

"Maybe it's the guys moving the equipment? Maybe they're letting them in?" Brent asks, grasping for an explanation.

"It's five degrees outside. There are no flies outside," I say. "They're literally coming back from the dead. I know it."

One of the guys calls out to see if Brent or I have a free hand. I duck back into the wide center hallway to help. Two men are struggling to unload what looks like a heavy wooden picket fence from a large case.

"What's this?" I ask, grabbing an edge.

"A marimba."

"A what?"

"A marimba."

"Oh."

Why the hell are they unloading a marimba for a formal New Year's Eve classical concert? I turn to head into the kitchen to tell Brent about this mistake.

"Hang on a sec," one of the men says. "Can you help a quick sec with this one too?" He's opened the other large black case, which seems to hold a metal picket fence.

"Another marimba?" I ask, trying to hide my confusion.

"Oh, no," the musician says. "This one is a vibraphone."

Back in the kitchen, I interrupt Brent from his fly chasing.

"What the hell are they doing with a marimba and a vibraphone in our front hallway?"

"It's for the concert," Brent says.

"A marimba/vibraphone concert?! Are you kidding?" I realize that I hadn't ever actually asked what kind of concert he'd arranged with our neighbor. In my mind I'd pictured a chamber music quartet, quietly playing "Auld Lang Syne" in the hallway while people mingled in formal dress and passed crudités. A concert not unlike one William Beekman would have hosted in the early nineteenth century. I had visions of little Mary Beekman spinning around on her tiptoes, waltzing by herself from room to room, with familiar Mozart and Tchaikovsky tunes making her forget that she'd been dead for over two hundred years. I pictured a lot of things for our final night at the Beekman. None of them included either marimbas or vibraphones.

"What? What's wrong with that?" Brent says.

"Do you even know what a marimba is?" I ask accusingly, even though I hadn't known exactly what one was until a few minutes ago.

"Not really," Brent says. "It's a jazz *something*, according to the press release."

I pick up the press release lying on the counter that I'd been ignoring for the last two weeks: "The Beekman Mansion hosts a New Year's Eve concert with a Grammy-winning improvisational jazz marimba/vibrophone duo . . ."

"They're improvisational jazz musicians?!" I say.

"They've won a Grammy," Brent says sheepishly.

"But they're *improvisational*," I say. "By definition that means any award they've won is because they just got *lucky*."

Suddenly a loud haphazard fury of sounds explodes from the hallway behind us. What I think is the marimba is playing a low bass melody, while what I think is the vibraphone is filling in any holes with a cacophonous repetitive pinging. It's a strange combination, unlike anything I've ever heard. And since it's so unlike anything I've ever heard, I can't really tell if I even like it. It sounds like the noise that would happen if the Love Boat ran full speed ahead into the Starship *Enterprise*.

It's so loud that I don't hear the reporter come up behind me.

"The music is . . . interesting," she shouts. I reach behind her and close the kitchen door so that I can hear her over the music. It's about as effective as using a rice paper screen to muffle a jackhammer.

"Yes, isn't it amazing? They've won a *Grammy*," I inform her, smiling. "Why don't you have a seat while I prepare dinner for us?"

It's not easy preparing a fresh-from-the-farm meal on the second to the last day of the calendar year. During the last two weeks we'd used up most of what was left in the root cellar for ourselves. Complicating factors, the reporter had informed us that she couldn't eat red meat for health reasons, which would have been fine a few months ago, when we could've slaughtered a chicken. But now the only meat we have left are some various unlabeled frozen packages of Cow.

"We've prepared a traditional winter farmstead meal for you," Brent explains, carrying a plate of homemade goat cheese that we'd aged in the basement. It was accompanied by freshly baked homemade rosemary crackers. As he sets the plate down, he expertly sweeps a small collection of dead zombie flies into his hand without the reporter noticing . . . hopefully. The flies are multiplying in the windowsills by the hundreds, as if making up for their absence during the last few weeks.

"A traditional what?" the reporter asks, straining to hear over what I've started thinking of as the marimbraphone.

"A *traditional winter farm meal,*" Brent says louder. "*Everything we're serving was grown at the Beekman.*"

"*How fun. Sounds delicious,*" she shouts. "*Can I ask you a few questions while we eat?*"

"Sure," Brent says. We're all shouting now.

"*So what made you two decide to buy the Beekman?*"

"Well," Brent says, "both Josh and I grew up in rural areas . . ." He's launching into the approved biography answer. It's not that there are conflicting stories, but the truth is that there is no one answer. There is no one story about anything that happens in the world. This is what people forget when they read nonfiction essays, journalism, or memoirs. Every second of every day, our heads are filled with millions of conflicting emotions and decisions. Compiled over a lifetime—or even a single day for that matter—it's impossible to have a truthful, accurate, and concise record of anything we do.

But the reporter has twenty-five hundred words with which to sum up her experience here at the Beekman. And those words will be forever recorded in the nation's newspaper of record as "the truth." A truth that has a beginning word and an end word, and exactly 2,498 others in between. And for the hundreds of thousands of people reading the eventual article, those words will be Brent's and my entire truth, from "once upon a time" till "happily ever after." Because every story ends with "happily ever after," right? As long as you end it at the right moment, it does. Most readers will never know more about us than what they read in this article, nor will they want to know more. They will all finish reading the last word thinking that they've read the whole, true story of us and the Beekman.

The reporter also knows that there is no one story. There's just the one she needs to leave here with tomorrow morning. The answer to why we bought the Beekman could fill the entire paper. Because we wanted a place to get away from the city. Because we wanted to grow our own food. Because the place looks like it belongs on the cover of a magazine, and we wanted a life that looked like the cover of a magazine. Because no one else in the area had the means to take care of such a high-maintenance historic building, and it seemed like a generous task to take on. Because I'm turning forty next year and wanted something to show for it. Because we're vain, kindhearted, ambitious, shallow, deep, humble, trendy, old-fashioned, rich, poor, proud, and vulnerable. Those are merely the beginning of the reasons we bought the Beekman.

But those are too many words for the reporter. She only needs one truth for the article. So we pick the one that sparkles most.

We bought the Beekman to return to a simpler life.

Truth isn't beauty. It isn't even always true. Truth is nothing more than consistency of message.

I learned that from advertising.

The marimbraphone is still sending its shattering call through the mansion as I pull some roasted vegetables from the oven.

"Mmmmm, those smell delicious," the reporter says. "What are they?"

"They're Chantenay long carrots, Sugar Hollow Crown parsnips, and celeriac," I answer. "It's one of our favorite combinations."

Actually, it's all we had, and barely at that. The first thing I did this morning was trudge out to the garden, shovel two feet of snow off a couple of the beds, and pour pails of hot water that I ferried from the barn over the frozen dirt. Eventually I was able to loosen these few vegetables up enough to pry them from the frigid earth. There aren't many, but artfully arranged on a plate they look more "contemporary bistro" than "postwar Scarlett O'Hara."

I was also able to find a few unfrozen spinach leaves in the corner of one of the cold frames that I'd rigged up months ago by propping an old window I'd found in the haymow on top of one of the raised beds. With it, Brent assembled a simple winter salad garnished with our own roasted sunflower and pumpkin seeds, minced pieces of dried apple, olive oil, and our homemade apple cider vinegar. For the "main course," we thinly sliced a few pickled green heirloom tomatoes and layered them on thick slabs of country bread that I'd made the day before. On top we spread a thick smear of homemade goat milk ricotta and some fresh ground pepper, and placed the simple "bruschetta" under the broiler.

Altogether the meal has a quaintly desperate cleaning-out-the-root-cellar feel to it that I'm sure the reporter felt was purposeful. We valiantly try to conduct the interview over the marimbraphones, but I'm sure she only catches about half of what we say.

As I clear the dishes, I hiss in Brent's ear.

"Can't you ask them to stop? They've been rehearsing for four hours."

Brent's trying to shoo zombie flies away from the homemade cherry pie sitting on the counter.

"You go ask them," he whispers.

"I mean, they're supposed to be improvisational. What's the point of rehearsing anyway?"

A zombie fly falls from the window straight down into a lattice hole of the pie. Brent turns his back to the reporter and tries to fish it out with his finger while I distract her.

"The cherries in the pie," I shout over the never-ending music, *"come from an ancient cherry tree that grows down by the crypt. We believe it's a variety that is no longer commercially available."*

The reporter looks up from her notes. She rubs her temples.

"You know, guys," she says. "I think I'll skip the pie tonight. I think I'm coming down with a migraine."

Shit. Between the zombie flies and the withered root vegetables and the marimbraphone, everything was falling apart. We never should have agreed to do this. A *New York Times* reporter comes all the way to Sharon Springs to write an article on our simple life of quiet country pleasures and instead we send her fleeing to her bedroom before the sun has even ducked below the horizon.

"We can pick it up in the morning," the reporter says. "Save me a piece of pie."

As if she's really going to feel like pie after waking up in a bed covered with hundreds, if not thousands, of flies. That's it. We've completely ruined our chances of selling the Beekman brand of country living to the most influential readership in the world. Whatever chance we had of saving the Beekman and turning it into a thriving farm business disappeared up the chimney alongside the smoke from the aged applewood kindling lovingly chopped with the hand-forged hatchet used to kill our heritage breed turkeys.

We failed. Again.

"Well, there's goes our last chance," I say to Brent, scraping bits of nubbly uneaten parsnips into the trash.

"What?" he asks over the music, brushing a zombie fly out of his hair.

"Never mind," I say. "Pay no attention to the homely drag queen doing dishes."

"Should we wake her up?" Brent asks, nervously wiping the counters of flies yet again. He'd awoken at 5:30 for fly patrol, to make sure the kitchen was clear by the time the reporter came down to breakfast. Usually the guests staying in the reporter's room were woken up by our rooster choir. But in the sub-zero weather, we'd shut them inside the coop with heat lamps. If everything was still, one could still hear the occasional, muffled *HERE COMES THE BRIDE!* from inside, but it was hardly enough to wake anyone up. Which was okay. I didn't feel much like sparkling this morning.

I'd managed to find two eggs in the chicken coop. With the shortening days, most of the hens had long since stopped laying. On the kitchen table, I'd laid out the country bread for toast and homemade pumpkin butter. I planned on poaching the eggs and garnishing them with some of the spindly parsley stalks from the cold frame. The last few potatoes from the root cellar were peeled and pared of their rotten spots, waiting to be turned into hash browns.

After yesterday's catastrophes, it was probably futile to try to woo the reporter back into our good graces, but we had to use up the food anyway. Potatoes rotting in the basement would probably affect the Beekman's asking price for when we had to sell.

A winter storm had moved in overnight, blanketing the yard with yet another fresh foot of snow, and it was still falling. It's conventionally pretty, but Brent and I were long past being affected by the Courier and Ivy–ness of the landscape.

Just as I begin to wonder whether to make noise outside of her door, the reporter descends the staircase and enters the kitchen.

"Good morning!" Brent chimes, jumping into breakfast action like Aunt Jemima on methamphetamines. He doesn't share my sense of surrender about our failure to impress. "How did you sleep?"

"Great," she answers. "Too well, actually. I think I might have overslept. My train is at eleven-oh-five."

I look at the clock, which happens to be directly above the window framing the blizzard outside. *Shit.*

"We'll have to leave right now to make the train," I say. "It might take two hours to get to the station in this snow."

"Really?" the reporter says.

"It's not like the city around here," I explain. "There are only two village plows. And one of them only seems to run during the summer months."

The reporter heads back upstairs to pack her suitcase and, I assume, probably take some photos of the fly killing fields for her editor.

"Shouldn't we at least make her breakfast before she goes?" Brent asks, grasping at straws.

"There's no time," I say.

"But she didn't even get a chance to eat dinner last night."

Why can't he just give it up?

"Just put a piece of cherry pie on a plate, and drizzle some honey on some yogurt for her to eat on the way," I suggest simply so that his feelings aren't hurt further.

I bundle up and head outside to try to shovel enough drifted snow away from the truck to enable me to back out. Overnight the drifts have piled up nearly to the door handles on the driver's side. Ten minutes later, the reporter emerges from the door, pulling her suitcase down the steps and through the two-and-a-half-foot-deep snow. I'm helping her into her seat when Brent appears at the door.

"Her breakfast," he hollers to me. I bound back up the steps to grab it.

"What's this?" she asks as I climb in the truck and hand her the plate.

"It's some homemade goat milk yogurt we made." I rev the engine and throw it into reverse. The truck lurches backward about two feet before the wheels start spinning in the snow. I shift into drive and rock forward. "The bacteria culture is from the very first batch we made when the goats first arrived at the Beekman. We've kept it alive for nearly two years." Reverse again. This time I make it about three feet. Forward. Gun. Reverse. Gun. "It's unpasteurized," I continue, "which means that none of the most beneficial enzymes was killed off with heat." Gun. Reverse. Spin. Forward. Spin. Reverse. "Of course, most health officials would say that no one should eat unpastuerized dairy products . . ." Forward. Reverse. Forward. Reverse. If she ever does manage to get a spoonful to her mouth, she's going to be too nauseated to keep any of it down. "But pasteurization laws really just exist to prevent widespread bacterial outbreaks from industrial agribusiness dairies." Forward. Reverse. Spin. Smoke from the gunning engine is beginning to come through the heating vents. "Naturally, people have been drinking and eating raw milk products from the beginning of time." Rock. Spin. Gun. The reporter is trying to aim the spoon into the small jar, but the rocking truck is making it near impossible. "Some people believe that raw milk products are so much healthier than pasteurized products that raw milk clubs have formed and have organized an illegal distribution system in New York City." ZzzzzZZZZZZZZZZ. The tires seem to be packing the snow down into pure ice. "And the honey is from our neighbors down the road. We also saved you a piece of the heirloom cherry pie from last nigh—"

Suddenly the truck catches the smallest bit of friction and careens backward. The reporter winds up juggling the pie plate, yogurt jar, and spoon as she tries to keep it from upsetting into her lap. If I slow down even the slightest bit, we risk getting stuck again. I jerk the steering wheel back and forth as the truck does a sort of reverse fish tail out the driveway. Every time the tailgate hits a drift, curtains of snow shower over the truck.

Finally we make it to the road, which is slightly clearer but not much. I can tell by the time we're only twenty yards away from the house that this trip is going to take much longer than I'd anticipated.

It takes two and a half hours, as it turns out, in four-wheel drive the entire way. Semis are jackknifed on the road, and the slightest inclines on the thruway have pileups of cars at the bottom, unable to make the icy climb. Even a large snowplow had pulled over under an overpass to ride out the furious snow.

The reporter, if she is at all nervous about my driving, never mentions it once. I'm sure her only goal is to find her way back into civilization by any means necessary—away from the squadrons of zombie flies, the Russian peasant meals, and the jackhammer marimbraphone. This couldn't have been the pastoral version of country life that she'd pitched to her editor. As a fellow writer, I sympathize with her. How she plans on eking the bucolic, aspirational weekend home story necessary for the Real Estate section's Great Homes and Destinations column out of this experience is beyond any skills I have. Perhaps she'll just back out of the project altogether. That might be the best Brent and I can hope for.

Once we reach the station, we wind up getting stopped at the bottom of the incline of the overpass that straddles the train tracks. The station is only a hundred yards away, but the pileup of cars at the bottom of the hill is blocking anyone from getting to the front doors. A few policemen are valiantly trying to push cars and cabs out of the way for the more able vehicles to pass, but every time they push a car in one direction, another one starts sliding into it from the other direction. Her train is parked just underneath us, already boarding.

"I think you might have to walk from here," I say. Normally I'd help, but I can't risk abandoning the truck in this pileup. I still have to make the long journey back to help set up for the party and concert tonight, if I'm lucky enough to survive the return trip.

"No problem," she says cheerily. The proximity to her escape must be buoying her thoughts. I hop out of the truck and grab her rolling bag from the back. If I were in her place, I'd be furious. What was supposed to be a fun little assignment for her turned into a literal migraine.

I watch her slight figure bravely struggling to pull her suitcase through the deepening snow and gusts of frigid wind. One of the policemen waves for me to reverse down the hill away from the spaghetti mess of stalled and stuck cars.

The reporter disappears in my rearview mirror, like most everything else this year.

It takes me even longer to return to the Beekman. What would normally be less than a two-hour round trip has taken me over five.

When I walk in the door, the mansion is a flurry of activity. Several volunteers are setting up the folding chairs in the grand hallway for the concert. The musicians are back practicing again, rehearsing a surprisingly familiar improvisational set. I'm not sure whether my percussive jazz knowledge is improving or my hearing is permanently damaged, but either way, today I'm finding the music much more palatable, even festive. Maybe it's just the knowledge that we gave the Beekman one last chance, and now that all is decidedly lost, I can finally relax and enjoy the final moments.

I walk in the kitchen where Brent is putting the finishing touches on two dozen votive candleholders that he carved from navel oranges. He'd cut each orange in half, scooped it out, placed a tea light in one half, and replaced the other half—with a hole cut out for smoke—back on top. One was lit on the counter. Nestled in a nest of pine boughs it was wonderfully beautiful— a glowing orange globe, studded with a few decorative cloves. And even better than it looked was the fragrance.

"These look beautiful," I say, putting my arm around him. "Perfect, even."

"I know we shouldn't have spent the money on oranges just for decoration. But I kept all the pulp. We can use it for juice."

"It's okay," I say. "The Beekman deserves a little festivity this season."

I hate seeing someone as wonderful and expansive as Brent make excuses about wasting orange pulp. He'd done his best this past year, and I hate that I'd made his life so miserable for most of it. It's not his fault that he strives for perfection as much as Martha does. I realize that of all the things that never quite reached perfection in this past nightmarish year, I was the biggest blemish of all for many reasons: for complaining, for not working as hard as he did, for pushing him away. When I think of how hard he tried to make my wishes come true . . . *My* wishes . . . Not his . . . Mine.

Okay. I can't think of that. I just can't.

I spend the next few hours sweeping up after the volunteers and generally trying to stay out of everyone's way. I carefully stack kindling and firewood in each of the fireplaces, and once finished, go room to room lighting each one.

When the sun begins setting, I head outside to take some pictures of the house exterior for posterity. Someday I'll look back, I think, and be able to appreciate that the Beekman was ours, if even for a short time.

Bubby struggles in the deep snow, trying to keep up with me as I walk around taking shots of the glowing house against the purple twilight sky from every angle. All four chimneys are puffing out picturesque columns of gray smoke, scenting the crisp air. Brent's placed a glowing votive in each window. The chandelier is framed perfectly in the tall Palladian window on the second floor. And the yellow lights from every window crisscross the snow in the yard, making illusory sidewalks of warmth, beckoning passersby to come inside.

If I didn't know better, I'd almost buy into the fantasy we've created. But I don't have the asking price.

The winter storm has passed, and only the lightest of breezes blows through the stately maple trees lining the road. Their frozen branches clack against one another.

"C'mon, Bubs," I say, reaching down to throw him up on my shoulder. He must weigh a good five pounds more during the winter months. He nestles into my neck, both of us happy for the shared warmth. "What do you think, Bubster? Pretty, isn't it?"

He pushes his purring head against my jaw. I take a close-up picture of his beautiful gold eyes.

"I'm gonna miss you, Bubby," I say.

Now it's my turn to cry.

Chapter Thirty-Five

It's amazing how quickly the house reverts to complete empti-ness.

Immediately after the caterer hauls the last empty tray to her van, shortly after 2 A.M., Brent and I turn the heat back down to 40 degrees. By force of habit, we start cleaning and straighten-ing. By 4 A.M. we've stacked all the borrowed chairs and folding tables on the porch for someone to pick up and return to Village Hall Gallery sometime in the next week or so. We've mopped the floors and trudged across the barnyard in the pitch dark with bag after bag of trash and empty bottles. We've washed, dried, and folded a load of dirty dish towels, and run the dishwasher three times.

By the time we make it to bed, we only have two and a half hours before Farmer John arrives to take us to the train station. We'll store our truck in the barn over the winter. That way, if we need to, we can sell it along with the house.

I sleep fitfully. Between the hard apple cider and the harsh reality of our situation, I toss and turn often enough for Brent to scold me several times during the short night.

John arrives in the morning immediately after finishing his morning chores. Brent enlists his help in baiting and setting dozens of mousetraps to scatter around the house. Without any activity in the place, the resident mice are likely to nest in the mattresses and couch cushions if left unchecked. I learned that from a Martha checklist.

"You should probably check one last time to be sure the crypt door is closed," Brent says. "Remember last spring when we found that the coyotes had been inside all winter and crapped all over the place?"

I really hadn't wanted to dress in full snow gear again. About the only thing that excited me about closing up the Beekman and leaving was that I would no longer have to stuff my feet into chunky boots and wear ski masks that froze over with snot vapor the minute I stepped outdoors.

The trek across the backyard is the most exercise I've had in months. The drifts are the highest there, being wide open to the vast pasture and winds that blow without impediment all the way from Cherry Valley. In some places I sink in the snow up to mid-thigh.

I'm completely out of breath by the time I make it around the slight berth to the entrance to the crypt. Because of the angle it was built, the stone walls lining the entry completely protect the doorway from the blowing snow, and the walkway is as clear as if someone had shoveled it. These are the little genius historical lessons that have been completely forgotten. In 1802, if half your family was wiped out by scarlet fever and the ground was too frozen to bury them, the last thing you needed to worry about was whether you could get the bodies somewhere safe until the spring thaw. So you angle your crypt away from the wind. I think of all the common sense that has been lost to history.

The crypt door has blown open a bit, which is fine, since after the trudging I need to sit down and rest for a second before making my way back to the house. I swing open the heavy iron door and step inside. I wait for my eyes to adjust to the dark before taking the one step down to the slate floor.

It's warm inside. Well, maybe not warm, but the earthen insulation keeps the inside of the crypt at least a few degrees warmer than the frigid winter outside. And it's completely quiet. Overall it's not, I decide, a bad place to spend eternity if one has to. Brent and I once fantasized that we, ourselves, would have our cremated remains entombed beneath the crypt's floor. Now it looks like we'd be even less than a footnote on the crypt's engraved obelisk.

I perch on the ledge that used to support the coffins—probably at one time William's and Joanna's. Maybe even Mary's. If I hold my breath, there's not even the smallest sound in the air.

"Well, William," I say. "Can I call you Bill?" There's no answer save for a clump of snow falling from a bough outside.

"This is it. We're outta here."

The emptiness of the moment hits me harder than ever. Harder than when I learned that Brent lost his job. Harder than when I lost mine. Harder than when the collapsing global economy made it clear that neither of us was going to find new jobs anytime soon.

Had this all been one big folly? There was so much that was left undone at the Beekman. So many of our plans that were now on hold, probably permanently. Sitting in the crypt, it's impossible not to be crushed by the huge weight of the unanswerable void that faces all of us eventually. Only my uncertain future is beginning right now. I have no idea what I'll do when I wake up back in the city tomorrow. For the first time in a long time, I don't know who I am supposed to be.

There is only one thing I was sure of, and that hurts me most of all.

I am sure that I loved my life here.

I am sure that I loved every thing we created. I loved growing my food. I loved the history. I loved the ghosts. I loved the goats. I loved Bubby. I loved learning from Farmer John. I loved being a part of a ghost town that long ago gave up any pretense of, well, *pretense.*

I loved the Beekman.

I hope it will find someone new that will love it as much as I did.

It deserves to.

The trip back to the train station goes far quicker than it did two days ago with the reporter. The thruway is completely clear of ice and slush as Brent, John, and I barrel toward the 12:05 train.

John is completely unaware that unless Brent and I find significant income in the next couple of months, we'll have to keep the Beekman closed to save money. And, eventually, we'll have to sell it. If we even can, given the real estate collapse. The next time we return to the Beekman will likely be in a moving truck.

With John's natural quietness, and Brent and I pondering our fates, the ride is mostly silent, with the occasional short exchange about weather, goat health, and *American Idol.* I keep searching for conversation topics—any topic—to distract myself from larger, darker thoughts.

Looking down, I spot a zombie fly stuck in a fold of my shirt.

"Hey, John," I ask, suddenly remembering. "Did you clean the house before we arrived for Christmas?"

John looks confused, as if it's a trick question.

"No, why?"

"Well, you know how there's all the flies in there all the time, right?" It feels like a relief, finally revealing our shameful fly problem to an outsider.

"Yeah."

"Well, when we first got up here last month, there wasn't a single one. Not one. And then all of the sudden they showed up again."

"So?"

"Well, isn't that weird?" I ask.

"Why?" John says, honestly puzzled.

"Well, why the hell would there be millions of zombie flies in the house every week for two years, and then all of the sudden there aren't any? And then," I continue, "they show up again the minute the *New York Times* reporter comes."

John takes his eyes off the road to look at me with the same weary, pitying look I've grown used to. His patience may be boundless, but his countenance can never find a place to hide.

"Because," he says, obviously holding back a sigh, "you had the heat turned down. Cluster flies only hatch when it's warm enough."

"Cluster flies?" I ask.

"Cluster flies," John confirms. "Every old house up here has 'em. They blow in off the fields and take up in the house. Probably first settled in the year the house was built. Once you got 'em, you can't get rid of 'em. You just have to get used to them."

"Cluster flies, huh?" I repeat.

"Yep," John says.

"Can't get rid of them?"

"Nope," John says.

It's particularly heartbreaking that flies can hang on to the Beekman for over two hundred years while we couldn't even hold on to it for two.

Epilogue

Atlanta, Georgia, 2009.

"We noticed that when you enter the canned goods aisle, you head straight toward the product without browsing any of the cans marked 'New Homestyle Recipe.' Why do you think that is?"

After asking the question, the no-nonsense focus group moderator peers down at her clipboard, waiting to record every word, gesture, and nuance of the answer.

The poor shopping victim, a slight woman in her sixties, pulls her pastel hand-knit cardigan more tightly around her. While the two-hundred-dollar focus group payment probably seemed like easy money to her a few days ago, I wonder how many thousands she'd pay at this moment to be rid of the three marketers, two ad agency Creatives, and the professional moderator who'd been pestering her about her shopping habits for the last hour and a half.

"I don't know," she stammers, as if looking for a correct answer. "Because I don't have my reading glasses on?"

The marketers nod at one another knowingly. I knew what that meant. The words "New Homestyle Recipe" on the label would soon read *"NEW HOMESTYLE RECIPE!"* in bold, italicized twenty-four-point type, most likely surrounded by some sort of starburst.

Five hundred miles away, the goats at the Beekman are contributing the final few inches of manure to their winter bedding.

In just a few weeks, the weather will be warm enough to begin mucking out the stalls again. Back in my hotel room this morning, I checked online and the forecast reported that Sharon Springs would reach 42 degrees today. There are probably only a few patches of snow left unmelted on the very top of Lookout Point— the highest spot on the Beekman property. In the flower garden the first green shoots of daffodils are probably poking through last year's fallen leaves. And even with the heat shut off in the mansion, soon the windowsills will grow warm enough in the spring sun to hatch the spring's first generation of cluster flies.

These last two months away from the Beekman have been, surprisingly, quite pleasant. The tidy 850 square feet of our city apartment was a welcome change from the 60 acres of never-ending chores of the farm. With no offices to escape to, we were initially worried about spending so much time together in such a small space, but we soon found that we actually liked each other's company. Again. We both spent our mornings writing our various projects, and then ate tuna fish lunches together at our kitchen table before returning to our respective chairs for the rest of the afternoons. We celebrated our tenth anniversary huddled under the bedcovers, listening to a howling snowstorm blanket the city, watching made-for-television movies, and eating the final roasted winter squash from last year's garden.

And then the *New York Times* article was published.

New York Times
February 26, 2009
. . . "We love our Internet friends," said Dr. Ridge, who on a recent day was watching a late-afternoon snowstorm from the kitchen. White drifts whipped over the frozen pond and

the goat meadow in the distance; already knee-high in places, the snow had transformed the landscape into a study in silver-blue.

Newly dug parsnips and celeriac were roasting for supper in one of the twin vintage-style stoves, and a pie made from Beekman cherries was cooling under a frost-rimed window. A soft cheese from Beekman goats was laid out with crackers and red wine . . .

There was no mention of marimbraphones and migraines. The reporter's pastoral tableau of country living made *me* envious of my own life.

Within minutes of the article going online the night before it was published and on the street, we started getting soap orders from all over the world. And within days, we'd closed on several large wholesale orders that dwarfed our combined sales from the entire previous year.

We'd also gotten a call from a network about producing another reality show about the farm. This time the series wouldn't be about "having it all," but two city guys "risking it all" to try to make it as farmers. We'd share the business struggles and the relationship challenges of trying to create an entirely new life for ourselves. This time it would be a reality show about, well, reality.

Our winter hibernation had come to an end.

Brent and I nervously called Farmer John to inquire when the new baby goats were due to be birthed. We needed more milk than ever. John reassured us that we'd be okay, and we solidified plans for launching a line of cheese and goat milk caramel later in the season. I started designing labels and a catalog. We expanded Beekman1802.com to include more how-to videos and guest blogs from Sharon Springs locals. Brent busied himself with spreadsheets and PR pitches. Heidi, the manager of the American, agreed to help send out orders while we were stuck in the city. Deb began manufacturing batch after batch of new bars.

But although the article and the resulting publicity were a massive second wind for the Beekman, the farm still wasn't going to be able to save itself. It takes more than a *New York Times* article and a truckload of soap sales to pay for a mansion.

One of us was still going to have to find work, somewhere, somehow. I began calling the contacts I'd made over my many years in advertising. Many of them were out of work themselves, but luckily, I was able to reconnect with the HR woman who first brought me to New York fifteen years ago. She was working at an agency that handled a large national brand of inexpensive prepared food products, and luckily, in a time of recession, inexpensive prepared food products were flying off the shelves.

Was I interested in a long-term freelance advertising assignment?

Was I?

I was.

I really am. In fact, I really want to. I know now that if I'm going to keep the Beekman sparkling—at least for the time it would be mine—I was going to have to dig in the dirt of corporate branding, planting seeds of television commercials and outdoor billboards and online banner ads, all for other companies. Companies like this prepared food brand. Each new headline that I write for some corporate giant helps pay to keep the Beekman standing and operating as a working farm for yet another day. And who knows? Maybe I'll someday even be able to convince giant prepared food brands that they should source more of their ingredients from local organic farmers. Or airline companies that they should do more to offset their carbon pollution. Or banks that they should make more loans to small businesses in small villages that are in danger of disappearing off the map forever.

Last year at this time I was counting the days until I could leave advertising. My only dream was to live the rest of my life at the farm, pickling, weeding, and mucking. It's what Oprah told me I should do, and what Martha inspired me to achieve.

But they were wrong. Actually, they weren't wrong. I just heard them wrong.

Martha isn't about achieving perfection—God knows she hasn't. It's about going back time after time trying to get there. It's about graciously, meticulously, fabulously hosting that last-chance *New York Times* reporter houseguest even when all you want to do is lie on a zombie fly–littered bed, read gossip magazines, and die.

And Oprah's call to live your Best Life isn't as simple as it seems. Your Best Life isn't necessarily your favorite life or the one you selfishly want. It's simply the life you're best at.

I happen to be best at making things sparkle. I always have been. And because of it, the Beekman is still here. I don't know for how long, but for now, it's here. And maybe someday soon you'll drop by, pick up a shovel, and muck some goat manure with us. Or weed the garden. Or pick some apples. Whatever you do best is what it needs most.

Will our hard work be able to save the Beekman? I don't know. But I just ordered seeds for the spring garden—lots of 'em. And just about the biggest sign of faith I can imagine is ordering seeds for a garden I don't know whether I'll be around to harvest. Maybe that's not faith. Maybe that's just farming. Or maybe that's just being middle-aged.

And Brent and I are still together. He's trying his best to create Good Things while I'm getting good at Living My Best Life.

And we never forget to say "I love you" before walking out the door. Because if you start forgetting to say "I love you" before you walk out a door, it's too easy to forget that you do.

With all your heart.

With love from the Beekman,

Josh, Brent, Farmer John, William and Joanna Beekman, little Mary, Bubby, the goats, the rooster choir, the zombie flies, and everyone in Sharon Springs

MICHELLE'S PINK STUFF

2 QTS HAND-PACKED (VERY IMPORTANT) STRAWBERRY ICE CREAM

4 SMALL PACKAGES OF JELL-O

4 CUPS BOILING WATER

1 CUP CHOPPED WALNUTS

2 BANANAS, SLICED

1 CUP RED GLOBE GRAPES, HALVED

2 CUPS MINIATURE MARSHMALLOWS

Dissolve Jell-O in boiling water. Add ice cream and stir until melted. Place in refrigerator for ½ hour. Stir in nuts, bananas, grapes, and marshmallows. Return to refrigerator. Stir every 15 minutes for about 2 hours to keep marshmallows from floating to top and everything else from sinking as it sets. Once firm-ish, refrigerate 24 hours.

SERVES INNUMERABLE "HORRIFIED" GUESTS

GARTH'S MOM'S CHRISTMAS EVE MARGARITAS

1 PT GRAND MARNIER

1 PT LIME JUICE

1 PT CRANBERRY JUICE

2½ PTS SOUR MIX

1½ PTS JOSE CUERVO (INCREASE ACCORDINGLY AS CHRISTMAS
    MORNING APPROACHES)

WILLIAM BEEKMAN'S SYLLABUB

From *American Cookery* by Amelia Simmons, 1796

TO MAKE A FINE SYLLABUB FROM THE COW [OR GOAT]

Sweeten a quart of hard cyder with double refined sugar, grate nutmeg into it, then milk your cow [or goat] into your liquor. When you have thus added what quantity of milk you think proper, pour half a pint or more, in proportion to the quantity of syllabub you make, of the sweetest cream you can get all over it.

Acknowledgments

Brent is a private person. If you are a private person, imagine having me as your boyfriend. Now you'll know how grateful I am that he's stuck around.

Farmer John is perhaps the most patient man on earth. His goats saved the Beekman far more than the Beekman saved them. I won't say much more because it'll embarrass him.

I'm also grateful that my parents made me pull weeds from our garden for hours on end in the hot summer sun. They were right. I was wrong. It did build character.

Martha Stewart probably won't read this far. She's a busy woman doing important things—which is why I've always admired, envied, poked fun at, and worshipped her. Thank you, Martha.

I'm surely going to forget to include at least one of my Sharon Springs neighbors in the following list. Please don't shun me at the Agway: Garth Roberts, Doug Plummer, Heidi Meika, Lee Woolver, Michelle Curran, Debbie McGillycuddy, Dan Fiske, Jason Paden, Tony and Vanessa, Ross Wasserman, Bob Sutherland, Suzann Kipp, Barbara and Peter Melara, Michael Whaling, Maureen Lodes, Megan Holken, George VanGarderen, Karen and Michael, Keith Bavolar, Karen and Peter Cookson, Harold and Barbara Hall, Rabbit Goody, Jim Feldman, Sharon and Bob, Jim and Norm, Dan and Dave, Rose, John and Steve, Mitch and Matthew, Pat and Eric Selch.

I consider these people my friends, family, and future fodder (lucky them): Papa and Pam, Jeannie O'Toole, James and Maya, Sally Kim, Carrie Kania, Andy McNicol, Anna DeRoy, Lauren Heller Whitney, Matthew Horowitz, Cecil, Max, Sophie, Linda, Angela Rae Berg, Laura Michalchyshyn, Lynn Sadofsky and the Planet Green team, Pyongson Yim, Fenton and Randy, the WOW peeps, Marty, Rob, Lenny, Mark, Lori Lum, Kenn and David, Andrew, and all our Beekman 1802 Internet pals.

About the Author

Josh Kilmer-Purcell was raised in rural Wisconsin before moving to New York City to work in advertising in the 1990s. His years moonlighting as a nightclub drag queen were recounted in the bestselling memoir *I Am Not Myself These Days*. Kilmer-Purcell and his partner, Dr. Brent Ridge, purchased The Beekman Mansion and Farm in Sharon Springs, New York, as a weekend home in 2007. With the help of John Hall and his goats, they launched their artisanal lifestyle company, Beekman 1802, in 2008. Kilmer-Purcell and Brent Ridge are the stars of the Planet Green docu-series *The Fabulous Beekman Boys*. For more information about life on their farm, visit Beekman1802.com.

— THE FABULOUS —

BEEKMAN BOYS

They're successful city slickers who know nothing about goat farming. So naturally they buy a goat farm. Tune in and see what happens next.

 Check your local listings

planetgreen.channelfinder.net